WINNING PRAISE FOR
THINKING BODY, DANCING MIND

"I enjoyed *Thinking Body, Dancing Mind* thoroughly: the calligraphy is beautiful; the points instructive and helpful; the affirming data convincing; the presentation lucid and fluent and Taoist." —R. G. H. Siu, author of *The Tao of Science, The Portable Dragon, The Master Manager,* and *The Craft of Power*

"An inspiring and valuable contribution, a great combination of ageless wisdom and practical techniques that will help anyone perform at peak levels in today's world and get more enjoyment and fulfillment in whatever game they are playing." —Robert J. Kriegel, Ph.D., author of *If It Ain't Broke . . . Break It!*

"This book is important!" —Michael Murphy, M.D., author of *Golf in the Kingdom* and *The Future of the Body*

"Unique, thought-provoking . . . beneficial." —*Booklist*

"*Thinking Body, Dancing Mind* is full of applications of Eastern philosophy that clearly relate to the needs and concerns of all of us in the West. There is something for thinking people in any walk of life—and particularly for elite athletes. Brilliant!" —Jim Hrbek, 1992 U.S. Olympic Coach, Women's Judo

"Jerry Lynch's Taoist-inspired techniques are so unique and effective. He provided me with a whole new way of viewing the real power I have within. I love the use of Tao and how it applies to all of sport . . . a refreshing, relaxing way." —Nancy Ditz, member of U.S. Olympic Marathon Team

"Jerry Lynch has gotten to grass-roots mental training for distance runners in his book *Thinking Body, Dancing Mind.* Application of his mental training techniques will take vital seconds off your time and assist in your becoming a competitive giant." —Harry Groves, Head Coach, Penn State Men's Track and Field / Cross Country Coach

THINKING BODY, DANCING MIND

TAOSPORTS FOR EXTRAORDINARY PERFORMANCE IN ATHLETICS, BUSINESS, AND LIFE

■

CHUNGLIANG AL HUANG

AND

JERRY LYNCH

BANTAM BOOKS
New York   Toronto   London   Sydney   Auckland

This edition contains the complete text
of the original hardcover edition.
NOT ONE WORD HAS BEEN OMITTED.

THINKING BODY, DANCING MIND
A Bantam Book

PUBLISHING HISTORY
Bantam hardcover edition published September 1992
Bantam trade paperback edition / June 1994

Book design by Lurelle Cheverie

ISBN 0-553-37378-1

Published simultaneously in the United States and Canada

Bantam Books are published by Bantam Books, a division of Random House, Inc. Its trademark,
consisting of the words "Bantam Books" and the portrayal of a rooster, is Registered in U.S. Patent
and Trademark Office and in other countries. Marca Registrada. Bantam Books, 1540 Broadway,
New York, New York 10036.

PRINTED IN THE UNITED STATES OF AMERICA

BVG   20   19

■

Dedicated to the spirit of Joseph Campbell,
who, as a world-class runner, personified the TaoAthlete
and recognized the significance of sport
as a spiritual journey applicable to all aspects of life.

CONTENTS

CONTENTS

CONTENTS

CONTENTS

CONTENTS

CONTENTS

Acknowledgments from Jerry Lynch

Paul Calandrino, author and friend, who willingly assumed a role very similar to that of midwife during the gestation and birth of this book by giving much love, support, encouragement, and timely imput.

Jan, confidant and spouse, whose belief in my work was a constant source of strength as she gently guided me back to the tao when I lost sight of the way.

Daniel, Sean, and Brennan, my three sons and tao masters in residence who, unintentionally, help me to remember what's truly important when I become too self absorbed.

And to Leslie Meredith, an editor of extraordinary sensitivity, dedication, vision, and persistence. Throughout each editorial phase, she inspired us to settle for nothing less than excellence. We feel blessed to have had her as part of this project.

Acknowledgments from Chungliang Al Huang

I gratefully acknowledge my Living Tao Foundation network who for nearly twenty years have shared with me the perennial learning and the humility in honoring the ancient lineage of the Living Tao as source for all human endeavors.

My wife, Suzanne Pierce, who lovingly and tirelessly interprets and edits all my initial "Chinese-English" thoughts into intelligibility. Together with my daughters, Lark and Tysan, remarkable women, they are my muse, reflection, and teachers for life!

PROLOGUE

by Jerry Lynch

As a young boy growing up in New York City, I had an unquenchable passion for sports. I lived ten minutes from Ebbets Field, home of the Brooklyn Dodgers. Duke Snider, Gil Hodges, and Pee Wee Reese were practically next-door neighbors. At the age of eleven, I had the thrill of seeing my first basketball double header at the old Madison Square Garden. I knew then that I wanted to play in that arena some day.

This ambition drove me to shoot hoops whenever possible. I even used to walk to the neighborhood schoolyard to shovel freshly fallen snow from the basketball court to squeeze in some extra practice time. As a junior playing high school ball, I had the opportunity to play at the Garden. My team was to open a twin bill there, preceding a pro game between the Knicks and the Celtics. All of my efforts seemed to have paid off. But three days prior to the game, I sprained my ankle. I would never get the chance again to realize my dream.

Even with this injury and disappointment, my passion for sports has never dwindled. I continue today to be involved with athletics, both professionally and as a competitive runner and cyclist. My intense love affair with athletics, however, has also awakened me to what is not right about this system—and other systems in the private and public sectors as well. For years, I have been concerned about the poor quality of leadership and coaching in sport and industry. Coaches and business leaders alike are obsessed with winning. They are intolerant of failure and see their competitors as an enemy they must annihilate. This attitude also breeds a high incidence of minor and major injuries that can discourage or destroy an athlete's body, hopes, and dreams. Because of my love for sport, I have sought ways to change these negative, harmful attitudes in order to help us all enjoy sports—and our lives—more fully and to reach the levels of extraordinary performance of which we are all capable.

What has evolved is TaoSport, an approach that combines my schooling in Western psychology with my passion for Eastern philosophy, specifically the precepts of Taoism. Gaining inspiration from visionaries such as Alan Watts, George Leonard, Michael Murphy, Tim Gallwey, and Fred Rohé, I devised effective strategies and techniques for dealing with the challenge of sports and the obstacles to optimum performance from what I had learned from the ancient Chinese book of wisdom, *Tao Te Ching: The Classic Book of Integrity and the Way*, by the great scholar, Lao-tzu. Written over two thousand years ago, the *Tao Te Ching* has much relevance for sports, business, and life today. Loosely translated, its title means the book (*ching*) of the way (*tao*) and power (*te*). Basically, it teaches that each of us possesses a limitless power and potential that we can use and realize when we act in accordance with the forces of nature, when we align ourselves with the natural flow of energy or events. The Tao teaches us to react to life's circumstances by yielding, by not forcing issues or energies unnaturally, and by following the natural path of least resistance.

All of us reach points in our sport, work, or home life when our actions and attitudes become joyless and unsatisfying. By using the Tao as a life-force in our pursuits, we can revitalize ourselves and our lives. Think, for a moment, of the freeze-dried food that hikers and campers use. Without water, the food is lifeless, inedible, and dull. Add a bit of water, and a nourishing meal appears. The Tao is like water; it makes possible life and vigor. It is liquid and yielding, yet it can be forceful and strong.

Cultivating the Tao in life, according to Lao-tzu, will bring you into harmony with your true purposes, resulting in greatness and fulfillment.

The Great Tao extends everywhere.
All things depend on it for growth,
And it does not deny them. . . .
It clothes and cultivates All Things,
And it does not act as master. . . .
In the end it does not seek greatness,
And in that way the Great is achieved.

When I followed Tao principles, I noticed how well I began to perform in all areas of my life. Excited by my own personal growth and improvement, I decided to incorporate my vocation with my avocation and created a number of TaoSports for improving performance in sports, work, and life.

I have already used the TaoSport concepts I describe in *Thinking Body, Dancing Mind* in training thousands of professional, Olympic, collegiate, and recreational athletes. All these athletes have enjoyed and appreciated the opportunity to see a new way (or Tao) of performance. One of my first successful attempts to involve others in this approach was at Stanford University in the early 1980s, where I team-taught an experimental seminar on human performance created by martial artist George Pegelow with former NFL standouts David Meggyesy and Guy Benjamin. Future tennis, baseball, and football athletes, were among the excited students in this class who were interested in a more Eastern approach to their sport.

From this encouraging beginning, I began to use TaoSport ideas as the foundation for all my work with athletes. It was quite exciting and encouraging to see elite athletes with whom I had worked at the U.S. Olympic Training Center adopt my approach to their sport and get positive results. Working closely with the University of California–Santa Cruz tennis team was equally rewarding. Many of the athletes claimed that TaoSport principles gave them the edge on their road to becoming the NCAA Division III National Champions.

Seeing the relevance of the *Tao Te Ching* to all activities in life, I incorporated many TaoSport principles into my courses and training programs at various corporations, such as AT&T and Public Services of Colorado, and my talks with business groups, such as the American Institute of Industrial Engineers and the American Institute of Certified Public Accountants. Many of these participants held managerial positions and applied TaoSport strategies to improve their working environments and the productivity levels of their co-workers.

After these successes, I decided to write *Thinking Body, Dancing Mind* to try to communicate this new approach and these helpful techniques to people who love sports but cannot attend my seminars. But my first draft of the book needed more of an underpinning in Eastern philosophy than I, a Western student of the Tao, could provide. Since I respected the insightful work of Chungliang Al Huang and his colleagues Alan Watts and Joseph Campbell, I decided to write to Al for feedback about the book. Al called me the very day he read my letter, four hours after the birth of my third son, Brennan. He was very excited about my work, and for the second time in one day, there was a birth in my family—the birth of *Thinking Body, Dancing Mind.*

As the primary author of this book, I have drawn on my own experiences to illustrate the principles of TaoSport. Hence, as you read and use the book and come across the words *I* and *we*, you will find that they refer to Jerry Lynch, not Chungliang Al Huang. But Al and I share all these ideas and wrote the book together in accordance with the collaborative, partnership precepts of the Tao that we present in our work. By combining our diverse cultural backgrounds, we have created a metaphorical marriage of East-West, yin-yang, dancing-thinking, body-mind, or TaoSport—a new concept and word that you can use as a touchstone for extraordinary performance in all of your activities.

We offer to you with humility and great pleasure the assembled gleanings from our lives. We hope you will be able to use them in your daily musings to achieve a life-game of good sense, humor, and aliveness.

PROLOGUE

by Chungliang Al Huang

We all participate in cycles of change. In traditional Chinese learning, the cyclic transformation of all aspects of life is understood as a process of constant movement. This process is the Tao—the Dance, the Sport, and the Business of our many ways of being in this world.

Almost two years ago, Dr. Jerry Lynch approached me to join him in a further exploration of the Tao. We undertook to use the Tao as metaphor and vehicle to break through old psychological boundaries and attitudes that limit achievement, to arrive at a new synthesis of East and West, to unite sport and the business of living. We wish to offer you a visual and kinetic language that will enable you to use your body and your mind as participants in a creative process, to become the best you can be, to engage the Tao in sport and sport in Tao—the TaoSport as the ultimate dance of life.

Sport is a whole-brain and -body activity. To be "good in sport" requires the presence and participation of your mind, body, and spirit in total synchronization, with the spontaneity and centered awareness attributed to ancient Taoist sages. The "ultimate" athlete is a "cosmic dancer," an "acrobat of God," the TaoAthlete.

Growing up in China, I was fortunate that my early learning was grounded in t'ai chi, a movement meditation that cultivates the unity of body, mind, and spirit. Later, Western sports such as basketball, soccer, and track and field were introduced into our school system as "physical education." Among these new sports was Ping-Pong, which was my and my friends' favorite and became a national game, perfectly in tune with our Chinese philosophy of the t'ai chi–yin-yang dance. I thrived and became a high school champion player.

Ping-Pong and t'ai chi, however, did not prepare me to cope with the vigorous muscle-strength emphasis of American sports, which I encountered when I came to the United States for college. My first year on a small Oregon campus was a shock. Fortunately, I discovered the folk, social, and modern dance courses, which were offered through the women's physical education department. In order to maintain my t'ai chi balance, I had to forgo imitating the macho image of most college men and submit to being one of the few males in dance classes. The unexpected reward and gratification was that not only could I boast about my intimacy with many lithe and beautiful women dancers, but we few men became instant leads in all the college musicals and dance concerts. (I was probably one of the first Asians ever to play Curly in Rodgers and Hammerstein's *Oklahoma!*)

In the early 1960s, after six years of acquiring the proper credentials, I began teaching dance at the University of California at Los Angeles. As the only male instructor, one of my first assignments was to initiate a course to entice men into the dance curriculum. I was keenly aware of the reasons so few men were attracted to dance—and of the misconception and stigma of dance and male dancers. So I made the most of my t'ai chi–kung fu training to show the young men that dancing is no sissy business! At the time, Bruce Lee was entering Hollywood movies with energetic heroism. I was able to catch hold of Lee's glory as a kung fu master to enter the American way of life as a Dragon, juxtaposing my Eastern philosopher-artist self with my pseudo-Western hero self (the jock with gracefully choreographed punches and kicks)!

Later, through the introduction of my good friend, philosopher Alan Watts, I joined the newly founded Esalen Institute faculty, to transmit the ineffable Tao. I was asked to participate in a project called the Sports Symposium, which was endeavoring to blend and synthesize East and West, the material and spiritual aspects of a new sport of the mind and the body. I was enlisted to infuse credibility and evidence into this new game, the TaoSport.

I designed lecture-demonstrations to show that sheer size and force do not necessarily mean power and strength, and that resilience, an ability to yield and rebound, is the Way (Tao) to be. One of my exercises demonstrated how a small person who is centered and yielding can safely catch a person twice his weight, jumping into his embrace. During one seminar, we proved one by one that this "Tai Ji hug" did indeed work. Everyone had great fun, with reassured personal power, except one extra-large, muscular man. He stood at the corner, looking at the jubilant group. I invited him to run and jump onto my hip. He thanked me for my brave consideration but declined, insisting that his weight would crush me. After some coaxing and reassurance, he hesitantly leaped into my embrace.

This huge man, as he was wrapped around my torso, was anticipating the thud of us both landing on the floor. I watched as he finally looked at me in disbelief, as I swayed and held him inside my arms. This event is etched in my memory: this extra-large, all-American male being cradled in simple human contact such as he probably hadn't experienced since he was a young boy. (He was David Meggyesy, a linebacker for the former St. Louis Cardinals of the National Football League. After nearly twenty years, we recently discovered each other again and relived this experience with fondness and new insights. David is currently with the National Football League Players' Association in San Francisco.)

In the 1970s, George Leonard (author of the seminal classics *The Ultimate Athlete* and *Mastery*, who at age fifty accomplished all the required skills to become an aikido blackbelt), George Pegelow (another martial artist), and I created an event called The Happy Martial Arts Festival. Launched in San Francisco's Grace Cathedral, it later was moved to the Frost Amphitheater of Stanford University. We brought together prominent martial artists and world-class athletes to share the essence of TaoSport. The promotion poster for the events showed a fierce sword-slashing samurai—except we replaced the sword he wielded with a picture of a giant chrysanthemum!

Along my journey into this TaoSport, I have enjoyed the works of other kindred friends. Michael Murphy, co-founder of Esalen Institute, wrote his groundbreaking classic, *Golf in the Kingdom,* and recently, the monumental *The Future of the Body*; Mike Spino and Fred Rohé shared their *Innerspaces of Running* and *The Zen of Running*; Denise McCluggage, her *Centered Skier*; Timothy Gallwey created the *Inner Games* of tennis and golf, and later, with

Bob Kriegel, of skiing. All these books expanded ideas of sport as the Tao in creativity, in work, and in everyday living.

Other than daily t'ai chi dancing and swimming, my contact with actual traditional sports has been mostly through my two daughters, who competed as runners in high school. They were both endowed with speed and strength, but sustained unnecessary minor physical and emotional injuries. It is obvious to me that school sports can be improved by incorporating a synthesis of Eastern and Western thought about the mind and body. I hope TaoSports will open the way for exploration of a more integral education for the young.

When Jerry wrote to me with his proposals for this book, I was intrigued and impressed by his professional and personal experiences with sport as a metaphor for life. His dedicated learning and intuitive understanding of Tao were evident. Jerry is both a romantic and a realist. He insists on looking at all of life with affirmative attitudes from the heart and the mind. His ability to absorb and digest the Tao teaching is remarkable. During the months that we conferred on this book, we have continued to agree on the inseparable unity of artistic play and the serious business of Life.

There are already many "Tao of" and "how to" books for succeeding in the world of sports and business. This book searches for the universal source of Tao in both. In the Chinese language, Tao is an ineffable open concept, the most profound and purest simplicity of being, in accordance with nature—the watercourse way. The everyday expression for "business" in Chinese, *shen yi*, is literally "the meaning of life/living." It is truly our business to make sure that our lives have meaning.

Thinking Body, Dancing Mind—TaoSports are indeed the new game in town, the timely and worldly juxtaposition and synthesis of the West and the East. This book is dedicated to Joseph Campbell. We hope that it will become an arena for the ultimate dancers of life!

THINKING BODY, DANCING MIND

■ I ■
BLUEPRINTS

■

AWAKENING TO THE TAO

The title of this book, *Thinking Body, Dancing Mind*, embodies a classic Tao paradox. It immediately encourages us to think differently by juxtaposing opposites. Ancient Taoist master-teachers often used paradox and metaphor to open up their students' minds to new ideas, new awareness, and profound understandings of deep forces and unseen interconnections. Does the body, indeed, think? It does when you cease to interfere with its deep-seated intelligence, known as instinct or intuitive physical response. Does the mind dance? It does when you free it to flow with life's natural processes, when you loosen your tendency toward critical judgment and control. A dancing mind is relaxed, visionary, and open to the full range of human possibility. "Thinking body, dancing mind" means that you have within you all that you need to be and to do anything you wish. The new attitudes and beliefs presented in this book will help you accomplish your goals and enjoy yourself in the process.

Part I enables you to begin your transformational journey by introducing you to the Tao and the concept of TaoSport. This process will lead you to extraordinary performance in athletics, work, and life. Here are guidelines—or TaoSports—for visualizations and affirmations for progressing along the way.

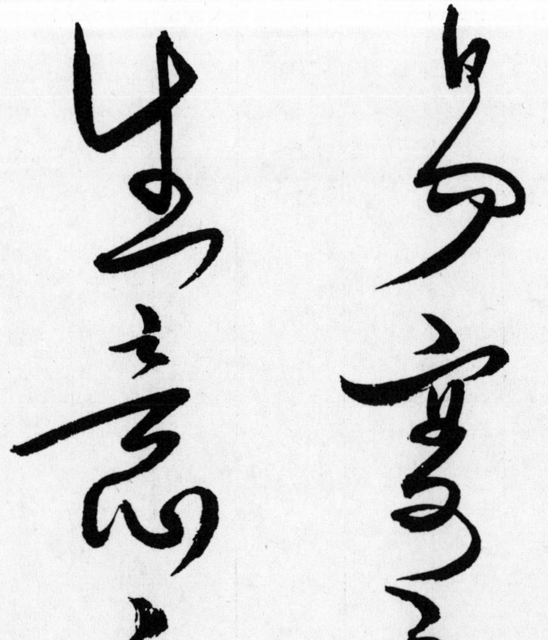

FROM WESTERN SPORTS
TO TAOSPORTS

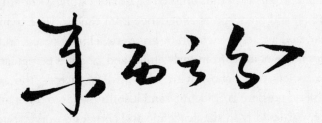

The Great Tao extends everywhere.
All things depend on it for growth,
And it does not deny them.

TAO TE CHING no. 34

I brought my son Daniel to his first organized baseball game, a Little League game, when he was at the innocent and impressionable age of five. My intention was to expose him to the wonderful excitement and joy of neophyte little leaguers and their enthusiastic, proud parents. Daniel and I were both enjoying our outing, when a routine grounder was hit to first with the bases loaded. In most cases, such a hit surely would have ended the first inning. Instead, the ball rolled through the first baseman's legs, and two runs scored. The subsequent behavior of the irate coach toward that vulnerable child killed Daniel's and my desire to participate in that league. "Smith— play first for Stevens!" shouted the insensitive coach, who proceeded to embarrass the child with harsh criticism and took him out of the game.

Danny was shocked and confused; he wondered why anyone would want to play such a lousy game. Even at his young age, my son empathized with the boy's pain. What Danny couldn't know yet was the potential aftershock

5

this incident could cause the heartbroken youngster, even well into adult-hood: Would he ever try to play again after such humiliation? What messages about his sense of self would he internalize? What would this memory do to his confidence, self-image, fear of failure, and vision of what he could or couldn't do in the future? Would he ever trust another coach? Would he ever play sports free of the anxiety and tension caused by this incident?

Unfortunately, this is not an unusual or isolated story. Most athletes in both individual and team sports experience from time to time tremendous pressure, fear, and anxiety generated by an overwhelming obsession to win. We learn this frame of mind from early childhood, and it is perpetuated by a competitive society that echoes with "the thrill of victory, the agony of defeat." Athletic pressure is epidemic, and it spills over into other arenas of performance, particularly in the academic and corporate worlds. Such atti-tudes undermine the very core of our individual integrity and values.

A recent *Sports Illustrated* interview with the president of Allegheny College, Daniel Sullivan, addressed the impact of this obsession with vic-tory, in a most powerful denouncement of college sports. "I cannot think of a single thing," he stated, "that has eroded public confidence in America's colleges and universities . . . more than intercollegiate athletics as it is practiced by a large faction of the universities in the NCAA's Division I and II. It is hard to teach integrity in the pursuit of knowledge or how to live a life of purpose and service, when an institution's own integrity is compromised in the unconstrained pursuit of victory on the playing fields." By contrast, the athletic department at Allegheny, he said, understands the role of sport in creating joy and fun while developing the athlete's potential as a human being.

The Western approach to sports has given rise to questionable ethical and moral means of competition and standards of success. The use of anabolic steroids in Olympic games, professional sports, and other athletic arenas has been widespread in all countries. Violence and cheating in sport reflect the "win at any cost" attitude. This pressure to win has a more devastating effect on overall athletic performance than perhaps anything else. The same attitudes toward sport carry over to the world of business and everyday life, making us ineffective in those arenas of performance, too.

This Western approach is also responsible for creating a number of major nonproductive, dysfunctional behavior patterns in athletes. Having worked with thousands of professional, Olympic, university, and recreational ath-letes, ages ten to seventy-five, I have seen how the following behavioral patterns, reinforced by our culture's competitive systems, stand in the way of their athletic and their personal joy, and their fulfillment and happiness in work and life in general. Most athletes today:

- constantly struggle for external recognition rather than internal satisfaction;

- measure their self-worth as an athlete or person solely on the outcome of their performances in sport, on the job, or in relationships of any kind;

- focus on attaining perfection in every task, instead of seeing life as a journey in search of excellence;

- treat their sport or goals as something to conquer, thereby expending valuable energy;

- have unrealistic expectations that result in frustration, disappointment, and distraction;

- blame others when things go wrong, and so feel out of control; and

- condemn themselves for their failures, setbacks, and mistakes, and so have a poor sense of self.

Athletics are big business, and athletes' well-being and health are often disregarded in the process. Athletes become statistics—living endorsements and walking billboards for corporate sponsors. A game's outcome, the result—"Who won?"—has become everything, supplanting the notion that sport is about passion and love for what you're doing.

In 1908, Pierre de Coubertin declared that "the goal of the Olympic Games is *not* to win but to take part." We seem to have gotten off track since then. Biased broadcasters during telecasts of the Olympic games, feeling a loyalty to the United States, exhibit a nationalistic bit of joy in the setbacks and mistakes of our close competitors; flags at awards ceremonies have become instruments of alienation and separateness rather than unification. The results of our overweening desire to be number one are the stresses, anxieties, drug use, and dishonesty that plague our sports and our society. Krishnamurti once said, "War is but a spectacular expression of our everyday life." So is sport an expression of our lives and attitudes.

PREPARATIONS FOR THE JOURNEY

行道

行道

A journey of a thousand miles
begins with a footstep.

TAO TE CHING no. 64

Playing a sport can be thought of as a spiritual journey that combines physical and mental activities. Unlike most physical sojourns, where you depart and arrive at a predetermined destination, the journey in *Thinking Body, Dancing Mind* is one of continuously new and exciting physical, mental, and spiritual beginnings and lifelong positive change. This journey has no final destination because you will be evolving and transforming constantly, thinking in new ways about how you work and play. By shifting your attitudes and beliefs about what is possible in your world, you will be able to redefine your potential, which is really unlimited, and unlock the extraordinary powers of your body-mind.

Sport also provides us with the perfect metaphor for understanding the dynamics of business and life. Athletic games are microcosmic dramas, with the same ups and downs, the jubilation and the sadness, the anger and the calm, the chaos and the peace, the success and failure that confront each of us in the macrocosmic drama of life. In sport, you experience every possible emotion and psychological state as you are forced to respond to myriad, constantly changing circumstances. As a distance athlete running marathons (26.2 miles) for many years, for instance, I have had numerous opportunities to enter into the states of mind of endurance, patience, persistence, fear, setback, and success in ways that are applicable in any of life's demanding events. By learning effective strategies and techniques for dealing with these fluctuating states of mind in sports, you, too, will be better equipped to handle parallel situations in business and life. Sports journalist Grantland Rice once said, "When that one Great Scorer comes to write against your name, he marks not that you won or lost, but how you played the game." To this I would add, "and how you lived your life day by day."

Philosopher Alan Watts used to say, "You don't dance to get to the other side of the floor." Nor, may I add, do we play to get to the finish of the event. Extraordinary performances and successes in sport, as in all of life, are created by our passionate moment-by-moment involvement. Our victories are natural by-products of this approach. Extraordinary performances come out of a process of continuous, regular physical and mental practice. The mindset of an extraordinary athlete is relaxed but focused and open to ever higher achievements. Real success or victory is measured by the quality of that very process of attention and mindful involvement, practice, and commitment.

THE EMERGENCE OF THE TAOATHLETE

The Tao of Nature is to serve
    without spoiling.
The Tao of evolved individuals is
    to act without contending.

TAO TE CHING no. 81

Taoism applied to sport enables you to notice and develop the inner strengths and personal qualities that can help you get into the mindset for extraordinary performance. It can help you learn how to react more harmoniously with the demanding situations you constantly face in athletics. In becoming a Tao-Athlete, you expand your repertoire of skills to meet the challenges of performance. TaoSport training provides you with a true understanding of the game, one that goes beyond the mere mechanical, routine ways in which

Western athletes tend to learn their skills. TaoSport training is a more dynamic, aware approach to overall excellence and success.

The New York City Marathon winner, Douglas Wakiihuri, epitomizes the TaoSport attitude. Born in Kenya and schooled in Japan, he brings an air of mysticism to athletics. In an interview following his wonderful performance in 1990, he stated that he could not separate marathoning from his search for the truths of life.

Consider the eloquent statement made by D. H. Lawrence in his classic work, *Mornings in Mexico.*

> Naked and daubed with clay to hide the
> nakedness, and to take the anointment of the earth;
> stuck over with bits of fluff of eagle's down, to be
> anointed with the power of air, the youths and men
> whirl down the racing tracks in relays. They are not
> racing to win a race . . . a prize . . . or show their
> prowess. They are putting forth all their might, strength
> in a tension that is half anguish, half ecstasy, in the
> effort to gather into their souls more and more of the
> creative fire . . . energy which will carry their tribe
> through the year, through the vicissitudes of the months.

In capturing the feeling of "breaking the four-minute mile," Roger Bannister, in his book by the same title, clearly displays a TaoSport attitude toward his event: "The earth seemed to move with me . . . a fresh rhythm entered my body. No longer conscious of my movement I discovered a new unity with nature . . . a new source of power and beauty, a source I never knew existed."

The Western approach to athletics emphasizes aggression, with the athlete a combatant and the game a battle. For the TaoAthlete, however, assertiveness replaces aggression and the physical game becomes the arena for the ongoing development of internal, psychological strengths. Tao-Athletes work to recognize and overcome "inner demons" that hinder their concentration and performance, all the self-imposed obstacles and limitations that they may have unconsciously erected.

A TaoAthlete's journey can be compared to the sacred path of the warrior, the heroic voyages in Homer's ancient epics, the Native American Indian vision quest, or Carlos Castaneda's envisioning of the impeccable warrior. Such warriors developed and exercised inner strength, integrity, and independence, but they also fought for a higher good beyond their own self-interest. TaoSport warriors, too, are ultimately in control of their destiny. They create inner and outer goals and strive to develop the skills to accomplish them—without seeking to destroy their competitors. The TaoAthlete

- is individualistic;

- has courage to risk failure, learn from setbacks, and forge ahead;

- possesses a multidimensional approach to competition;

- focuses on how the game is played (process) as opposed to outcomes (product);

- uses the event to gain greater self-realization;

- trains the mind to see through the complexity of outer trappings of athletics into its essence;

- knows his or her vulnerabilities and trains to strengthen them;

- creates balance, moderation, and simplicity when possible;

- sees competitors as partners who facilitate improvement;

- sees success as one part of the process of sports;

- understands that performance is a roller coaster and has the patience to ride the ups and downs;

- blends with forces so as not to create counterforce;

- has vision, and dreams things into possibilities; and

- enjoys sport for the pleasure it gives.

The TaoSports you learn in this book will facilitate your journey on this inner heroic path in athletics. They will help you create passion in your sports practice of extraordinary performance. They can help you redefine your athletic and human abilities and potential to take you to new levels of achievement. Your sport can become a way to practice the positive, holistic attitudes of the TaoAthlete. And since the way you meet challenges in sports is also how you usually approach challenges in life, you can learn to transfer Taoist principles from your game to the rest of your life as well. In fact, you could use the reverse approach and practice these TaoSports first in your work and relationships and then apply the principles to your game.

Although written about sports, this book is not meant only to be read by athletes or sports enthusiasts. If you are simply a sometime athlete, you may find yourself becoming enthusiastic about a sport as you read this book. Your sport may take on a totally new dimension when looked at from the perspective of the Tao. Athletes on many levels of play will benefit, as will directors and coaches, who can all use these TaoSports for more effective leadership. TaoSports will also help parents of children who play sports or who are thinking about becoming athletes. TaoSport concepts will guide and teach youngsters healthy ways to participate in athletics so that sports become a stage for learning valuable lifelong lessons. Finally, TaoSports are for all managers, supervisors, leaders, and business people who seek effective ways to attain levels of extraordinary performance and for all of us who desire to accomplish our daily routines with a new, refreshing view of life. Many doors open to the one Tao.

Keep in mind that no athlete or other person will ever be permanently focused and aligned with the qualities of TaoSports. When you lose touch with the mindfulness and balance of the TaoAthlete, however, know that you can return by, first, using the meditative and reflective techniques in this book to identify your problem or block and, then, by referring to the TaoSport strategy in this book that deals with that particular issue or concern.

Steve Gottlieb, an all-American tennis star from the University of California, practiced and trained using the principles of the Tao. Using TaoSport strategies, he improved his performance more in six months than in his previous ten years of playing tennis. When he graduated, he decided to go to law school and began preparing for the Law School Aptitude Test. He came in for an appointment with me because he was struggling, fighting, and forcing the process of preparation for the exam. He said he felt anxious, tense, tight, and unable to concentrate. The only thing I needed to say to him was, "Steve, you are a national champion and an all-American." To which he responded with glee, "That's right, it's the same thing. It's like preparing for the national championships." He left that day ready to "train" for this event using the precepts of TaoSports, just as he had for tennis. After months of committing himself to inner work and TaoSport practice, he needed only a single reminder to become re-aligned with the Tao and its power for performance. Relaxed, focused, centered, and balanced, he visualized his path and achieved his goal. The process was a joy; scoring well on the test was the bonus.

TaoSports provide a sense of yielding to forces in nature, as well as a much-needed balance to the incredible demands placed upon each of us in sports and everyday life. Being in a TaoSport frame of mind is, in a sense, an ideal way of being in the world. It is living an enlightened lifestyle, aligned with a Universal Way, aligned with the Tao or Way of Nature.

When you align with the Tao in all things, you hold the key to joy, success, and fulfillment in whatever you do. Following the Tao requires no special knowledge or learning; you simply need to follow the laws of nature. For example, we fight against making mistakes. But mistakes are a natural process; to be alive is to make mistakes. To align with the Tao, try to consider mistakes as nature's lessons from which you can learn, recover your energies, and forge ahead. According to the *Tao Te Ching*, setbacks are natural and inevitable. They are gifts that provide opportunities to improve your performance.

By reading *Thinking Body, Dancing Mind*, you will learn to develop a conscious awareness of the laws of nature, act in accordance with them, and in the process evolve as a more empowered, successful performer. TaoSports will help you discover your true dynamic self, your integrity as an athlete and person.

TaoSports provide immediate pathways to joy, fun, and excellence in sports. They are alternatives to Western attitudes that limit or hurt your performance and can enable you to create opportunity from failure, a heightened sense of confidence from negative self-image, and consistency in all aspects of play. The numerous recommendations in this book can redefine your full potential and free you to achieve it.

The *Tao Te Ching* functions as an alchemy in this modern Western world. Those who align with the principles of TaoSport begin to transform themselves, transcend the ordinary, and experience an inner freedom that enables them to become extraordinary in other arenas of life.

Olympic marathoner Nancy Ditz has had some extraordinary experiences using the principles of TaoSport. "The TaoSport approach has provided me with a whole new way of getting in touch with the real power I have within. TaoSport not only applies to all of sport, but to all of life as well. It is a refreshing, relaxing way to view performance."

Vince Stroth, offensive guard for the NFL Houston Oilers football team, claims that "TaoSport works so well that I have overcome many obstacles that haunted me for years. My game has improved immensely. I now have a more expansive view of myself and my capabilities."

Successful head tennis coach Bob Hansen of the University of California NCAA national champions, sees TaoSport as "the icing on the cake. It has given us the edge we needed." He recommends this approach to anyone who desires a complete, well-rounded approach to sports.

Terry Schroeder, captain of the 1984 and 1988 U.S. Olympic water polo team silver medalists, claims that these techniques help to create an excellent balance between body, mind, and spirit. "I have achieved beyond what I thought were limits not only in athletics but in all parts of my life."

Just as an athlete needs physical workouts, you will find that you need to practice these inner TaoSports regularly to get their maximum benefit. Changing attitudes is not easy. As Gandhi said, "Life is a constant vigil." If you purchase state-of-the-art carpentry hardware and then leave it all in the garage, nothing will get built. Use these tools for transformation diligently. The Russian novelist Fyodor Dostoyevsky once said, "A new philosophy, a way of life, is not given for nothing. . . . It is only acquired with much patience and great effort." According to the natural way, the Tao, these changes in your life and sport will be gradual and small at first. However, the payoff of your vigilance and practice will be a life of fulfillment and success in all arenas of performance. Persist on the journey, and greatness is yours.

HOW TO READ THIS BOOK

You may read this book gradually, chapter by chapter, from beginning to end, so that you gradually learn the skills and mindsets of a TaoAthlete. The book begins with a discussion of how to develop and keep an open "Beginner's Mind," and it adds inner skills and practices to take you to advanced TaoSport levels. Each chapter is also an entity unto itself, however, so that you can open the book and randomly select a particular topic that seems appropriate to your problem or question or frame of mind at any given time.

We've structured the six major parts of *Thinking Body, Dancing Mind* to reflect the steps involved in constructing a home. This metaphoric home will house your new thinking body and dancing mind. Once you learn the inner skills—the inner structure of this home—you can always return to it. And this is one house in which you can always play ball.

Each of the chapters within the larger parts mirrors one basic precept of the Tao. The introductory quotation for each chapter gives a teaching of the *Tao Te Ching* or the *I Ching* (the ancient Book of Change), and the chapter itself relates the teaching to sports. Using anecdotes, stories, affirmations, visualizations, and exercises, each chapter helps you train with and practice TaoSports first in athletics ("TaoSport Training for Athletics") and then in business and life ("TaoSports for Business and Life").

We urge you to read slowly and visualize the relevancy of each TaoSport exercise to your performance issue. See yourself, in your mind's eye, adapting a new way of thinking and feeling, in alignment with the qualities of the Tao.

To help you feel the spirit, the essence of TaoSports, we have provided a flowing energy with Chinese brush calligraphy. Let your mind play with this beautiful artwork if you find yourself stuck in your process of TaoSports. Meditate on the characters. You may find that the images and their beauty and strength will come to you in moments of crisis or when you need to draw on your spirit for extra effort and success. The images help you pull together TaoSport ideas into a visual, holistic symbol.

We hope that this book will also prompt you to go to the original Chinese source, the *Tao Te Ching*. Many people, when reading a scholarly translation of the *Tao Te Ching*, feel lost about how to apply its teachings. To help you, we have included excerpts from the *Tao Te Ching* and the *I Ching* and shown how these teachings are useful in sports, business, and everyday life.

VISUALIZATIONS

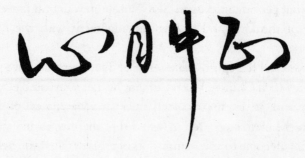

Meditation can renew both mind and body.
By pacifying stress that is based upon projection, true
relaxation can be attained. What springs forth
will be in accordance with your real needs.

I CHING no. 52

Learning to visualize is essential if you are to practice the TaoSports in this book. Visualization is an active form of meditation in which you relax and choose to view images in your mind's eye that will influence your emotions and energy. Visualization is a natural process. It lets you tap into your inner sources of peace and calm so that you can respond positively to events in your life. What you see in your mind's eye can strongly influence your beliefs and achievements. Our central nervous system does not distinguish between real and imagined events: It sees and accepts all images as if they were real. For example, close your eyes right now and imagine a juicy, sour lemon. In your mind, cut a big wedge from the lemon and place it in your mouth. Bite down, and let the sour juices permeate your entire mouth. Did you find yourself puckering or salivating?

In sports, the action in a game, the losses and the victories, is the result of the visions and images that the players carry with them. If you have an image of yourself blowing a lead, fumbling a ball, or missing a shot, you will create

16

tension and anxiety that, in turn, will contribute negatively to your performance. On the other hand, if you carry around with you images of success, you create an inner state of calm, confidence, and relaxation that contributes positively to actual success.

In the words of George Bernard Shaw, "Some people see things as they are and ask 'why?'; I dream things that never were and ask 'why not?' " In visualization exercises, you dream or visualize about your sport, work, and life. Think of how you look and feel when all goes well. When you are about to perform in a sport, take an exam, or give a presentation, imagine all the wonderful possibilities that may occur. Tapping into these memories and thought patterns mitigates tension, anxiety, and fear and improves your ability to perform well.

Golfing great Jack Nicklaus, in his book, *Golf My Way*, talks about having very sharp, distinct images in his mind prior to each shot. "First I 'see' the ball where I want it to finish, nice and white and sitting up high on bright green grass. Then the scene quickly changes and I 'see' the ball going there: its path, trajectory, and shape, even its behavior on landing. Then there is a sort of fade-out, and the next scene shows me making the kind of swing that will turn the previous images into reality."

Olympic gold medalist Mary Lou Retton used visualization and imagery prior to all of her splendid performances and has recalled, "I always pictured myself positively. It gave me confidence. It was especially helpful in the Olympics, which were so important to me. I did all the routines in my head the night before competition. Since I usually had trouble on the balance beam, I'd review that in my mind a lot, picturing myself landing straight on the beam."

Elizabeth Manley, silver medalist in figure skating at the 1988 Olympics, believes that the visualization process was the key to her success. "In learning to execute the difficult triple Lutz jump under tremendous pressure, for example, I would stand at the side of the boards, close my eyes, and picture myself doing the jump perfectly in my mind. Nine out of ten times I would successfully do it by preparing this way."

Sue Holloway, a member of the 1976 Canadian Olympic ski and kayaking teams and a 1984 silver and bronze medalist in kayaking, believes "There are no bounds to what can be done mentally." As she has stated, when she rehearses her race starts, if she makes a mistake, she goes back and starts over until she gets it down perfectly.

Visualization is not magical or psychological hocus-pocus—it is a learned skill. When you practice it regularly, it will enable you to perform up to or beyond what you perceived as your potential. It works because it acts like a dress rehearsal. It is a form of practice that makes you familiar with the script for the task ahead of you. When the time comes for the actual performance, you have a sense that you have already experienced this moment or action and everything seems easier, familiar. In addition, visualization clears the mind of interfering, negative images that block your efforts to perform well by replacing them with images of success. You may be the best at what you do, but negative images can create anxiety and tension to hinder you. Positive images relax the mind and body and allow you to perform well.

GETTING STARTED

The TaoSports in this book give you numerous ways to use visualization. Here are some pointers in getting started: Before you begin each visualization exercise, find a quiet place, close your eyes, take five deep breaths, and relax. To get into the state of deep relaxation you need for visualization, I recommend a technique called Deep Abdominal Breathing (DAB). While there are many ways to become relaxed, the DAB method is easy to learn, quick, and effective. I've used it successfully with thousands of people. After practicing this three times a day for two to three weeks, you will be able to create a state of deep relaxation within fifteen seconds.

Practice the following DAB method with each exercise in this book. Some people have difficulty closing their eyes at first. Do what's most comfortable for you. You can partially close your eyes, or just fix them on a single object to narrow your field of vision and block out all external visual stimuli. In time, you'll be able to close your eyes.

Exercise: Deep Abdominal Breathing

• Breathe only through your nostrils (unless they're clogged); mouth breathing is not relaxing.

• Inhale very slowly; as you do, push your abdomen out as far as you can, as if it were a balloon expanding. As a result, your diaphragm will move downward, allowing full lower extension of the lungs. Breathe deeply, but not forcefully, since this may defeat the purpose of relaxing as well as cause you to hyperventilate. If you feel dizzy during the initial practice sessions, simply take slower, shallower breaths.

- When your abdomen reaches full extension, slowly and smoothly draw back your shoulders and raise your head. Continue to breathe in and fill the upper part of your lungs as much as you can.

- You have used your entire respiratory system. Now hold the breath for five seconds.

- Release, exhaling slowly through your nostrils. Draw in the abdomen, holding for two seconds before taking the next breath.

- *Repeat* this process for five breaths (more if needed), and as you do, count down 5-4-3-2-1, saying one number on each exhalation. "Feel" yourself getting deeper and deeper into relaxed calmness.

- What is the first image that comes to your mind about the relaxed state you're in? Some people see steady, glowing lights filled with potential energy. Others see calmly flowing waters, or tall, strong trees, or an animal or person whose character they admire. Remember this image as a source of inner peace or strength for you.

- When coming out of the relaxed state, count slowly 1-2-3-4-5. At five say, "I am relaxed, alert, and in fine health." Avoid abrupt transitions, if possible.

- As you become more adept at this technique, try using just three deep breaths.

Use this method to become deeply relaxed prior to each visualization in this book or any imagery exercise that you create for yourself. Since you are developing a new skill, it may take you a week or so to activate the imagery process. After some practice, you'll be able to create a deep, relaxed state and the images will begin to flow freely.

Some people have a tremendous capacity for imagining immediately, while others require more time before the images begin to flow. If you experience difficulty, here is a way to help yourself improve your capability. Look out the window of your home for two minutes, noticing everything in detail. Now, close your eyes and recall and re-create as many details as you can. See the scene as vividly as you could with your eyes open. Practice this once a day for three days.

Visualization: A Quiet, Tranquil Place

It often helps the visualization process if, before you take your five deep breaths, you begin by entering a mental sanctuary, an imaginative place that provides a feeling of calm and tranquillity during your visualizations. Choose a beautiful, favorite natural environment for this "home." You may picture a house in a high mountain meadow or a place nestled among beautiful sand dunes looking out to the expansive ocean. Create the protected, quiet environment of your best fantasy. Practice DAB with this visualization.

Picture yourself in a quiet place. With your eyes closed, take five deep breaths and relax. Mentally look around and notice all the details, sounds, smells, and beauty of the peaceful environment around you. It is your ideal space. Arrange it any way you wish. Perhaps you have a large deck— see yourself standing on it looking out to the beauty of nature. Or your home looks out into the shaded, cool beauty of a forest or onto a warm, sunny meadow. This sanctuary is under your total control. You choose who comes, who stays, and who goes. Begin to feel comfortable. Know that you have control over your life here and that what you decide will happen here can happen when you return to the outside world. If you decide you want to take the peace and calm you feel in this safe home with you into your interactions with family, friends, and colleagues, know that you can do so. You can create an inner sanctum, an inner peaceful home for yourself at any time of the day or night. You can enter this place whenever you need a moment of peace or whenever you have a problem or issue you want to meditate on or resolve. You can also create an image or a picture of any object in this inner sanctum that makes you calm and happy, that, when you think of it during work or play, will make you smile, remember this inner peace, and relax.

Now, begin to come out of your relaxed state. With your eyes closed, count slowly from one to five and feel yourself becoming more aware of

your actual surroundings with each number you
count. Slowly open your eyes when you reach
five, and tell yourself, "I am relaxed, focused,
healthy, and strong, ready to face the day and the
task at hand."

WHEN TO USE VISUALIZATION

Your imagination can be trained like a muscle. If you wanted to build up your body, you wouldn't go to the gym only once a week and expect results. So, too, you need to work out mentally and consistently. Current research suggests that extraordinary athletes and other achievers practice their physical *and mental* skills regularly and consistently.

Begin to form a habit of using visualization daily. Set aside ten to fifteen minutes a day, either when you rise in the morning or at the end of the day before bed. It's best to visualize before eating or two to three hours after a meal. Personally, I find the morning hours quiet and peaceful. When I begin my day with a visualization and mental rehearsal of that day, the events unfold according to my outlook.

A question I am often asked is, "Isn't it dangerous to get my hopes up by visualizing the positive and risk being disappointed? Maybe I should prepare for the worst and if everything turns out okay, great." It's true that preparing for negative possibilities will prevent disappointment, but such thinking also contributes to negative outcomes that weren't necessarily inevitable. Disappointment will not kill you; why not increase the likelihood of positive results through the use of visualization?

> Cherish your vision and your dreams as they are the children
> of your soul—the blueprints of your ultimate achievements.
>
> —Napoleon Hill

USING ANCHORS

To create an instant, positive state of mind for a performance, whether you need to be relaxed, calm, focused, centered, patient, or any other state, you can use what I call an anchor as a reference point or cue. Like Pavlov's dog, who would salivate at the sound of a bell, you can relax, focus, or be whatever you choose if you associate that feeling with a word such as *relax* or *calm* or *focus* while you are visualizing a favorite image.

When you are in a relaxed state in your inner sanctum, repeat the anchor word over and over, telling yourself that when you recall it during a real performance, you will become what that word signifies. As you say your anchor word during a visualization, feel peaceful and calm throughout your entire being. You now have a reference point for relaxing immediately.

Another way of anchoring uses a physical stimulation instead of a word. For example, press your thumb against your index finger to form a circle, or make a fist. While you are visualizing and relaxing, hold your fingers or fist in this way, and tell yourself that when you do this, you will be centered, assertive, positive, detached, passionate, or any other quality that you need to rely on for strength. Be sure to feel that centeredness, assertiveness, or passion in your relaxed visual state as you make that particular physical anchor. Then, when you're waiting for a pitch, changing sides in a match, or going to the foul line or in a huddle, you can form the anchor and produce an instant positive mindset to help you perform.

AFFIRMATIONS— THE LANGUAGE OF TAOSPORTS

Affirmations are very important tools for awakening to the Tao and living with its forces. They are strong, positive statements about something that is already true or has the realistic potential for becoming true. If you're having a hard day, for instance, tell yourself, "I am calm and happy in the moment." Just by being open to this thought and saying it to yourself, you will allow yourself to become nearer to this positive state of mind and even to *become* calm and happy. To replace the random, endless, negative, or positive chatter that filters into your mind each moment of the day, affirmations are conscious, preplanned, positive thoughts to direct your actions and behaviors in a productive way. Unless you direct your own thoughts, you leave much to chance. With affirmations, you can change patterns of negative thought that, like tape recordings in your head, continue to play old, counterproductive tunes. Affirmations help you develop your full potential with new, positive phrases. Words truly can transform the quality of your existence.

People often have difficulty with affirmations because they feel as though they are deceiving themselves when they make statements about something that may be true in the future but is not true now. An athlete, for example, may have this difficulty when he or she affirms, "I am a national champion," before he or she has actually become a champ. What we all need to remember is that affirmations are not self-*deception*, they are self-*direction*. They point your feet in the direction you wish to travel and enable you to be more willing to do all you have to do to reach your goal. Even if you affirm greatness but fall short of your potential or your best showing, you still will have gone further than you would have if you hadn't set your sights high.

Application of Affirmations

In his book *Human Options*, Norman Cousins emphasizes the importance of language—our words—for performance. "The principal language of this age," he states, "must be concerned with the awakening of vast multitudes to the possibilities rather than the limitations of life."

I suggest that you write your affirmations on three-by-five-inch index cards and strategically place them in areas that you visit frequently during the day: the bathroom mirror, the refrigerator door, the dashboard of your car, next to the telephone. Recite the affirmations when you notice the cards. After some practice, you will have memorized them and be able to recall them when you need them. Keep the cards visible as reminders to yourself to think about your direction in sports, business, or life.

Affirmations are most effective if, as you recite each one, you take thirty seconds to visualize what the affirmation is saying. If you affirm, for example, "I am a national champion," see yourself winning an important event. Feel what it would be like to be such a star.

The chapters in *Thinking Body, Dancing Mind* suggest many affirmations from which you can choose to help you align yourself with the Tao and improve your performance. You may even be inspired to create your own affirmations for yourself. In sport—as in all activities—affirmations are quite useful in turning fear into confidence, increasing your concentration, preventing you from pushing yourself too hard or becoming more frustrated, reducing self-criticism, sharpening your skills, helping you cope with fatigue, treating injuries, and carrying out any other performance tasks that you may need to address.

In life outside sports, you can help yourself create a more positive self-image through the use of affirmations. Perhaps you want to create real changes in your physical appearance. Seeing yourself as you desire yourself to be will facilitate your movement toward that dream. Affirm to yourself: "Slim and thin, I run to win." During times when you are particularly self-critical, if you consciously choose loving, caring phrases, you can help yourself change the negativity you feel. Tell yourself, "I am talented, intelligent, and creative," or "I deserve the best," or "I am abundant and have a lot to offer."

Use affirmations to become more self-accepting, to feel good, to develop relationships, to become more creative—or even to relieve boredom.

Guidelines for Creating Personal Affirmations

Use the affirmations provided in this book or that you create on your own to suit specific situations. The following guidelines will help you formulate workable, powerful affirmations:

1. *Be positive.* Affirm what you want, not what you don't want. Avoid negative statements. Don't say, "I will not overeat today," because it may be picked up by the brain as, "I will overeat." Instead, say, "I am eating lightly today."

2. *Be present.* Frame your statements as if the future were now, not as if it were still coming. In this way, you transform the future from a wish that is always coming but never arriving into a present reality. Rather than saying, "I will be happy," say, "I am happy"—even if it's not true yet. Act "as if," and it will keep you on track.

3. *Be concise.* If your affirmations become too wordy, you tend to become lost and confused with the verbiage, and so will your mind. Simplicity is also the key to remembering the affirmations.

4. *Be rhythmic.* A cadence and rhyme will tend to deeply impress affirmations into your central nervous system. For example: "I'm in position to strike and get what I like," or, "Better every day in every way." Phrasing your affirmations this way will help you remember them more easily.

5. *Be conscientious.* It's better to repeat affirmations fifteen times, twice a day, than to wait for Sunday and devote one full hour to them. "Every day I say the way" is a good affirmation to help you become consistent in your practice.

■ II ■

THE
FOUNDATION

ENTERING THE TAO:
THE BEGINNER'S MIND

A successful businessman went to a Zen master and announced he had come to learn all about Zen. The master invited the man to sit down and have tea. As the master poured the tea, it overflowed. The businessman shouted, "It's spilling, it's spilling!" To which the master replied, "Precisely—you came with a full cup. Your cup is already spilling over, so how can I give you anything? Unless you come with emptiness, I can give you nothing."

Your journey into TaoSports begins when you empty your mind of all the overused and undernourishing ideas you have inherited about athletics, business, and life. By opening your mind and being receptive—a mindset called the Beginner's Mind—you invite many new attitudes on which you can build your TaoSport approach to all of life. Using your Beginner's Mind, you will see things in a refreshing, exhilarating way, and become aware of a multitude of alternative avenues that lead to extraordinary performance.

Come into these TaoSports with an empty mind. Open yourself up to your unlimited potential for achievement. This is your initiation into the eloquence of the thinking body and the grace of the dancing mind.

志ちえ

BELIEFS

信不足焉
有不信焉

Those who lack belief
will not in turn be believed.

TAO TE CHING no. 23

Your attitudes and beliefs influence what you experience in life. Personal power is directly related to your mindset. What you believe, you become.

An athlete's mindset is crucial in every aspect of performance. In the words of psychologist John Lilly, "Beliefs are limits to be examined and transcended." Stated differently, Henry Ford once proclaimed, "Whether you think you can, or think you can't, you're probably right."

In 1954, the entire sports world believed that it was humanly impossible to run a mile in faster than four minutes. Their limiting belief was supported by research reported in more than fifty medical journals throughout the world attesting to that "fact." We now know that Roger Bannister challenged and broke through that barrier. What is not so well known is that the sub—four-minute mile was achieved by more than forty-five runners within the next eighteen months. It is difficult to believe that all those athletes increased their performance within that short amount of time. A more likely explanation is that once the four-minute barrier was broken, they all be-lieved it could be broken again.

If your mind believes "I can't," you will sabotage your own efforts. You won't do what's required to realize the goal. But when you use the Beginner's Mind, you believe, "I can," and you follow paths of behavior and thought that help ensure that the dream will be fulfilled. The psychology of dream fulfillment includes the mindsets of hope, motivation, commitment, confi-dence, courage, concentration, excitement, and observation.

As the *Tao Te Ching* recommends on the previous page, you need to work to renounce your restrictive beliefs about what you can and can't do in sport. Your power as an athlete starts with the awareness that you have unlimited potential once you align yourself with the belief "I can." Remember that acting "as if" you can achieve something is self-direction, not self-deception. It places you on the road of excellence. As you forge ahead, you can learn from your setbacks and mistakes.

Hard opinions about yourself distort the truth about your potential. The Tao teaches you to be flexible in your beliefs: Rigidity will block your growth. The *Tao Te Ching* (no. 49) simply yet powerfully states: "Evolved individuals have no fixed mind." Fixed mindsets obscure the unlimited boundaries of your potential. Keep your mind open; keep a Beginner's Mind.

TAOSPORT TRAINING FOR ATHLETICS

When you are in the Beginner's Mind, you act as if you can accomplish something. After I conducted a series of workshops with the cross-country team at Anderson University in Indiana, I was presented with a T-shirt that said in bold print: ACT AS IF. The team all acted as if they were champions—and they fulfilled the prophecy, producing several all-American distance stars.

Most athletes on all levels of play, from the recreational enthusiast up to the professional, utilize far less than half of their potential to achieve. Why should you believe anything other than "I can"? Approach each free throw, putt, pitch, fly ball, pass, stroke, spike, or technical maneuver with a positive inner belief of yes—act "as if," and activate your concentration, confidence, and courage.

The Tao teaches us to neutralize an extreme force with its opposite force. Fight fire with water; fight anger with love; fight "I can't" with "I can." Our ability to neutralize extremes gives us the power to alter reality. Beginning to believe you can rather than can't is your ultimate power to alter your game and win. Simply act "as if" you can.

Exercise: Acting "As If"

Vince Stroth, an offensive guard with the NFL's Houston Oilers, once came to me in order to improve his mental game. I asked him how he desired to play each game. He replied, "I want to be consistently alert and 'on top' of each down; to be persistent, 'dig in,' and keep the pressure on; to never go away and to make my presence always felt." I suggested to him that this sounded like a description of an animal—actually, like a badger. Vince got excited as I told him to act "as if" he were a mean, wild badger. The very next game against the Los Angeles Raiders, Vince the Badger played in a way that is rarely matched by anyone at his position, culminating when he played a major role in two scoring drives.

This "as if" exercise is similar to exercises that actors do. Choose a person (perhaps a well-known athlete) or animal that possesses a quality or trait that you'd like to emulate. World-class runner Jon Sinclair, for example, exudes confidence and mental tenacity. He runs with the fluidity and grace of a tireless deer and never lets up. Jon's an excellent model for me, as a runner, and I imagine, always, what it feels like to be him as I run. I imitate him in all respects as an athlete.

Once you choose your symbol or image, pair yourself with it during your visualizations. Then, prior to any performance, act as if you were that model.

Affirmations for Believing in Self

To develop strong beliefs in yourself, construct a number of affirmations that make firm for you what you must believe to achieve. A forty-year-old tennis client, for example, wanted to believe he could be ranked in the top five in his age group in Northern California. He actually had the right stuff, but mentally he couldn't quite believe in himself. I suggested he repeat over and over, "I am one of the top five players in Northern California" and "I am the California state champion" (even though this was a definite stretch for him). With such self-direction, he acted "as if" he had already secured his position. He wrote these affirmations on cards and posted them everywhere. When he did his daily visualization, he imagined himself playing as if he were this champion. When he practiced, he reminded himself, "I am a champ and I play like one," even when he wasn't keeping score. He eventually earned a number-two state ranking—a place much higher than he had believed possible prior to his TaoSport training.

Affirmations like the following will help you reinforce the power of your belief in yourself:

- *"What I believe, I receive."*
- *"I am ———."* (*Fill in the blank to reflect your direction or who you are.*)
- *"Beliefs are limits; stretch and go beyond."*
- *"Fixed minds detract from potential. Flexible minds are the essential."*

Visualization: Expanding Beliefs

William James, the great American philosopher, once said that the greatest discovery of his generation was that "human beings, by changing the inner beliefs of their minds, can change the outer aspects of their lives." What you believe, you will achieve. In *The Art of Strategy*, R. L. Wing says, "Your inner opponent's greatest advantage is your lack of belief in your ultimate triumph." Do not doubt yourself or your ability to succeed.

> Find a quiet place, close your eyes, take five deep abdominal breaths, and relax. Recall a situation where you've told yourself, "That's too hard, I could never do that—no way." Now, understand that if you've learned to walk, you probably can accomplish most athletic skills. See yourself performing "as if" you were an athlete with great skill, dexterity, and talent. See yourself doing what you believed you couldn't. Feel "in the groove" playing as a natural for this particular sport. Feel yourself concentrating as you confidently accomplish the goal. Feel the sense of elation, and now believe that you are capable of such achievement.

TAOSPORTS FOR BUSINESS AND LIFE

I have learned much about how self-limiting beliefs work from my seven-year-old son, Daniel. On one of our afternoon walks, Dan noticed a beautiful apple tree atop a twelve-foot brick wall. "Dad, climb up there and get us some apples," he enthusiastically requested. I immediately gave him five reasons why I couldn't, but he wouldn't buy any of them. "C'mon, Dad, you can do it—I know you can." "Danny, boy, no way—I can't." To which he responded, "Please." I thought to myself, Okay, I'll start going up to the wall and prove to him that, indeed, I can't do it. As I reached the wall, I noticed that the bricks were protruding slightly. I gingerly gave the climb a shot—step by step, holding the edges of bricks with my fingertips. As I crawled over the top, I heard Dan yell: "Way to go, big guy! I knew you could do it!"

This challenge illustrates perfectly how our beliefs can limit or open our lives. How many of us face obstacles or walls in the way of progress and let the belief "I can't, no way" block our journey? We have to practice refraining from making these judgments and assume "I can" until we're proven wrong. As we approach and try these seemingly insurmountable hurdles, we just might discover the incremental steps we need to take to get over them.

Affirmations for Expanding Beliefs

Keeping a Beginner's Mind about your potential in sport is no different from how you should travel your path in business and daily life. Your worst enemy is yourself; the greatest obstacle is your mind and its beliefs about what is possible. Activate these psychological processes by assuming "I can." We often hear inside of us the same voices of the people who drilled our limited beliefs into us from birth. To help silence these negative voices, you can use the following affirmations:

- *"I say 'I can' to my dreams that seem impossible."*
- *"I question authority when I am confronted by the harsh limiting beliefs of so-called experts."*
- *"The past is no indicator of what I can do in the present. I believe!"*
- *"Believing 'I can' is self-direction, not self-deception."*

- *"If I shoot for the sun and miss, I'll become one of the stars."*
- *"When I 'act as if,' I get a lift."*
- *"Labeling is disabling. I don't judge or limit the outer boundaries of my potential."*

Exercise: Mitigating Irrational Beliefs

Here are some of the more common irrational belief statements that reinforce "I can't," thereby preventing us from experiencing our full potential at work and in other aspects of life: "I'm too old, short, fat, tall, skinny, stupid." "I'm not ready." "They're so much better than I am." "I'm incompetent, unprofessional." "I don't deserve to win." "I don't deserve happiness."

Take the example of someone who feels incompetent at work because she failed to complete an assignment to her manager's satisfaction. She begins to doubt her own abilities as a result. By asking herself the following questions, she will be able to shed light on the truth of her beliefs:

1. "How valid is my belief that I am incompetent? Do I not complete tasks well all the time? Isn't this just one mistake in a long history of good performances?" Probably her self-doubt has no validity when she views her setback in this larger context.

2. "How would I feel if I changed my belief about myself to reflect the truth?" She might restate her belief by saying, "Generally, I'm quite competent and very professional. Occasionally I make errors, but that's human. I do my work as well as, or better than, anyone else." By thinking in this way, she experiences less pressure and anxiety, and consequently can work even more effectively.

POSITIVE THINKING

Those who identify with the Tao
Are likewise welcomed by the Tao.
Those who identify with Power
Are likewise welcomed by Power.
Those who identify with failure
Are likewise welcomed by failure.

TAO TE CHING no. 23

According to the Tao, the words you use to express yourself are the seeds of your future experiences. If you think negatively, you'll fail; think positively, and you'll succeed. As we saw in the preceding chapter, deeply ingrained beliefs or attitudes can be uprooted and changed by using the power of positive thought and words. This chapter will help you become more aware of how to use positive thinking to create change. A Beginner's Mind is a positive mind.

In sport, athletes' negative thought patterns create mental and physical resistances that greatly hinder their performance. Try the following test: Hold your arm out straight, while a friend tries to push it down. Resist the pressure as you say out loud, "I love my sport," over and over. Now change the phrase to "I hate my sport," and compare the strength you experience.

Notice how much stronger you are, and how much better your performance is, when you vocalize "I love"—a positive thought pattern.

Imagine the implications for your performance when you repeatedly verbalize that you hate hills, wind, exercise, weights, sprints, practice, traveling, playing away, and any other items you generally dislike. Simply changing the statements to "I love" will provide you with more physical strength and energy, resulting in a more powerful, natural performance. Try to discover some things about what you detest that you can "love" and focus on those. Many runners hate hills, for example, but these wonderful obstacles offer them the opportunity to develop their strength and increase their heart's efficiency.

I was recently invited to the Penn State University campus to work with the athletic department's track-and-field team. During one of my clinics, I emphasized to the team members the importance of their viewing hills in cross-country meets as positive partners for gaining an advantage. I even asked them to begin to love hills. The following week, in a race against ten other universities, Penn State was running shoulder to shoulder with an opponent whose team featured three all-Americans. At mile four, they came up against a gruesome hill. It was anyone's race at that point. All of a sudden, a voice out of nowhere screamed, "You love hills! You love hills! You love hills!" Penn State's head coach was reminding them of the lesson they learned in the clinic. Penn State "dropped" all their competitors at that precise moment and ran away with a sweet victory.

Athletes increasingly discover the power of positive attitude and thought. Triathlete Mark Allen, for example, attributes his spectacular victory in the 1989 Ironman over Dave Scott to his Zen-like ability to focus on positive thoughts. Scott, by contrast, simply refuses to fight the negative chatter in his head or let go of the negative by replacing it with the positive.

Positive attitude and thought are conveyed to the body-mind in the language of affirmations. Strong positive statements "make firm" what is already true or has the potential to become true. Since your athletic achievement is usually a reflection of your images, and your images follow from your thoughts and words, it pays to construct a language of affirmation that complements the positive pathways of the rest of your training. By so doing, you replace negative inner chatter and counterproductive mental tapes with a fresh, clear, helpful inner coach who can lead you to success. In neither Taoism nor in t'ai chi practice does allowing positive thoughts to propel our actions mean that we ignore the difficulties of life's circumstances. Rather, the Tao balances the negative with the positive, and life's difficulties and seemingly negative occurrences often become lessons that show us how to forge ahead.

In his book *Inner Game of Tennis*, Tim Gallwey states, "I know of no single factor that more greatly affects our ability to perform than the image we have of ourselves." Part of positive thinking is having a positive self-image. Each athlete carries around a mental blueprint of self, based on a rigid belief system formed by past performances. All your actions mirror this image. Most of the time, your performance is a reflection of how you see yourself.

We are all born natural athletes, yet some of us are told as children that we are uncoordinated and clumsy. If we believe these labels imposed on us, we usually avoid physical activity, and this avoidance then perpetuates the unathletic characteristics since we never give ourselves the chance to develop our physical selves. Even the best athletes carry around internal signs that say, "My backhand is weak," or "I can't spike," or "I buckle under pressure."

You can work to free yourself of these negative labels. Get in touch with the real athletic you.

The performance of Chris, a runner, is totally determined by his opinion about himself. "I'm not athletic," he says. "In my younger days, the neighborhood kids would never pick me for their team. At the age of thirty-four I took up running to get into shape and shed some pounds—now I'm hooked on the sport. I've been training diligently for two years and I still can't get below 43 minutes for a 10,000-meter race. I'd love to run faster, but I guess I can't. I'm a bit clumsy, slow, and awkward—I can't help it. I've always been that way. Really—I don't see myself as a runner. I don't know why. Have I reached my potential?"

Chris has clearly not come close to his potential. But he has created barriers to his further achievement rooted in his childhood that he has to get past. He can change from awkward and slow if he is determined.

To begin the process of forming an accurate, positive image of yourself, remember that like the Tao, you are a natural process: You grow, blossom, and unfold according to the principles of nature. You will experience a powerful new image by nurturing your inner, true self through the use of positive affirmations and visualizations. Your athletic performance will begin to mirror this new image rather than the more limited version. Be sure to re-create your positive self-image as your performance improves. When you set a personal, school, or national record, reset your image of yourself to reflect the new you. If you fail to do so, you will not continue to perform up to this new level; your results will vary according to the image.

TAOSPORT TRAINING FOR ATHLETICS

Prior to the 1988 Track and Field Olympic Trials, a world-class runner was concerned about making the U.S. Olympic team and came to me to see if I could help her performance. She knew that her negative thought patterns would virtually destroy any hopes she had of going to Seoul. I suggested to her that she rephrase her negative thoughts about not making the team to: "I am a member of the 1988 women's 1,500-meter Olympic team." I asked her to write this positive thought on three-by-five index cards and place them in various places: on her bathroom mirror, the dashboard of her car, her track bag, the refrigerator door, and her purse. For six months, every time she encountered one of these cards, she was to recite the phrase and imagine it to be true. Essentially, she was "brainwashing" herself, cleaning her mind of the negative and replacing it with the positive. Not only did she make the Olympic team, she ran her best during the part of the race she had previously hated, and she set a personal record in the process.

Affirmations for Positive Thinking

- *"I am in control and ready to roll."*
- *"Calm and confident, I play well."*
- *"Expect success, I'm one of the best."*
- *"I love my sport!"*
- *"Positive thinking will stop me from sinking."*
- *"Think high if you want to fly."*
- *"Positive thoughts awaken me to possibility."*
- *"I am an athlete who sees the positive side to all outcomes."*

Remember that affirmations tap into the Tao. The TaoAthlete moves away from negative, resistive thinking and into close harmony with the reality of positive possibilities.

Visualization: Positive Results

The following visualization exercise will help you to turn a negative situation into a positive one. Remember to find a quiet place, close your eyes, take five deep breaths, and relax.

> Imagine a specific personal situation in sport that has strong negative overtones for you. If you're a runner, for example, see yourself getting a cramp halfway into the race. Experience every aspect of the scene, and when you feel yourself getting anxious and tight, say *"Stop!"* and erase the scene and the negative feelings. Empty your Beginner's Mind. Breathe in and out three times.
>
> Now, re-create the same scenario, but this time design it in such a way that you know you are in control. You are positive, and you see yourself responding to the situation in a helpful way—exactly the way you would want. Perhaps you see yourself running through the cramp and it dissolves. Or you give yourself an image that will carry you through fatigue. Once you obtain a clear new image, forget the negative problem and continue to practice this new, productive exercise mentally twice a day for six weeks, until it works for you in your sport. Remember that you need to confront and work at changing old habits for at least four weeks before you can really say that they've been supplanted with new positive behavior.

Visualization: Positive Self-Image

As an athlete, you are probably familiar with the replacement drinks that replace the valuable electrolytes lost during strenuous exercise. This visualization will help you to replace vital positive "imagelights" (highlights about the real you) lost during life or after a poor performance.

Imagine numerous athletic water bottles (the kind you see on bikes will do) on your training table. Each bottle contains an ingredient that when ingested will create itself within you. See and read the labels: self-confidence, patience, strength, gracefulness, fluidness, quickness, excellence, calmness, courageousness, and any other qualities you'd love to possess.

> As you drink from each bottle, see and feel the
> ingredients flowing through your entire body.
> Feel them being absorbed into your skin and
> organs. Imagine looking into a full-length mirror
> and seeing yourself become this athlete. Affirm:
> "My performance in sport is aligned with this
> wonderful self-image." See yourself performing
> your sport according to this new portrait; feel the
> joy and satisfaction. Affirm: "I now release all
> images from the past that limited my potential. I
> am, and play in harmony with this changed
> image."

Affirmations for Self-Image

These affirmations will help you remember the connection between your positive self-image and performance, and that you have control over your self-image.

- *"How I see me, I will be."*
- *"My performance is a perfect mirror of my image of self."*
- *"I have a strong positive self-image as a powerful athlete."*
- *"How I see myself is my responsibility. Work at making it work."*
- *"I become what I imagine."*
- *"I imagine an unlimited self."*

Exercise: Remembering Your Greater Self

In your journal, training log, or notebook, make a list of every single success you've experienced in sport, from as far back as you can remember. Reaching goals, winning championships, titles held, awards won, teams selected for, a timely hit or basket to win a game are but a few. Keep this list and add to it periodically. Read the list to yourself during moments of self-doubt and affirm these accomplishments as indicators of who you are as an athlete. You may even consider re-creating the feeling of success you had by visualizing one or more of these past experiences.

TAOSPORTS FOR BUSINESS AND LIFE

Most of us are bombarded with negative comments in our lives at the daily rate of about fifteen to one. Keeping focused on constructive thought patterns is a tremendous challenge for anyone. It's unrealistic to expect yourself to always be on the right path. Once you become aware of your negative patterns of thought and behavior, however, you can counterbalance them with positive actions more easily. You can enhance your performance on the job, at home, and in social situations when your mind and heart are positive.

A work team at AT&T in Denver, Colorado, was tired, burned out, and unhappy as a result of their department manager's "habit of negativity." Whenever a worker did something positive, the manager would be silent and exude a "that's only to be expected" attitude. But if a worker slipped up, he'd assault him with put-downs and criticism. Naturally, in this environment the workers' productivity was dismal. As a group, they composed a letter to the department manager stating that if he "accentuated the positive and eliminated the negative," he would see less absenteeism and illness and would encounter happier, more productive employees. They told him specifically how he could accomplish this: by being constructive when setbacks occurred, and by helping workers to correct their errors. They asked him to give them monthly statements that first emphasized those areas that were positive, then critically assessed how to change those things that needed changing. He accepted their advice, and the subsequent turnaround was miraculous. One of the more powerful changes he made was to institute a morning class on the last Friday of each month for three hours on company time. Here he discussed with the group ways to work more effectively and smartly. This was followed by a group lunch to give themselves a chance to be together socially, away from the workplace.

Guides for Positive Thinking and Positive Acts

- If you have children, give them lots of loving, positive images and statements each night just as they begin to fall asleep. They are most receptive to such comments in this relaxed state. Tell them, for example, "Joey, you are a wonderful boy, I love you. Jessica, you're terrific, and I'm happy you're part of this family. Mark, you're a handsome, healthy guy." When they awaken the next morning, they seem to be more loving and peaceful. Vary what you say to keep it interesting and relevant to what's presently happening in your lives.

- To foster greater allegiance, cooperation, and communication among those with whom you work, find sincere, truthful ways to encourage and compliment their positive attributes. You can always find something good to say about someone—just notice it and act upon it.

- To affirm your professional, personal, parental, physical, and social self—since positive currents start from within—maintain a pack of index cards containing positive personal phrases. Read a few of these at the beginning of each day. When I do this, things usually go well.

- To deepen your level of intimacy with your friends, use positive statements affirming their greatness and importance in your life when the opportunity presents itself. When they're being negative, gently infuse them with a dose of tender love, then redirect the downward spiral. For instance, you might say, "Yes, Larry, it has been a tough day, but I love you. How can I help you?"

- To transform negativity, remember that every cloud has a silver lining. Every aspect of every day in everyone's life has simultaneously a negative and a positive charge: The glass is both half empty and half full. Notice how much better you feel when you focus on what's there rather than on what's missing.

Visualization: Overcoming Self-Doubt

The following visualization will help you to turn a negative situation into a positive situation when you are approaching a new job or work situation, or a social encounter:

Imagine you are in a situation that will create self-doubt for you, prior to its occurrence. Feel the anxiety and fear build. Imagine what these feelings would look like if they were an immense and threatening figure looming over you. As you come face-to-face with this personification of self-doubt, imagine that you fire laser beams at it from your eyes. You score a direct hit, and the self-doubt specter disintegrates into a smoldering heap of rubble on the floor. Now, open a bottle of "confidence-enriched" victory juice and drink deeply. You speak articulately, and you look poised in the formerly stress-filled situation. Imagine that those around you are very impressed with your total being. Hear them give you wonderful, powerful, positive compliments. Know that you are highly valued and are seen as the perfect person for this situation.

RELAXATION

In focusing your Influence,
Can you yield as a newborn child?
In clearing your insight,
Can you become free of error?

TAO TE CHING no. 10

When you practice physical relaxation even while you are playing a sport, your heart's arterial pathways open for better circulation, and your lungs expand to increase your oxygen consumption. Your muscles become more flexible and fluid, and your performance improves. If you soften and relax your mental approach to athletics, as well, you reduce the anxiety, tension, and stress that could inhibit your success. As the Tao passage above indicates, when you focus your breath (or influence) and relax (or yield) like a baby, you can see your way clear to establishing a firm footing for action.

Coaches and athletes are notorious for pushing to the max for success. They often use the expression, "Give it all you've got." They speak such words with warm-hearted encouragement, and they mean to help you bring out your best. Most of us really believe that if we try hard, our efforts will be rewarded. Yet these "going-all-out" attitudes actually create enormous tension, stress, and anxiety in us that impede our performance. The ancient Japanese art of aikido teaches that the less resistance you create, the more efficient and effective your action. You can feel the difference for yourself: First try to do some pushups with your arms tensed, then do a few with your muscles relaxed. The implication for sport is simple but powerful: Relax in order to max. Yet like all things in life, more isn't necessarily better.

I had the opportunity, before running an important race, to practice yoga with an incredible teacher. After two hours of various postures, I found myself extremely relaxed—so much so that I barely made it to the race before the start. Three miles into the ten-mile event, I realized that people who are normally a minute per mile slower than I am were floating past me. Yet I was so relaxed, I didn't even care. By mile five, the adrenaline "kicked in," and I surged, reeling past all who had previously passed me. I never did kick in enough to win, though. I was too relaxed. This was a lesson in moderation. One has to learn how to use relaxation and find a delicate balance.

As he observed the ways of nature, Lao-tzu noticed, as has Western science, that force in one direction tends to trigger the occurrence of an opposing force—or, every action has an equal and opposite reaction. As you compete or perform, relax. Don't force your muscles. Let them yield, not harden. Think of the image of water when you begin to feel tension and anxiety, whether in sport or in life. Remember, water is fluid, yielding, and soft, yet strong. In athletics, tension and stress are rigid and hard; they are obstacles to achievement. You soften this hardness when you relax your body and mind.

The Taoist paradox "soft is strong" was followed religiously by Bud Winter, coach of many prominent Olympic athletes. He developed what he calls the "ninety percent law," which says that running or performing at ninety percent effort stimulates relaxation and results in faster movement, more strength, sharper vision, less fatigue, and an improved sense of well-being. His classic book, *Relax and Win: Championship Performance in Whatever You Do*, supports the notion that relaxation is the most widely ignored aspect of athletic training programs in the United States, yet is the most crucial. A relaxed body-mind is a common characteristic of all great athletes in all sports throughout the world. Their optimal performance occurs when their physical, mental, and emotional selves are relaxed and working harmoniously together prior to and during a performance.

TAOSPORT TRAINING FOR ATHLETICS

Many techniques are available that can help you to experience such states of relaxation. Experiment and find one that works for you from those we recommend in this chapter.

In athletic environments where people take themselves and their sport very seriously, it is difficult to relax. Anxiety levels rise when people place a life-or-death price tag on the outcome of an event or game. Yet in the grand scheme of things, no loss or setback will ruin your life. Create an environment for yourself where you take your task seriously but not yourself or the outcome. Oftentimes, an astute coach can help you.

Harry Groves, head track and cross-country coach at Penn State University, is a master at this. He sees the bright side of everything, so it's relaxing just to be around him. He seems to pass this attitude on to his squad, creating an ideal, relaxed environment for performance. At a recent Penn relays championship, a team member approached Coach Groves concerned about how his father would feel if he didn't run a good race. Groves quietly replied, "Look, if you run the race of your life, your father will definitely love you. But if you don't run well, your father will still love you, and so will I. Now, go out there and have a great time."

The young man did just that and, in the process, brought home a wonderful victory. With the pressure off, he ran the race of his life.

Visualization: A Warm Ray of Sunshine

Try the following Beginner's Mind visualization exercise for relaxation. Be sure to find a quiet place where you will not be interrupted. You may need to disconnect the phone and close the door to your room. Soft lighting will help, as will loose-fitting clothing. If it is convenient to recline, do so.

> Imagine a strong, radiant yellow beam of sunlight entering the top of your head. "See" and "feel" it permeate your skull, neck, and shoulders, move out your arms to your fingertips and into your chest cavity, and continue to flow throughout your entire body, down to the very last cell.
>
> Notice how it nourishes and nurtures each molecule, bringing with it enormous health,

beauty, vibrancy, and energy. "See" yourself
being transformed into a relaxed being, full of
joy and happiness.

Affirm to yourself, "I am relaxed and calm and
am getting better every day in every way." Count
from one to five slowly. As you reach five, open
your eyes and remain relaxed.

Anchor for Relaxation

To develop the ability to bring about a state of relaxation instantly, create a
cue or signal for yourself, as we discussed in Part I. Alternatively, repeat the
"Warm Ray of Sunshine" relaxation exercise. When you are in a deep
relaxed state, decide on a physical cue, such as making a fist or forming a
circle with your index finger and thumb. Feel the sensation of being relaxed
as you perform the cue, and tell yourself that you will return to this state of
calm whenever you perform this cue. Practice this a few times, and the cue
will become an instant reference point for relaxation. During moments of
tension or anxiety in athletic contests, revert to your personalized cue and
experience the calm you need for optimal performance.

Affirmations for Relaxing

Memorize any of the following affirmations to use during times of athletic
tension and pressure, either prior to or during a performance:

- *"Relax. Relax to achieve the max."*
- *"To perform without flaw, use the ninety percent
  law."*
- *"I am so relaxed, I see my skin draped on my
  bones."*
- *"Relax my jaw and get so much more."*
- *"Look inward, smile, and relax."*
- *"Calm, calm, calm, calm, tranquil, tranquil,
  tranquil, tranquil." (Repeat these words over and
  over again, slowly.)*

TAOSPORTS FOR BUSINESS AND LIFE

Harry, a divisional manager from Public Services of Colorado, was concerned about his workers' output. He attended one of my classes on enhancing performance. When I talked with him about the benefits of relaxation, I mentioned that fifteen minutes of deep calm before working can make one more proficient and productive during the day. Harry was concerned that he already was too short of time for all the work he had to do; taking fifteen minutes away from his already tight schedule would not be feasible. Even the division meetings that he chaired, although necessary, cut into other work he needed to do, he said. I asked him to try to relax for fifteen minutes just before the meeting at nine o'clock the next morning and to visualize the group working well together and resolving the issues at hand. He was to see his workers posing and solving specific problems. He said he would follow my suggestion "just this once." The next morning, in a deep relaxed state, he imagined his workers being swift, efficient, and effective at the meeting just ahead.

When I returned the next week, he reported excitedly, "Jerry, I can't believe it! What normally takes an hour was concluded in twenty minutes! It was the best conference I've ever had. I think I'll have everyone relax before tomorrow's meeting. What else can I do to improve my work?" Harry is now a believer in relaxation for life. I have known many other people who relax prior to jobs that they expect will take three or four hours, only to complete them more efficiently in half that time.

Guides for Relaxation

You can use the following keys and strategies to create a Beginner's Mind state of calm before and in the midst of competition, work, or family upheavals.

- Develop a personalized anchor, as explained in the "Anchor for Relaxation" exercise, to help you during times of upheaval.

- Develop your own visualizations, images of calm and tranquillity, that particularly affect your central nervous system and mind. Draw on these images when you need them.

- Take three deep breaths and count backward from ten to one when you are faced with potential flareups at work or home.

- Avoid caffeine, alcohol, and sugar. Fortify your body with foods and supplements rich in B-complex vitamins. Your diet can help you maintain calm.

- Before you make any presentation or perform any professional activity, visualize yourself doing it in a relaxed and calm manner. Run through all the possible positive scenarios in your mind. See how many routes you can envision to a successful outcome.

- If anxiety-producing situations loom on the horizon, take time out for a hot tub or sauna. While you are experiencing the heat, breathe deeply and visualize. Soft music and commercial or self-made relaxation tapes can help you become calm before sleep. Classical, Baroque, and Native American compositions are quite helpful.

- Exercising on a regular, consistent basis will help you to better regulate the impact that anxiety and stress have on your life.

Exercise: Relaxing the Body

The following technique was developed by Edmund Jacobsen in the 1930s and is called Progressive Muscle Relaxation. Take a reclining position, and breathe in and out three times. Prepare to contract and relax each and every major muscle group throughout your body. Begin at your feet. Tense your feet, and clench your toes. Hold for five seconds, and relax. Tense your calf muscles, raise them a couple of inches off the floor, tense, tense, and relax. Let your legs drop to the floor. Tense your knees, and proceed to the lower and upper legs, then to the abdomen, buttocks, chest, back, shoulders, arms, hands, neck, and face. Contract and hold for at least ten seconds, then release. The idea is to become aware of what tension feels like and to experience the relaxation that follows when you release or "let go." Whenever you feel tense in a game or at work or home, try saying to yourself "let go" and recall the feeling of relaxation you received from the daily practice of progressive muscle relaxation.

VISION

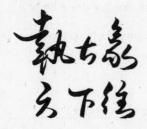
Hold fast to the Great Image,
And all the world will come.

TAO TE CHING no. 35

Besides positive beliefs and thoughts, we also need positive visions in the Beginner's Mind. As a young boy enthusiastic about becoming a great basketball player, I recall watching Boston Celtic star Bob Cousy making all the right moves on TV. Following the game, I'd go to the schoolyard and imitate his style; I played my best basketball on those days. The reason is very clear in retrospect. When I introduced positive pictures, images, or movies of Cousy into my mind as a model for my actions, my central nervous system accepted them as real and my body responded to them.

The "Great Image" referred to in the Tao is the image of going beyond limits. What you can conceive, you will achieve. As an athlete, you create and direct your own performance. If what you visualize doesn't materialize, you must be flexible. Follow the ancient Taoist philosophy that encourages the Beginner's Mind by holding on lightly to your dreams. Do not become absolute or rigid, even in terms of your dreams.

During my own competitive years, I used visualization on a daily basis. Before I ran the 1982 Summit Marathon in California, I drove in my car over the entire course and obtained images of strategic spots where I would need to surge. I ran short segments of the course to get a physical and mental feel for the environment. And I raced over the final two miles, crossing the proposed finish line with my arms raised in victory.

With all these accumulated data and images, I visualized—twice a day for two consecutive weeks—every mile of the course, exactly as I planned to run it on the marathon day. I felt the surges; I saw myself leading from mile ten and eventually crossing the finish line in triumph. When the day finally came, it was no accident that the event unfolded precisely as I had rehearsed it. I felt as if I had actually accomplished it all before. And I had, in my mind's eye. I ran totally relaxed for each and every mile, without the slightest doubt or hesitation, and achieved one of my most rewarding victories.

If an athlete can picture in advance each movement of an event exactly as it should be, in a relaxed meditative state, the greater will be the chances that he or she will carry out those movements during the actual performance. Lee Evans set the world record in the 400-meter race at the 1968 Olympics in Mexico City after two years of daily visualization of each step of the event. Chris Evert, Jack Nicklaus, Dwight Stones, Steve Scott, and hundreds of other elite and professional athletes create sharp, vivid images of success before each performance—the list of the faithful could fill a book. Refusing to leave the outcome of their sport to chance, they train mind and body synchronously.

Perhaps one of the most convincing pieces of research to verify the power of imagery in sport was an experiment performed with two groups of basketball players who were trying to improve their free-throw percentage. One group shot one hundred free throws every day for three weeks; the other group simply visualized doing the same. The study found that the visualizing group showed significant improvement over those who actually shot the ball.

TAOSPORT TRAINING FOR ATHLETICS

Visualization: Anchor for Improved Technique

This visualization exercise shows the power of visualization to transform erratic performances into consistently successful play in your sport. Choose a particular facet of your game that you see as problematic or improvable— your backhand tennis technique, the form of your swing with a bat or golf club, your flip turn, the point at which you release the discus, your dismount from uneven parallel bars.

> In your mind's eye, see yourself repeatedly
> performing in the way you would like. Create a
> cue device that can signal to your body that it
> should execute the perfect form or play. Such a
> cue, for example, can be making a strong,
> impenetrable fist with your hand, or forming a
> gentle circle by lightly joining your index finger to
> your thumb. As you form your cue, visualize the
> action you want it to affect. Visualize this
> improved facet of your performances, and tell
> yourself, "I can recall and repeat this stroke or
> play or form on command in the future as I use
> my cue."

Now, having practiced this a few times in your mind, give yourself the cue and perform the improved skill in actuality. Notice that the visualization has helped you improve your performance. In the future, when you get off track, use the cue, signal, or anchor to bring you right back to your desired level. Practice this exercise until it becomes a habit.

Visualization: Optimal Performance

Another valuable use of visualization is to rehearse mentally a time when you played or performed at an optimal level. This visualization exercise gives you "the feeling" of playing like a champion. You can use it either before or during an event to boost your performance.

> Again, close your eyes and take five deep
> breaths. Remember a game or time when you
> performed flawlessly. Re-create the scene, and
> watch yourself as you play. Become aware of
> your surroundings; see who is there, who is
> playing with you. Hear the sounds, and smell the
> smells. Now, move back into yourself and see
> how it feels to play at this level where you can

do no wrong. Focus on each wonderful
sensation, each aspect of this excellent
performance. Notice the pleasure and
confidence you experience when you play at this
level.

Remember these feelings of optimal
performance, and know that you can call them
up the next time you participate.

TAOSPORTS FOR BUSINESS AND LIFE

You can use visualizations to create positive images and pictures in your mind that will strongly influence your work and home life as well. Your visions are the blueprints of your reality.

One of my favorite stories about the power of visualization concerns a navy pilot who was incarcerated in Vietnam for many years. To help himself stay sane, he drew six lines on a two-inch-wide flat stick to resemble the neck of a guitar. He had never played guitar, yet his cellmate, who did, taught him in their free time. The pilot practiced compulsively under the tutelage of this friend, who showed him the appropriate finger positions on the "neck" and sang the notes. For hours every day, he visualized the chords and heard the sounds in his mind. By the time he was released, he had become an accomplished guitarist.

Visualization is also used as an aid to maintain wellness and speed the healing of injuries and illness. Pioneering doctors have used visualization techniques to treat patients diagnosed with cancer. Carl Simonton and Bernie Siegel, two such prominent physicians, use visualization in conjunction with other therapies; they show remarkable rates of success in helping patients become well again.

In the corporate sector, more and more business people are using visualization as a tool to facilitate the achievement of major tasks and company goals. A wonderful example of this is recounted by a manager at the Martin-Marietta Company. He and his team of engineers were in a position to bid for a lucrative government project, yet the team had little hope of getting the contract. Their motivation and enthusiasm were quite low, and they even considered withholding their bid. But rather than "throw in the towel," the manager held a meeting and told the team they needed to change their negative attitudes and images. He asked them to create positive pictures instead, seeing themselves working harmoniously as a team, doing terrific work, making the bid, and getting the contract. Thereafter they met once a week, and the manager led them in visualization (which he had also used successfully in his personal life). Their level of excitement and enthusiasm rose exponentially as they took on the challenge in a positive way. He told them that regardless of the outcome, he would consider them a success because of the incredible work they were doing. In the end, they did get the contract, and they continued to have monthly visualization sessions to keep their morale and motivation at a high positive level.

Visualization: Abundance

The following visualization exercise is a favorite of mine; I use it with clients who are short on self-esteem and want to change themselves from within and create abundance in their lives.

> Enter your relaxed state, and envision yourself in a positive way: intelligent, beautiful, healthy, vital. How does it feel? Next, "see" yourself in wonderful, comfortable clothing, the kind that makes you feel confident and relaxed. You look good. "Feel" the personal power within you. You are emotionally balanced, spiritually grounded, and peaceful. You are creating harmony in your world and in the world around you.
>
> You are receiving an abundance of recognition and support for all that you do. Financial rewards are comfortable and appropriate for your lifestyle. If you are having a problem or need to make an important decision, look at the situation calmly, from a distance. See if you can shed light upon your situation by asking yourself, "What do I need to know? What do I need to do at this time?" Wait for an answer to come to you. If nothing comes, ask again the next time you do this exercise.
>
> You live in a home that matches your values and interests. You have created an environment that gives you all the love and comfort that you

deserve. If something changes to make your
home uncomfortable, see yourself pull back and
calmly put it all into perspective. Life has its
cycles, and change is certain. Perhaps you need
to accept what is going on and realize that things
will change again for the better.

See the relationships in your life; they are
warm, kind, and generous, and they reflect the
world you have created. "Feel" the tremendous
amount of love and joy that they offer and that
you accept. If conflict arises between you and
someone you love, see this as a natural part of
life and look objectively at the situation. Resolve
the conflict calmly, peacefully, in a way that
benefits everyone involved.

Tell yourself that this is a wonderful world and
that you deserve a most joyful, fulfilling life.
There is enough good for everyone, and you will
do what you can to see that this good is
multiplied for all.

Repeat this exercise every day for three weeks. As you touch upon all of
the areas the exercise mentions, be sure to take the time to actually imagine
the positive "as if" it were so. Notice how your relationship to yourself and
your world transforms in real life.

Guides for Vision

- When you are faced with a difficult business negotiation or are trying
  to secure an important contract, visualize the situation unfolding
  exactly as you'd like it to. See yourself presenting it in a most beneficial, successful way.

- Before you have an interview, phone conversation, or attend an important meeting, compose your thoughts and use positive mental images
  to be better prepared.

- If you're having trouble accomplishing something at work or at home,
  create a clear image of what you wish to accomplish with this affirma-

tion: "This situation or something better is manifesting for the good of all involved."

- After you have prepared adequately for an examination at school or anywhere else, and before you enter the exam room, visualize yourself doing extremely well, answering each question appropriately and intelligently.

- When you are ill or injured, use images of healing and wellness to help relax your body and allow your immune system to function more effectively.

- Visualize peace at home, and see your children playing happily. Even if they are acting up, the image will put you in a better frame of mind to accept the craziness. According to the Tao, feelings of inner peace ripple outward toward the other people in your life.

- Focus on images of fulfillment and joy rather than misery; this will make you less stressed.

- Create positive images about yourself, and focus on the wonderfulness of those around you. You will begin to feel more loving and confident.

FOCUSING

執古之道
以御今之有

Hold on to the ancient Tao
Control the current reality.

TAO TE CHING no. 14

When Soren, a sixty-four-year-old ultra–distance runner, reached the finish line of the Western States 100-miler, a reporter asked him how someone his age runs a hundred miles. Soren replied, "I don't run a hundred miles; I run one mile—a hundred times." By focusing on one mile at a time, Soren can go the distance. If he focused on the whole distance, the mere thought of such a task would distract and fatigue him.

Focus your thoughts and your actions on one small aspect of the present, and you will create personal power. Giving full attention to the present moment is energizing and enables you to control the current reality. You must be present in order to win. For athletes, focusing on the moment is key to the Beginner's Mind for achievement.

Olympic medalist swimmer Dara Torres has stated, "Luck isn't what makes the difference when competition is really close. It boils down to who is more 'on' that day, who has the focus, the will to win at that moment."

Centering, discussed in the next chapter, is the thought process of understanding how every aspect of your game contributes to your overall development and growth as an athlete and person. It is a kind of concentration that is all-encompassing. Focusing, by contrast, is the process of narrowing your concentration in order to eliminate specific unproductive or distracting occurrences. It is a method of fine-tuning your span of attention so that you stay in the moment, in the here and now.

You can focus on that backhand volley you missed, on the strike you looked at, on the pass you dropped in the end zone, on the shot you blew at the buzzer, on your failure to surge the last two hundred meters of the race, on the putt you almost made. You can focus on past and upcoming problems forever. But this will only put pressure on you and impede your concentration on the next move, play, or shot you make. The only way to make something positive happen is to focus on the present moment.

Concentrate on what you have control over. You can't control your competitors, or your teammates, or the weather, or the crowd. But you do have control over your own performance. As former Olympic diver and now coach Janet Ely-Lagourge has said, "All too often we get wrapped up in the pressure, and suddenly it's not fun anymore."

Developing the power to devote full attention to the present is one of the most valuable Beginner's Mind skills. Athletes who perform optimally are totally engaged in the moment. Their effectiveness is directly related to how well they focus on being present. In his book *The Tao of Leadership*, John Heider says, "Expeditions into distant lands of one's mind . . . distract from what is happening. By staying present . . . you can do less yet achieve more."

Mark Allen, one of the greatest triathletes ever to compete, has said that it's a mistake to focus on how much more there is to go when doing the Ironman Triathlon. He attributes much of his success to focusing in the moment—to giving his attention to his form, stride, and breath. He focuses on his reasons for doing the race, on why he is here on the Big Island of Hawaii competing in this ultra-event, on his deep urge to move and run. By focusing on the joy of movement, you take yourself deeper into the present moment, down into your motivation, and past any fleeting distractions and discomforts.

Single-mindedness accompanies excellence. Athletes become absorbed in their actions, oblivious to what's around them. They are childlike in their absolute absorption: they feel no guilt about the past, no fear of the future. They play and get lost in the present. This oneness with their sport yields a "high," a sense of being in a time warp, a flowing state without any conscious need to control; it's an ecstatic, trancelike level of concentration. You can feel things move along in a natural rhythm, the way they're supposed to.

We all have varying degrees of concentration. But with the Beginner's

Mind, visualization and meditation processes can train you to develop greater powers of attention. No one can maintain this state for very long periods of time, but you can learn to focus to provide yourself with the proper mental environment to develop your athletic skills rapidly. You can learn to discipline a wandering mind that diminishes your performance through distraction and diversion of energy.

> It is of great importance to achieve an inner peace
> which will allow you to act in harmony with the times. . . .
> Hold your thoughts to the present. . . . Actions that
> spring from this attitude will be appropriate.
>
> *I CHING* no. 52

TAOSPORT TRAINING FOR ATHLETICS

I was trying to help my three-year-old son Sean improve his batting skill by having him focus his attention in the moment. I explained that he needed to keep his eye on the ball as I pitched it. He took the ball and held it up close to his eye, saying, "Like this, Daddy?" He was—literally—in the moment. Later, he transferred this literal close focus to following the ball's movement toward him and the bat, just as you will learn to keep your attention focused by using strategies and Beginner's Mind games during an athletic event. In tennis, consider playing each point as if your ranking depended upon the total number of points you won in a certain period of time—a game, a match, a season. This will force you to focus on the point in the present. Sometimes saying the mantra "Bounce, hit . . . bounce, hit" helps keep your mind from wandering. In many sports, such as distance running and skiing, this focused state comes over you naturally. The key to activating focus at will is to choose a small aspect of your activity in the present and dwell on it. Focus on the seams of a ball as it is pitched to you; tune in to your form, rhythm, pace, or fluidity; feel yourself at one with nature as you ski down a mountain. Concentrate on your tennis racquet, golf club, bat, lacrosse stick, or bicycle as if it were a natural extension of your body. When shooting basketball foul shots, focus on the front part of the rim, and see the ball slip perfectly over it for the point.

Learning to focus your mind requires practice and time. The mind will always wander, regardless of how much you practice and how mentally strong you are. It is impossible to remain permanently focused—and it is actually not necessary. Look for opportunities to give your mind a break from the rigors of concentrating: change your side of the net in volleyball, sit in the dugout or on a ski lift, or walk to the next tee—these are all examples calling for slight but purposeful distraction.

Visualization: Stopping Distraction

A collegiate basketball player finds himself on the foul line with two seconds left in the conference championships and his team down by one point. The fans sitting behind the basket are yelling and waving towels to distract him. He ices the victory with two foul shots. After the game, he is asked how he blocked out the incredible noise. He says he never heard a sound. To focus himself, he had watched the seams of the ball spin perfectly off his fingertips, up and over the front rim.

As an athlete, you must learn to recognize your own personal patterns of distraction. Under what circumstances does your attention wander? When do you begin to think about external happenings, at work or among family or friends? Do you go inside yourself and obsess with your fatigue or the error you just committed, or perhaps brood on how you wish an event had gone? When you identify your patterns of distraction, try the following visualization:

> Imagine yourself playing in an upcoming event.
> Visualize yourself as clearly as possible,
> participating as you would hope. Simulate, in
> your mind's eye, various distractions: noise from
> the crowd, a bad call from the referee, an
> obnoxious play by the opponent. As these
> distractions occur to you, tell them that they can
> stay if they wish or step aside and leave, but you
> must immediately attend to your play or
> performance. Imagine yourself dismissing them,
> that they have left. Focus your vision on the ball
> or road or slope or water itself. See its shape and
> texture. Look for the writing between the seams
> of the ball (or in the cool air or water). See the
> ball spin, feel it in your hands. Stay focused on
> this image for two minutes, no matter how
> difficult it is.

Practice this exercise twice a day. The object need not be a ball; the image of any significant, tangible object related to your sport will do.

Affirmations for Focusing

Choose any of the following affirmations, or create your own to repeat during those times when distraction sets in before or during an event:

- *"I stay in the here and now, so I'll take a bow."*
- *"Think less, achieve more."*
- *"Single-mindedness creates happiness."*
- *"Like a child at play, I ask my mind to stay."*
- *"Focus, focus, focus, focus."*
- *"Follow through, and I am true."*

TAOSPORTS FOR BUSINESS AND LIFE

Visualization: Training the Mind to Focus

In your state of relaxation, return to your natural breathing patterns. Focus entirely on your breathing. Notice that each inhalation carries oxygen that will bring peace and calm throughout your body. As you exhale, notice that your breath carries away not only carbon dioxide but all your tension and anxiety. Watch it float away. Count from one to ten, and then repeat the process when you get to ten. Do this for a total of five minutes once a day. Be patient, since this may take time to master—don't become discouraged. Notice how much you improve in seven days.

Exercise: Focus from Distraction

Create a state of total distraction for yourself by intentionally introducing a wide variety of thoughts and issues. Think about your work, problems at home, financial issues, what to have for dinner, where to go for a vacation, paying your taxes, and on and on, until your mind jumps from place to place, spinning endlessly like a wheel in the mud. Then return to a relaxed state, and discipline your mind by using the visualization on the previous page, "Training the Mind to Focus." Once focused on each breath, allow your mind to choose one thought and think about it, then go on to the next, until each has had an opportunity for attention.

By practicing in this way prior to any athletic, work, or home-related task, the mind becomes more adept in maintaining attention. If you find yourself distracted while doing the task, use deep breathing to relax, then begin to visualize yourself attending to business once again. See yourself fully concentrating on one small aspect of the task and able to maintain this focus on a specific area of concern. Be present, and tell yourself that when you're finished, you will give your attention to the distractions.

Exercise: Candle Focusing

This is an easy, quick way to strengthen your ability to focus and be present in the moment, in the Beginner's Mind.

Stare at a candle at the base of the flame (do not stare directly at the light) while you focus on your present feelings. Exclude all other thoughts. Just focus your body and mind on your sensations. If your mind wanders, bring it back to the present moment and feelings by saying, "At this very moment, the candle flame and I are the center of life. I focus on the brilliant light that enables me to feel peaceful and calm. That is all there is in this moment."

Guides for Focusing

- When you have many important items to attend to in the present, rate them in order of importance. Focus on the first, and mentally see yourself stacking the rest, with the most important on top, in a file box. Tell them that their turn will come in time, that you will focus on them when it's appropriate.

- When going for a job interview or an important meeting or presenting a talk, you will be more focused and "tuned in" if you visualize, prior to your arrival, the physical environment where the event will occur. See how you'll be dressed, imagine the other individuals who will be present, define your goals, and see yourself acting as if all went according to plan. Feel the exhilaration of having focused perfectly and the reward of accomplishment.

- Take a walk in the forest or any other natural setting. Stop and listen to the sounds; smell the vegetation; feel the texture of the trees; focus on birds in flight—particularly hawks, eagles, vultures. This will help you to attend to the present.

- When you are cleaning up after meals, get into the Tao of dishes. Experience the textures of the soap on the glasses and plates. Focus on doing a thorough job, as you enjoy the quiet time alone and away from the intense energy of your children or other activities. Place the clean items neatly on a rack to dry. See how they glitter. Clean the sink so that it sparkles after rinsing. Act as if this were the most important job now—and it is.

- Cooking can be a way to focus and concentrate. Focus on the textures, colors, and tastes of the food as you prepare it. Have music playing in the background, preferably Zen meditation sounds or Classical and Baroque—these help to focus on the task at hand.

CENTERING

What is skillfully established will not be uprooted;
What is skillfully grasped will not slip away.
Thus it is honored for generations.

TAO TE CHING no. 54

Performance in sport or any other arena of life is greatly influenced by one's ability to remain centered within. An extremely talented potter was explaining to me why her creations were sometimes inconsistent. The quality of her work is directly related to how external events in her life affected her. If they throw her off-center, her pottery becomes asymmetrical. When she remains centered and inwardly calm, she throws balanced, beautiful pottery. Centering is the condition of remaining true to yourself and performing up to your capabilities, regardless of the changes in your external world. It is a Beginner's Mind state of being open at all times to the pain, fatigue, setbacks, and fears, as well as to the joy, exhilaration, and victories that athletics provide. See your sport as a microcosmic stage where you create the opportunity to discover your limitations and go beyond them for all aspects of your life. This vision will keep you centered.

Being centered will help you perform as you would like to amid the changes in your environment during the event. Distracting noises, weather variations, unfair rulings or judgment calls, and any other unexpected situations will have less effect on you physically and emotionally if you are coming from a centered self. The Tao speaks of centeredness, metaphorically, as a deeply rooted tree. When attacked by hostile forces, the tree withstands them, remaining unmoved by negative energy. External aggressive tactics are basically ineffective against a centered person or athlete because that person understands these forces as part of the process of learning the bigger lesson of life.

Centered TaoAthletes can enjoy wins, accolades, and awards more fully, as by-products of excellence rather than as ends in themselves. They do not measure identity and self-worth by the result, score, or rating of a performance. They see victory as just another component of playing the game, one that will provide inner guidance for future experiences in all of life. Setbacks do not create fury and unhappiness and are seen as natural occurrences in all performance situations. Centered TaoSport athletes enjoy the game as a process of self-learning and maintain a healthy perspective.

They succeed and do not boast.
They succeed and do not make claims.

TAO TE CHING no. 30

TAOSPORT TRAINING FOR ATHLETICS

Tod was a talented tennis player, but one bad call by the linesman could throw him off-center for the rest of a match. If he remained at the mercy of such reactions, he would never fulfill his potential in the game. He came to me at the request of his coach to see if he could learn to control his temper. Our work together emphasized the joy of the process of playing tennis rather than the outcome of the game. I asked Tod to think of himself as a giant rock, solid and unmovable. Whenever a situation would annoy him, he had to repeat the phrase "Solid as a rock, I cannot be moved away from center" five times. He became, in his own words, the "rock jock." I also told him that he wouldn't be all-American material until he could see bad calls as something everyone gets. It all balances out in the end.

In Tod's first match after these sessions, a set-point ball was called out against him that easily could have been called in his favor. He went over to the line judge and shouted, "I am a rock jock! That call doesn't shake me." That way, he got his frustration out without losing his cool. He eventually won the set in a tie-breaker and won the match two sets to love.

It is important to realize that no one can maintain the Beginner's Mind or be centered at all times. Knowing this and acting in accordance with it is, in itself, being centered. The key is to be conscious of the times when you are off-center, when you are fighting the natural occurrences in your game. Then you can decide to return to a more helpful, healthy position.

Affirmations for Centering

These affirmations are centering tools to help you become more effective during unpredictable changes in your sport:

> In a relaxed state repeat one or more of the following, five times each. Then, during an athletic event, be sure to recall and repeat any of these when things begin to deteriorate:

> - "I am open to every play in every way."
> - "Centered and strong, I play right along."
> - "Like a deep-rooted tree, I'm centered and free."
> - "Regardless of how things unfold, I refuse to let go of my hold."

Visualization: Centering

This visualization exercise will give you a chance to practice Beginner's Mind centering to help you during difficult competitive situations:

> After you enter your state of relaxation, imagine being disturbed by a poor call or decision from a referee, or perhaps becoming outraged at an

opponent for playing unfairly. Feel your anger
and frustration. Immediately affirm: "To control
this game, I must remain tame." Know and
reaffirm that this simulation will help keep you
centered. Imagine yourself "keeping it together"
and finishing out the contest exactly as you
would wish.

Handling a negative event in a positive way is an experience that can become a touchstone for future encounters.

TAOSPORTS FOR BUSINESS AND LIFE

After I have been away from home on a business trip, I usually return feeling quite centered, with all of life in perspective—until I walk in the door and encounter three young boys. This transition often brings chaos and stress. Recently, I was returning from the Olympic Training Center in Colorado, feeling relaxed and wonderful after five days of rewarding work. Knowing how difficult the transition can be, I decided to take ten minutes during my flight to San Jose and visualize my arrival at home and how I intended to remain positive and centered. I saw myself greeting the family and responding to my environmental change in a balanced, satisfying way. I imagined being thrown off but coming back to center. After two hours at home, Jan, my wife, asked, "Where have you been? You seem so different." To which I jokingly responded, "I had some brain surgery." In fact, I truly had altered my usual patterns of interaction by mentally seeing myself centered and things going smoothly—and they did, exactly as I had envisioned. When the kids began to act up, rather than overreact, I handled the situation in a quiet, calm, effective way.

Visualization: Coming Back to the Center

Know that regardless of what happens in business and life, you can survive and make it. You can cope with the ups and downs. This visualization exercise will help you get through everyday setbacks and crises, such as disappointments with colleagues at work and family problems or arguments:

Picture yourself in an uncomfortable situation on the job, one that throws you off-center into a reactionary mode of behavior. Notice the surroundings, the expressions on people's faces. Feel the tension in the air. Say to yourself, *"Stop."* Here is an opportunity to practice centering. Affirm: "I refuse to give others permission to take me off-center." See and hear yourself responding and performing the way you'd like, with wonderful ease, confidence, and poise. Notice how rewarding it feels to act with balance. Use this visual experience as a touchstone for future centering during setbacks and crises.

Guides for Centering

- Remember that we are never as great as our greatest victory or as bad as our worst defeat. Knowing this helps to keep our internal and external judgments in perspective. Victory and defeat are ephemeral. Enjoy the accolades and recognition for work well done, but see them as detached from who you are. Our greatest achievements are our relationships with our families, our co-workers, and our children.

- Visualize how you can have more meaningful relationships as a worker, a spouse, and a parent. See yourself when you get off-center, and imagine how you can return. Congratulate yourself for being aware of it.

- When you are taken off-center, rather than become self-critical, remind yourself that you're only human. Only God—or the Tao—is itself all the time, without effort. To accept your human shortcomings is to be centered.

INTUITION

聖人不行而知
不見而名
不為而成

Evolved individuals know without going about,
Recognize without looking,
Achieve without acting.

TAO TE CHING   no. 47

Intuition is direct knowing without the conscious use of reasoning. To learn to "know without going about" is important for anyone's personal development. When you use the intuitive Beginner's Mind, your actions will follow the natural, correct path and provide you with greater power. After you have learned by heart how to do something, how to play or work, you can begin to rely on a natural sense of timing.

In sport, your skill level is directly related to your ability to use your Beginner's Mind to trust and listen to your intuitive self. Athletes have come to know this by various names: as instinct, impulse, feeling, insight, sixth sense, or automatic response. Such intuitive knowing is essential to fast-paced activities that demand the cooperation of body, mind, and spirit. To be good at basketball, for example, one must constantly be in position to make an instantaneous response. Intuition provides immediate understanding of a developing situation and the ability to know how to react to it.

No one better portrayed the intuitive athlete in basketball than Magic Johnson, of the Los Angeles Lakers. His uncanny knack for throwing passes blindly to spots that were not yet occupied by intended receivers created pandemonium in arenas when Lakers showed up out of nowhere to catch the ball for an easy slam-dunk. He's not called "Magic" for nothing. His intuitive sense as an athlete enabled him to dominate the National Basketball Association for more than a decade.

In cycling, I respond quickly and intuitively to a sprint or "attack" on a hill, giving it no thought whatsoever. Those who refuse to follow such instincts generally fall behind the lead riders. Ignoring your instincts in sports can result in a serious setback or even physical injury (particularly in the high-risk sports—skiing, hang-gliding, mountain climbing). One athlete, while cross-country skiing during a race high in the Colorado Rockies, heard a tremendous thunderlike noise, a common sound in that area since storms frequently roll in at lightning speed. She instinctively turned and raced away. Within five seconds, the spot she had vacated was covered with tons of snow caused by an avalanche. Because she had practiced many times in her mind what action she'd take if she were confronted with such a natural threat, her intuitive sense moved her away from the opening to safety in the trees.

Whether you are predicting the delivery of a fastball, knowing the precise moment to surge in a race, being in position to receive a pass, responding to unpredictable offenses, or reacting quickly to unfamiliar defenses, you call upon and employ your intuitive self almost unconsciously. You have no time to think. In such situations, analysis is paralysis. We all possess this instinct, yet few of us trust it to the extent we must to be successful consistently.

Act out the laws of your inner Self,
trust the inherent correctness of your instincts. . . .
In this way you will meet with success.

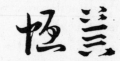

I CHING no. 32

TAOSPORT TRAINING FOR ATHLETICS

To improve your athletic performance, cultivate and develop your instincts and intuition by practice. When you intuitively feel "this isn't the best time or way" or "throw it, throw it"—follow your instinct, observe the outcome, and see how you feel about it. When you cannot see or understand what's happening or developing in the moment of play, don't push for the answer. Relax and look with soft eyes; become calm, and go with the flow of your intuitive self. This is what TaoSport teaches.

One of the most powerful ways to develop and strengthen intuition as an athlete is serious, focused practice. Always practice your sport as if you were in the middle of an important game or event. If you watched professional athletes from any sport practice, you couldn't distinguish that level of play from their level on game day. By practicing so assiduously, they condition their brains to respond at the highest level. They program themselves so that, under actual game conditions, they instinctively respond.

Timothy Ferris, in his book *The Mind's Sky: Human Intelligence in a Cosmic Context,* describes the premotor cortex in the brain, the part of the mind that allows you to coordinate sequences of actions instinctively. Talking about quarterback Joe Montana, Ferris says:

> Montana could check off two covered receivers and
> throw to a third man, sometimes even finding a way to
> get the ball to a covered receiver, in part because he
> didn't have to reflect on the situation at the time. . . . To
> introduce conscious decision-making into the process
> would wreck his timing. As Montana remarked, "If I
> ever stopped to think about what happens, after the ball
> hits my hands, it might screw up the whole process."

The process Montana describes is the same for any sport. A player who has practiced diligently will respond instinctively to any number of variables that develop in a situation. In a baseball game, for instance, with no outs, bases loaded, and a ground ball hit to first, there's no question how the play will evolve for the first baseman: throw home, back to first—a quick, efficient, intuitive response. The key is always to practice how you plan to play, and then you'll play as you practice.

Affirmations for Intuition

The following affirmations can be used as touchstones for excellent, more intuitive performances in sport:

- *"Thinking body, dancing mind."*
- *"Analysis is paralysis. Act, don't think."*
- *"I trust the inherent correctness of my instincts."*
- *"Intuition creates fruition."*
- *"I'm in sync, I use instinct."*
- *"I follow my heart, and that's the best part."*

TAOSPORTS FOR
BUSINESS AND LIFE

It was twenty minutes after the hour and my four o'clock client had not shown up. I gave up waiting and decided to leave the office. Two miles away, I felt a strong urge to turn around and go back. Without hesitation, I followed the feeling, but as I pulled into the office driveway, I still saw no sign of him. I felt ridiculous for having followed my intuition and prepared to leave once again. As I backed out, my client pulled in. He had been delayed in traffic.

Many books are being written these days about the use and value of intuition in corporate circles for the purposes of decision-making and the setting of policy guidelines. My favorite story on this topic is that of a group of twelve managers who unanimously agree on the direction their company should be taking, but because the move is so unconventional from traditional patterns, they become paralyzed with indecision. They search for more data to support and justify a move that they know intuitively is right. Finally, the chairperson takes charge and says, "The average age of the twelve of us here is forty-five years. This gives us 540 years of experience and wisdom. If we all feel the same way, let's go ahead with these ideas." They followed their inner wisdom and made the decision on that basis. That year, the company tripled its profits, thanks to intuitive management.

In business and life, decision-making doesn't usually require immediate and split-second reactions, as it does in sport. Because of this, you can usually take the time to consult your intuition when you're confronted with a problem, question, or decision. The following exercise will help you to contact your inner self.

Visualization: Finding a Spiritual Guide

Although it may seem rather strange to you at first, this exercise will give your intuition a tangible identity so that you can call on it for guidance anytime.

In your mind's eye, create a "spiritual teacher" who will help to give you input into questions or problems that you must address or decisions you must make. This teacher could be totally fictitious, a figment of your imagination, or a real person—a friend, or perhaps someone famous that you do not know personally but you admire. Your choice could be anyone, a historical figure or someone alive today, someone you admired in your childhood or youth, or an ancestor you never knew. See this teacher as a very wise person, with much integrity, insight, clarity, humor, and kindness. Give your teacher a name, and invite him or her to your place of peace for consultation.

This teacher is your true inner voice, a reflection of what's happening inside of you, a mirror reflecting what you feel at the moment. In establishing this contact, you create a powerful source of balance and energy.

My own adviser is a fictitious very old Taoist, who doubles as a nurturing father as well. He lives very simply and is available to me at a moment's notice. We often "meet" and discuss issues of concern. He always has wonderful advice (intuitive data) on my decisions, problems, or questions. Sometimes we "play" together like two kids. His laughter is contagious.

Once you have chosen your teacher, make contact on a regular basis during your visualizations. Invite this sage to come to you during your deep, relaxed state.

Structure your dialogue by thinking of a question you have, a problem to be solved, or a decision to be made. Present one or all of them to your adviser and say:

What do I need to do?
What do I need to know?
What do you think is the answer?

The most immediate response is normally a good indication of the direction to take. Trust the feeling; trust what you "hear," and act on it. If your teacher does not respond, you may need to take more time to deal with your issue. Thank your teacher, and plan to meet again soon. Perhaps your intuition isn't clear at that moment, or you are simply not ready to move on the issue at hand. Either way, it's your inner self talking to you, and your intuition knows what you need and when.

When you are satisfied with the dialogue, tell your adviser that you appreciate the input and look forward to talking again soon. Stand up, hug each other, and depart.

Exercise: Becoming Conscious of Who You Are

Now that you have found your spiritual guide whom you can consult during times of doubt or when you need information, you need to understand his or her specific attitudes.

Make a list of five people whom you admire. They can be living or dead, known or unknown. Do not read any further until you have created the list.

Now: Are you on that list? Think about why or why not. If you failed to include yourself—and most people do—write your name as number six.

Next, list all the qualities and attitudes that you most admire in each of these people. Try to come up with four or five per name.

Chances are, you chose these people because you possess traits that resemble theirs. Notice the similarities—you may possess these qualities in latent form if the similarities aren't immediately apparent.

Exercise: Staying to the Left of Your "But"

Many of our intuitive desires are nullified by our rational thought or judgment. Notice how often your inner voice speaks to you, only to be followed by "buts" and excuses for not following your "whims."

A gifted psychotherapist, George McClendon, gave me the following exercise, which has enabled many of my clients to choose what they want rather than what they "should" want in life.

When you make the following statements, stay to the left of the "but." In other words, do what you initially say, and forget what follows the "but." Here are some examples.

- "I could really use a vacation, but that would be irresponsible with all this work to be done."

- "I'd love to go to the party, but I need to get up early tomorrow."

- "I really think things could be done more effectively, but they'll laugh if I make the suggestion."

- "I know I deserve a raise, but he'll just refuse."

- "I want to leave this meeting, but I might be criticized."

- "I need to rest, but there's too much to do."

- "I'd really like to get in shape, but there's no time."

- "I really want to take that class, but I might get too tired."

- "I'm really hungry, but I shouldn't eat yet."

- "I really want to sing, but I'll look like a fool."

- "I'd love to ask her to dinner, but she'd probably refuse."

- "I want to quit this program, but people will get down on me."

Exercise: Using Intuition for Snap Judgments

On many occasions in business and life, you are required to come up with an instantaneous response to a question, problem, or decision. When this happens, try doing the following:

> Take one deep abdominal breath, and imagine
> yourself as a wonderfully enlightened human
> being. You have everything within you right now
> to resolve the problem, answer the question, or
> make the decision. What would you do, how

would you act, if you were enlightened? The
answer is your intuitive self speaking. Trust it!

Practice your intuition by trying to predict certain daily occurrences. Ask yourself questions throughout the day: Who is calling on the phone? Who's at the door? What is the color of the car approaching from the rear? What will my spouse make for dinner? These and similar queries will train you to respond instantly and instinctively.

Unlimited amounts of potential and information are available to you when you choose to tap into your intuitive storehouse. Whether you are confronted with a major crisis, stressed by a major decision or problem, or simply looking for an alternative to everyday, mundane realities, your inner voice can help matters work out. It is your most reliable guide.

Logic is based on the known. Go beyond this limit to unlimited pastures of the unknown—your unlimited intuition.

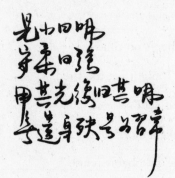

To perceive the small is called insight.
To remain yielding is called strength.
If, in using one's brightness,
One returns to insight,
Life will be free of misfortune.

TAO TE CHING no 52

Develop a sense of life's patterns and movements through the cultivation of insight—the intuitive mind.

REFLECTION

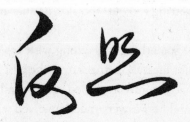

> Your inner stillness will bring enlightenment by
> objectifying your impressions. . . . Through objectivity
> you will know when to act and when not to act. In this
> way you make no mistakes and suffer no consequences.
>
> *I CHING* no. 52

If centering and focusing are mental techniques that affect your performance by controlling your immediate thought patterns, reflection is a process that enables you to take time out and "check in" with your progress as an athlete. As an athlete, you are constantly bombarded with input. The continual dramas of life and sport obscure your awareness of where you are, from where you came, and to where you are going. You have to be able to know and interpret such data to grow and develop, as well as to appreciate how far you've come and why.

Practicing silent reflection or inner stillness helps you to understand yourself better, your perceptions and impressions, as well as the world around you. As a result, you come to know what to do and when to do it. Your timing improves so that you minimize your risks of error, setback, and failure. Periodic reflection is a way of tuning in to your body, mind, and spirit and assessing your training and competitive performances. It helps you to see what you need to polish and what you need to change. It also helps you to observe the relationship between your personal and your athletic lives.

Dave was the Northern California number-one-ranked singles tennis champion in his age group, fifty and over. He was highly competitive for years, but one day he came to me concerned that his game had seriously faltered. Could he be getting too old, too slow? What had happened to his serve?

Rather than assume something was wrong with his game, I asked if he had undergone any major lifestyle changes over the past two years. It turned out that his workload had recently increased substantially, he had remarried and moved his home, and he was very much involved with his one-year-old son. Many responsibilities required his time and attention. I suggested he take time to reflect silently for thirty minutes a day, thinking about his priorities in life, what was important to him, and how he would prefer to use his time each day. After a week of such reflection, Dave returned with a powerful insight. He realized that tennis was no longer crucial to him. He was no longer willing to play long and hard to maintain his position on the ladder. His work and new wife and child gave him joy that far exceeded his tennis ranking. Realizing that his focus had shifted, he ceased to get down on himself for his lackluster performances. Paradoxically, without the pressure, he played better tennis. Most of all, reflection taught him that performance is the result of his priorities, not his abilities.

Your sports performance will have its ups and downs, subject as it is to the natural cycles of life. No athlete can compete without periodic fluctuations in performance, and neither can you. But much is to be gained from reflecting upon these natural cycles.

The process of Beginner's Mind reflection allows you to become more astute in reading and understanding the natural patterns of your performance. By aligning yourself with these rhythms, you gain personal power over your performance. If you are at a low period, accept this low period consciously, and you will stop fighting it. Just as Dave did, you will also improve your performance.

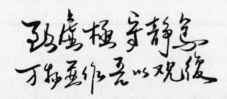

Attain the highest openness;
Maintain the deepest harmony.
Become a part of All Things;
In this way, I perceive the cycles.

TAO TE CHING no 16

The Tao teaches us to notice life's patterns, to reflect upon what is happening. Reflection can lead to positive growth and change.

This could be a time in your life when you are making an inner voyage, exploring new ideas, fantasizing new experiences, new career or role. It may be that you see situations in a strange new light.

I CHING no. 56

Reflection takes time and practice. As with any skill or habit, you get better the more you work with it. Reflect upon your feelings about sport, its patterns and rhythms as they present themselves to you. Work at understanding the deep relationship between your personal and your athletic lives. Their interaction contributes directly to your performance fluctuations.

TAOSPORT TRAINING FOR ATHLETICS

For five days, an extremely talented athlete consistently failed to keep up with other cyclists. Normally, he would have had no trouble outriding them. He seemed rather despondent over the matter. I asked him how his life outside of sport was going. He reflected for a minute and said he had no time to train because work was demanding. He hadn't slept through the night in months because a severe bike injury made him uncomfortable. His ten-month-old child kept him awake for many hours. For a week prior to riding with his friends, he had been nursing a flu and had lost much of his strength. Once he told me about his life, he realized, "Aha! I'm physically drained. No wonder I can't keep up." Reflection helped him get a grip on reality. He was no longer discouraged, having realized that the events in his life were responsible for his poor performance.

Affirmations for "Tuning In" to Your Life

- "When I travel inside, I can move outside— reflect!"
- "Stop, look, and listen—what's going on?"
- "Reflection will enlighten me."

81

- *"I am open to understanding how everything relates to my performance."*

Exercise: Inventory

This exercise will help you understand the relationship between your life and your sports performance. Complete this inventory during periods of low energy, poor performance, and decreased motivation and commitment. During the past year:

- Have you experienced changes in sleep patterns?

- Has there been a death or a loss of a close relationship?

- Have you experienced unusual stress at work or home?

- Has your family grown, bringing an increase in responsibility?

- Have you become involved with new interests or hobbies?

- Has your social life taken on new dimensions?

- Has your interest in sports changed in any way?

- Have you been excessively ill or injured?

- Have you had an increase in financial responsibility?

Answering yes to one or more of these questions suggests that your personal life is affecting your physical capabilities, as well as your change in attitude toward sport. Use this reflection as an opportunity to become aware of where you are, from where you came, and to where you are going.

TAOSPORTS FOR BUSINESS AND LIFE

John, a professor of Chinese philosophy at the University of Colorado, had some colleagues who didn't consider him serious enough for the academic life. They objected that he sojourned every other quarter to the Sonora Desert, the Olympic Peninsula, or other peaceful locations, to try to understand the relationship of the Tao to life. According to his peers, his publication output was below standard. John, however, realized that the real essence of philosophy and the love of knowledge could only be experienced away from the antiseptic setting of the university environment. His travels catalyzed stimulating new thoughts, stories, and ideas, which he brought back into the classroom to inspire students to reflect, as John had, upon their journey in life. To the dismay of his detractors, John's classes about Taoism constantly overflowed. Students would line the hallways outside his filled classes to hear him speak.

Whenever times got difficult while at home or on the job, John would seek solitude by running thirty miles or spending the night alone in a tent to reflect upon life's happenings. He refused to ride the windowless train, metaphorically traveling through life blindly, only to get off at the last stop and wonder, "Where have I been? What was this all about?" Not only did John believe in taking time to smell the roses, he ate them.

Guides for Conscious Living Through Reflection

The mundane realities of daily existence will often cause you to disregard the value of inner stillness, but you will notice that life is much more meaningful when you take the time to reflect. Conscious living is a conscious choice. These reflections may help you come to terms with different choices and challenges that you face in life.

- When you feel self-absorbed and obsessed with life's pain and struggle, take the time to reflect upon what you already have or will have rather than on what you lack at the moment. This will give you a positive perspective. Remember that a partly cloudy forecast is also partly sunny. The dawn always follows the darkest part of the night.

- If you become ill or injured, take the time to reflect upon your lifestyle to see how diet, sleep patterns, or lack of exercise could be contributing to your problems. For example, try to see the relationships between an illness and the kinds of foods or drugs you may be ingesting. Are you exercising too hard or too long? Are you not getting sufficient rest each day?

- When failure or setback come your way, reflect upon the lessons they potentially offer. Learn from them—your performance may improve as a result.

Exercise: Reflection

This basic exercise will help you to take the time necessary for reflection so that you will be better able to cope with life's patterns, cycles, crises, and setbacks.

> While you are relaxed, say the words, "I trust my feelings and perceptions about my present world."
>
> How are you feeling emotionally? Feel your sadness, anger, excitement, peace, frustration, happiness, confusion, disappointment. Why are you feeling this way? How do these feelings impact on the rest of your life, at work or at home?
>
> How are you feeling physically? Experience the feeling, be it tired, energetic, calm, relaxed, cold, hot, weak, or strong. Why are you feeling this way? How do these feelings affect the rest of your life?
>
> How are you feeling spiritually? Are you empathic, caring, and loving? Do you take time to reflect and be inner directed rather than be unconscious and concerned with the external aspects of life? Why are you feeling this way? Do these feelings impact your life?
>
> How are you feeling mentally? Are you alert, clear-thinking, and decisive? Or do you feel dull, unclear, and hesitant? Why are you feeling this way? How do these feelings impact on your life?

THE
OBSTACLES

GOING BEYOND BLOCKS
TO THE BEGINNER'S MIND

You may sometimes experience resistance to getting into the positive Beginner's Mind that is conducive to practicing the TaoSports of Part II. The TaoSports of Part III will help you recognize the most common obstacles to the Beginner's Mind and show you how to overcome them. You will learn to see many of these obstacles as opportunities in disguise.

FEAR

All things in the cosmos will be aroused to movement
through fear. This movement will be cautious,
and cautious movement will bring success.

I CHING no. 51

While recently cycling downhill one wet, drizzly morning, I had a serious cycling accident. The bike slid out from under me, causing multiple skin abrasions and sore bones and muscles. Afraid of having another accident, I avoided riding for weeks. The first time I was back on the bike, I descended a hill with a group of my training buddies, feeling like a beginner. I mentioned to someone that I was quite fearful of falling on sharp turns. His reply: "It's good that you have fear—you need to be cautious." He was right. I had not been cautious enough when I had fallen. My new fear helped me ride carefully and successfully in the downhill portion of the ride. I noticed that when I tried to fight my natural fear, I experienced a lot of tension in trying to force it away. This behavior would have eventually led to another accident.

Fear is a natural emotion. It indicates that you need to be alert. It is a survival instinct. Fighting or forcing away fear creates a counterforce that makes you tense and anxious and interferes with your performance.

Fear is intrinsic to certain sports that have real physical risks.

Many athletes seek out such sports because they love the element of fear that accompanies the event. Curious about this attraction I asked a sky diver why he chose his sport. He replied, "The adrenaline rush that I get as I'm about to exit the plane is the greatest rush in the world. It's better than sex. I feel so alive."

He invited me to observe one of his free-falls and I took advantage of the opportunity. When I watched the jump, I noticed that two bodies were attached to each other. Why did he jump holding on to another person? Because he would be too frightened to jump alone, without his instructor. "I didn't want to be *too* fearful," he said. He took on only as much fear as he could handle. Mountain climbers, sky divers, downhill skiers, kayakers, gymnasts, cyclists, and athletes in various other potentially life-threatening sports all feel this fear. In each case, the fear presents the athlete with the impetus to compete, yet it can also create an obstacle to performance. What you resist will persist. Resistance is quite common among neophytes in these arenas of sport. They, too, tend to fight such fear and force it away.

TAOSPORT TRAINING FOR ATHLETICS

While I was living in Boulder, Colorado, I was fortunate to be able to work and play with many outstanding rock climbers. I joined two of them on a climb up the cable route of Long's Peak (14,000-plus feet). I realized, however, that I had taken on more than I could handle. Frozen to the slate with the threat of a two-thousand-foot drop, I held on for my life. I tried to fight my fear by saying, "What's wrong with me? Why am I so scared? The other climbers did it, so why can't I?" But I couldn't move. "Damn this fear," I thought. But the fear persisted. One of the other climbers realized how frightened I was and reassured me that the fear I was experiencing was nature's way of saying, "Don't continue." He climbed down to my position, and in a slow, relaxed fashion he guided me back to a safe place.

I realized when it was all over that by fighting my own healthy fear, I had caused it to increase so much that it incapacitated me. I learned that I need to take the first sign of fear as an indication that I may have overstepped my skill level, that I may not be ready; I may need more training. If I can relax in that moment of fear, my ability to perform will improve.

According to the teachings of the Tao, cooperating with the forces in nature will create an advantage for you in your sport. Because fear is a natural part of life, it doesn't go away. It can either paralyze you or give you an opportunity to assess the risk you're facing and prepare for it properly. Fear is a friend that you must acknowledge and embrace. If you feel endangered or fearful, ask yourself why you're feeling that way. Have you prepared well for what you are doing? Do you have all the information you need? Are you thoroughly equipped? Are you out of your comfort zone? Let yourself be afraid—accept fear's friendly word of advice.

The TaoSport approach to fear is in the principle *wu wei*—let go. Like practitioners of the martial art aikido, you can actually "defeat" your opponent—your fear—by blending with its own force. Philosopher Alan Watts states, "The other side of every fear is freedom." Transcending fear is the ultimate freedom, because once you transcend it, you realize that anything is possible, given the proper preparation.

Remember that you are not alone. Every athlete—even the greatest of the great—has fear.

Visualization: Releasing Fear

If you have double-checked that you are completely prepared to progress with your event and yet you still feel fear, here is a visualization to help you embrace and then let go of your fear.

> Go to your imaginary safe place and breathe
> deeply, in and out, five times. Once you are
> relaxed, picture the fear as a person. Give it a
> face, a personality, a posture, and a demeanor.
> Know that this entity is a natural friend. Talk to it
> as if it were real: "Hi, fear. I understand you are
> here to help me be a better athlete." Listen to
> fear's response. Then, ask your new friend,
> "What do I need to know or do at this time to
> feel more confident and relaxed?" Hear what
> fear has to say. Listen to your friend's wonderful
> suggestions. Reassure fear that you will abide by
> the input, thank your friend for being in your life,
> bid farewell, and tell this friend to come again in
> time of need. Fear smiles and waves "good-bye,"
> turns, and walks away. Sense how relaxed and

wonderful you feel. You are fortunate to be able
to discover and receive such help from a good
friend.

Exercise: Subdividing Tasks

We often feel fear when we are overwhelmed by the enormity of a task we
have undertaken. Whether climbing a rock, skiing a steep mountain, running a marathon, or performing in a triathlon, we fear we just might not
make it all the way. Rather than looking ahead, try dividing the task into
small, manageable segments. Can you climb another two feet up? Can you
ski just to that tree? An Olympic marathoner once told me how frightened
he was that he'd blow his lead and possibly not finish. Rather than dwell on
that, he focused on running relaxed to the next mile while holding the lead.
He did this for each of the last four miles, and to his surprise, he finished
with energy to spare. Looking at the whole picture can be a frightening
experience. Taking one step at a time reduces your fear as you relax into the
shortened task.

Affirmations for Fearlessness

These fearless affirmations will enable you to think more positively about
your fears prior to their occurrence. Think about the typical fear-producing
situation in your sport, and recite these affirmations:

- *"Fear is my friend who helps me defend."*
- *"Thank you, fear, for helping me here."*
- *"The voice of fear is healthy to hear."*
- *"Courageous athletes feel the fear and go
  beyond. I am courageous!"*
- *"I respect and stay within my comfort zone."*

TAOSPORTS FOR BUSINESS AND LIFE

Remember the story of Beauty and the Beast? The heroine was given the
choice of moving in with an intimidating monster or witnessing the death of
her father. She chose the former to save her dad's life. Then, confronted by

her enormous fear of the beast, she discovered that a kind, gentle soul resided within his threatening exterior. It's a powerful lesson for all of us as we prepare to go beyond the fears that limit our lives and achievements.

At a recent "Risk Taking for Success" seminar, one of my corporate clients and I were talking about overcoming the fear of speaking before a large group. One of the participants claimed that this wasn't an issue for him. "It's no big deal," he said. When asked what his secret was, he replied, "Just as I'm about to go onstage, I look at everyone and see them as little toddlers running around naked in the sand. It reminds me of how we're all basically nice, playful people with common origins. I can't help but laugh." By taking ourselves too seriously, we create fears about having to live up to the very serious images we create of ourselves. If you can lighten up, you can enjoy the fact that we all have more in common than not.

Visualization: Changing Fear to Comfort

Certain situations related to business and work can create counterproductive fear or anxiety: talking with a boss, presenting a talk before a group, confronting an irresponsible employee, being interviewed for a new position, negotiating with a client, and handling crises. These are but a few that may be relevant to you. This visualization exercise will help you reprogram your associations from fear to comfort.

> Imagine in full detail your most fearful scenario, one that stimulates all the fear centers of the brain. Perhaps, in the past, you experienced a trauma during such circumstances. See the scene in complete detail: the people, the place, the sounds. Now, take one more deep breath, relax, and re-create a similar situation. But this time change the way you act. Respond with a more positive, powerful posture. See yourself being calm, confident, and "on top of things." Notice how smoothly the event unfolds.

Practice this new scenario for a minimum of five minutes, twice a day for one week prior to the day when you are to perform a task that frightens you. You will find yourself able to change the fear into a positive experience.

Guides for Handling Fear

- Take a close look at your fear. Ask yourself, "What is the worst thing that could happen if I followed through on this fear-producing situation?" If you can live with the worst-case scenario, you can go beyond the fear. If not, wait and collect more information until your fear of going forward is less than your fear of standing still.

- Remember that fear can be helpful to you, alerting you to where you need to be careful and prepared. Assess the risks and prepare properly. Information-gathering is a wonderful way of releasing fear. The unknown is fear's fuel.

- If you're afraid to interview for a job, to make a presentation, to take an exam, or to perform any task, you probably haven't prepared adequately on some level. Fear helps us plan the work and work the plan.

- Vigorous exercise coupled with relaxation or meditation helps to put fear into perspective. You will come to understand its message more clearly. You may discover that you really have nothing to fear, that the fear is an illusion or an irrational obsession.

- Seek out others who have had similar fears in their lives and ask them what they did to cope with them. Experience is a great teacher—perhaps you can take advantage of the life learning of others.

FEAR OF FAILURE

In the Natural Law some lose
and in this way profit.

TAO TE CHING no. 42

In the Western world, "winning isn't everything—it's the only thing." Many respected coaches, parents, and teachers believe that losing represents failure and is an abomination to be avoided at all costs. To many athletes, losing is so devastating that it causes them to discontinue their efforts or quit sports altogether. Players are traded, coaches are fired, athletes are benched or "cut" in the wake of error, setback, failure, and loss.

This mentality is responsible for much of the fear of failure that athletes experience at all levels of competition. Viewing failure as shameful creates unnecessary anxiety, tension, and pain. Failure cannot be avoided. The greatest of the great have failed at times, and so will you.

A wonderful Buddhist saying states, "The arrow that hits the bull's-eye is the result of a hundred misses." You perfect your game through adversity and failure. Lao-tzu taught that we must align with the forces of nature. Look at failure as a lesson from which you can learn. Seeing failure as an opportunity for improvement makes it more tolerable and will help you relax and figure out how to go beyond your present level of performance.

Just as the tumultuous chaos of a
thunderstorm brings a nurturing rain
that allows life to flourish, so too in
human affairs times of advancement are
preceded by times of disorder. Success
comes to those who can weather the storm.

I CHING no. 3

As a child, you learned from repeated failures to master one of the most difficult and challenging of athletic skills: walking. Watching my son Sean learn how to walk was a painful process. His first four steps ended in a fall that brought his forehead into the corner of a small table and gave him a vicious half-inch black-and-blue welt. Two days later, he repeated the fall, with another, equally painful bump. When he screamed uncontrollably, I picked him up and held him tightly, saying, "Oh Sean, my boy, I love you so much. I wish you didn't have to feel such pain. Don't worry, you'll be walking soon." Following these words, he calmed down and immediately tried again. Within five days, he had it down.

Sean's two painful bruises were indicative of major setbacks. When adults get banged up that badly, they often consider it sufficient reason to quit. Such failure and physical trauma is enough to call a halt to further attempts. But Sean kept on going, learning from each mistake. Failure was his teacher. He mastered the skill because he received lots of love and support during the setbacks, and more important, no one ever said he couldn't do it. How many times, when I've experienced failure, did I tell myself, "I'm no good! I can't do it! What's the sense in trying?" My failure was so damaging, I refused to try again. I've taken up cycling at the age of forty-eight and I'm progressing rapidly in spite of my own accidents because, fortunately, I've learned from Sean—and the Tao!—that setbacks are only lessons in improvement. They're the only way we can progress in sport.

The *Tao Te Ching* challenges us to see the way things are and accept the truth about them. Evolved TaoAthletes do not fight failure; they tolerate these experiences. Sometimes they're "on" and sometimes they're "off" just as sometimes singers are "in voice" and sometimes not—but they view each as a natural state.

For example, Olympian Joan Benoit ran a series of progressively slower marathons prior to her fastest performance in Boston. By the third time she ran a slow marathon, she may have thought that her days of improving were over. It's easy to lose confidence in yourself when you try as hard as you can but continue to do worse. Rather than get discouraged and quit, however, Benoit learned something new from each "failure." She put it all together and finally ran the race of her life, setting a world record for the 26.2-mile distance.

Michael Musyoki, the number-one road-runner in the world in 1982, reflected upon failure and setback after one of his poorer performances. Most people had expected him to win the important 10,000-meter race, but he was edged out at the finish line by Jon Sinclair—someone he had beaten a number of times before. After the event, when reporters asked him to what he attributed his failure, he responded very matter-of-factly, "One day you beat someone, the next week he'll beat you." Like Joan Benoit, he exhibited a trait common among all champions and TaoAthletes: a high tolerance for failure and setback, as valuable pieces of data. They realize that what they learn from defeat is more valuable than a victory.

In the martial art aikido, the fighter blends with the direction of an opposing force, moves with it, and uses its power to defuse the attack. This offers an interesting perspective on failure: If you see your setback as an opposing force, you can still accept and blend with it and internalize its lessons to your advantage. By doing this, the power of the opposing force no longer exists. You redirect the force and forge ahead.

TAOSPORT TRAINING FOR ATHLETICS

As a competitive runner, I've often experienced setbacks while running important races. One day, a stiff wind was backing us at the start. I could have taken advantage of that wind by going out faster—I then could have expended less effort to run more quickly. Instead, I ran my usual opening pace quite comfortably, even effortlessly. At the turnaround, I headed back into the gale, but I was never able to make up the valuable minutes I had lost. I have since used this information on how *not* to pace myself in such a situation. Each experience we have yields us a treasure of knowledge—if we choose to see and accept it that way. The lesson here is to redirect failure and setback so that they work for you, not against you.

Affirmations for Reframing Failure

These affirmations, if you recite them daily, will enable you to use failure as a positive force for athletic improvement:

- *"Failures are lessons from which I learn and forge ahead."*
- *"Success does not guarantee happiness; failure need not guarantee misery."*
- *"Performance is a roller coaster."*
- *"STOP, LISTEN, and LEARN."*
- *"Adversity leads to inner strength. I am a better athlete because of it."*
- *"Tomorrow's another day!"*
- *"I silence my need to control outcomes."*
- *"I act, I don't react—I learn from failure."*

Exercise: From Failure to Opportunity

This cognitive restructuring technique can be used when you experience disappointment as a result of a poor performance, setback, or failure.

1. Record the objective facts about the event: for example, "I dropped out at mile twenty-four of the marathon."

2. Record your subjective judgment of your performance: for example, "I'm a terrible athlete; it's awful not finishing."

3. Record your emotional response to this judgment: for example, "I'm depressed. I'm devastated."

4. Record the objective data that support the subjective judgment you made in Step 2: for example, "There is none." For any objective data you do find, record the good counterinformation that is always there.

5. Record what you've learned from setback: for example, "I need to pace myself at the start, hydrate regularly, and change my training runs."

6. Based on Step 5, record how you feel now: for example, "I'm still

disappointed but I'm okay. I'm a better runner because of it, and I look forward to my next race."

Visualization: Self-Focus

If you have experienced a disappointment or setback, this visualization will help you focus on your next performance rather than dwell on your competitor's abilities. Let go of any desire to control the outcome of your next performance.

> In your state of relaxation, affirm, whether or not you are victorious, "I am in great shape, and I'll perform like a champion." Take a few minutes, and imagine yourself performing as well as you can, making all the right moves and exhibiting the strength, grace, and fluidity of an incredible athlete. See yourself in this moment as the epitome of excellence. Say to yourself, "If anyone is going to beat me today, they'll have to be at levels they've never before reached." Feel yourself forcing others to be at their very best. Dwell totally on your game, knowing that the outcome will take care of itself. If you happen to fail (according to the scoreboard), you are now open to advancing your level of play, as a champion would, by learning from any errors or setbacks.

TAOSPORTS FOR BUSINESS AND LIFE

Did you know that when a plane flies from San Francisco to Hawaii, it is off-course ninety percent of the time? It eventually reaches Hawaii because the pilot corrects for the interference and errors caused by the prevailing winds and other variables.

I was giving a seminar on "How to Turn Failure into Success" to a large group of industrial engineers at Stanford University. The division leader had just won the Manager of the Year award for exceeding expectations for productivity. His secret, according to the engineers, was his attitude toward failure. Rather than becoming obsessed with negative outcomes, he simply rewarded his workers for finding the solutions to inevitable setbacks, errors, and failures. Of course, with the pressure of always having to succeed removed from them, the employees were more relaxed and less fearful of failure, and as a result, their performance improved as well. Here is a perfect example of visionary leadership.

As in sport, failures and setbacks in business and life can be opportunities that show a better way without us realizing it. You and I must simply notice that, and be good to ourselves and others when adversity sets in.

Guides for Coping with Adversity

A very good friend desperately needed a job. After receiving a series of rejections from potential employers, she became devastated. Within two weeks of her latest setback, a most incredible job became available, one that was perfectly aligned with her talents and dreams. She applied, and after a few interviews she was one of two finalists. Learning from her previous interviewing mistakes, she decided to be more assertive and tell the prospective employer that she was the perfect choice for them, then give a list of reasons why. She got the position. What's interesting in retrospect is that her previous setbacks were, in the long run, really necessary for teaching her how to eventually land the ideal job. Had she been offered one of those other positions, this perfect job would not have been available for her.

Many of us are critical and unkind toward ourselves when we experience setbacks. The Tao has helped me focus on failure as a positive, natural, inevitable process. These positive thoughts might help you deal with adversity.

- It is absolutely impossible for anyone to be thoroughly competent and achieving. Failure is part of the process of living.

- If your performance at work is lackluster, think how you can improve something for the next time.

- Patience and persistence will bring you from failure to success in most ventures.

- Real failure is the unwillingness to take the chance to improve life.

- Find the opportunity latent in setbacks and failure by asking what you have learned from this experience. How would you do it differently the next time?

- Expectations with regard to outcomes are setups for failure. Establish strong preferences, instead, and then do everything within your capability and power to bring those preferences to fruition.

Exercise: Breaking "Failurephobia"

To set the stage for success in most competitive business and work situations, set yourself realistic, challenging, short-range goals. Since you are likely to achieve these goals frequently, you will build in the psychological message that "I am a winner; I am successful; I accomplish what I set my mind to doing." This will build courage, confidence, motivation, and commitment for future directions.

Exercise: Shattering the Myths of Failure

Since childhood, you have learned three basic myths about failure that make it intolerable. These myths are self-imposed limits, and there are ways to cognitively change them.

MYTH 1
IF YOU WORK HARD ENOUGH, YOU CAN AVOID FAILURE.

Not so! The greatest of the great could not escape failure, so why should you? I've worked with top-ranking Olympic athletes and performers from every walk of life. They all experience failure on some level. Failure, like so much of what we resist in life, is simply nature's way of expanding and teaching us.

MYTH 2
FAILURE IS WORTHLESS.

Failure is a necessary prerequisite to success. It teaches us much more than success if we learn from our mistakes, which are crucial to growth and development. Very successful, creative people have a higher-than-ordinary tolerance for their own errors, mistakes, and failures. They are willing to learn from their setbacks and push through those temporary "schooling" experiences.

MYTH 3
FAILURE IS DEVASTATING.

Disappointing, yes! But the feelings that result from setback and failure are generally exaggerated. Some people can find success to be more disappointing than devastating.

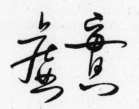

From the Taoist point of view, an educated man is one who believes he has not succeeded when he has, but is not sure he has failed when he fails, while the mark of the half-educated man is his assumption that his outward successes and failures are absolute and real.

LIN YUTANG, *THE IMPORTANCE OF LIVING*

FEAR OF SUCCESS

Holding to fullness is not as good as stopping in time.
Sharpness that probes cannot protect for long.
A house filled with riches cannot be defended.
Pride in wealth and position is overlooking one's
    collapse.
Withdrawing when success is achieved is the Tao
    in Nature.

TAO TE CHING no. 9

Following his spectacular victory over Bjorn Borg at Wimbledon, John McEnroe became the number-one-ranked tennis player in the world. His adjustment to this new crown was not smooth; he seemed to find it more of a burden than an accomplishment. After his victory, his level of play noticeably fell. In his own words, "I couldn't handle it well, and I don't know why." McEnroe had made his mark as one of the best ever to play tennis, yet the pressures and fears that accompany that lofty position seemed to take their toll.

Cycles and change are constant. After a victory must necessarily come some kind of decline. When we are successful, when we win an event, we have the illusion that we have "arrived." After the initial heady rush of happiness at our success, this illusion fades. Just as you don't dwell on times you did *not* win, don't dwell on your victories. Enjoy your moments of triumph, and let them support you during the challenges that follow. Some winning athletes worry about always having to defend their position at the top. Accepting the Tao will relieve you of that kind of pressure and strain. You do not need to fear success. Setbacks always follow success.

The zenith is usually brief. . . . When decline
approaches, the superior man does not consciously
anticipate it, for he expects such cyclic changes. He is
concerned with making the best of matters at hand.

I CHING no. 55

In his essay "Those Wrecked by Success," Sigmund Freud wrote that some people have difficulty dealing with the happiness of fulfillment. Such "success-phobia" is rampant in sport. Most athletes who would readily claim that they desire success subconsciously sabotage their own efforts. Many have a pattern of becoming ill or injured on the brink of making major breakthroughs. Because of the enormous stress associated with success, their performance suffers; they become erratic and inconsistent.

Some athletes at the top of their sport experience much anxiety over the numerous negative competitive factors: the envy, the sniping, the performance pressure. Success becomes an albatross for them, so weighty and strangling that they avoid it at all costs. Whenever they do well, they fear the inevitable failure that will always come after success because, they know, superior performance is transient. Remember that everyone fails at some time or other on the journey to excellence. Learn from your setbacks, and become more polished in the process.

This doesn't mean that you should look for or desire disaster and failure. If you do, you will find them, albeit prematurely. You can reach great heights without falling backward, but if your mind is focused on setbacks, you will create unnecessary and inhibiting tension and anxiety.

A subtle negative association with success is that it threatens other aspects of life: job, family, friends. After all, if you are really good, you may be tempted to devote more time to the sport to become even better. This means spending less time on your social and financial responsibilities.

Gayle Barron, the 1978 women's winner of the Boston Marathon, shed some light on this problem during one of my seminars at a running camp.

She related how difficult it was for her to be a pioneer (prior to this, women were not allowed to run Boston) in her field. Many of her friends believed that women should be at home with their families. She found little support among them for her avocation. When she succeeded, it forced them to look inward and evaluate themselves. They didn't appreciate this and showed their disapproval. She wondered how much she may have held herself back and sabotaged her true potential to win her friends' approval.

The truth is, in all of society, everyone who tries to succeed experiences pressure and tension. By breaking away from their stereotypical roles, many feel guilty for achieving beyond the limits society has conveniently ordained.

TAOSPORT TRAINING FOR ATHLETICS

I collected this story of the fear of success while I was working with a track and field program at a major university. The highly respected head coach told the entire coaching staff that "things have been going fantastically. We're off to a great start—the best in years. Be very careful because that is when something crazy usually happens. . . . Keep your eyes open for something that may go wrong." Sure enough, they found it—something did go wrong. The coach's negative attitude was transmitted to the entire team, and as he had predicted, it was "too good to be true." The coaches really didn't believe they deserved success (or they believed they deserved to have something go wrong because they were too fortunate), so neither did the team. None of the talent lived up to their potential that year, even though they easily could have won the NCAA championship.

Exercise: Uncovering Fear of Success

The Tao encourages you to discover whether you have any of these fears of success. Understand that they are quite common and natural among athletes. Answering the following questions will help you uncover any fears that may be preventing you from enjoying success—a yes response to them indicates a possible fear of success. You may find it valuable to visualize yourself during a successful performance, then during a problematic performance. Stay with the feelings you experience in each case and consider these questions:

1. If you had succeeded in the problematic performance, do you think you would have experienced pressure from yourself or others to perform as well or even better in future contests?

2. If you had succeeded, do you think you would have become more accountable to a greater number of people? Would this, itself, be frightening?

3. If you had succeeded, do you think your life would have become more complicated in an unpleasant way?

4. If you had succeeded, do you think you would have feared the inevitable decline from your ephemeral lofty position? Are you really afraid to fail, ultimately?

5. Do you fear the enormous amount of work it may take to commit yourself totally to being successful?

Visualization: Discovering Fear of Success

Having answered these questions, you are now ready to experience any negative feelings you associate with success. Visualize the following, and notice the reactions you have to your success. Anxiety, tension, or pressure will indicate a fear of success.

> Imagine yourself successful in your sport. See yourself rise to the top. Now that you are a success, how does it feel? Take a few moments to dwell on this feeling. What concerns do you have with regard to your future, your new life as a success? Do you have any anxiety or tension related to expectations or inevitable failure in the future? See and feel yourself experiencing all feelings associated with this place of success.

Remember that the Tao sees options in nature; if you fear success, you may choose to avoid going forward altogether. You may consciously decide to "stay put" for now and not "go for it" at this time, leaving your options open for the future. Having the ability to be a successful athlete is not the sole reason to become one. You can decide for yourself just what level of success makes you happy, but make sure that you are making a conscious decision, and not one based on false beliefs about your talents and potential.

Visualization: Embracing Success

This visualization will help you accept and embrace success in advance of an event. Practice this for several weeks before an event, twice a day.

In your state of relaxation, bring to mind one or two important goals that you can attain in your exercise, sport, or event. In order to achieve these successfully, what work do you need to do? Focus on the process of the work and exercise you need to do. Feel the joy and excitement of simply doing it. Being excellent in the process is also true success. See how much you improve, and notice how much higher your level of play is. You feel tremendous satisfaction in the moment of preparation, regardless of the outcome.

Now, in your mind, test your skills and achieve your goals. Feel yourself playing at levels beyond your custom and habit. See yourself fulfill each goal effortlessly. Now bask in the warmth of success. Say to yourself, "I deserve all of this. It's my moment, and I enjoy the entire experience. All who know me celebrate this accomplishment, knowing that they too will have their turn."

Affirmations: Beyond Fear of Success

- *"I deserve and am entitled to the very best there is."*
- *"There is plenty of success for all of us."*
- *"I give myself permission to develop my full potential."*

- *"I enjoy the bliss of fulfillment."*
- *"Although decline is inevitable, the thrill of victory is worth it."*
- *"I would rather succeed and then fail than never succeed at all."*
- *"Every athlete has their day. I welcome mine whenever it comes."*

TAOSPORTS FOR BUSINESS AND LIFE

The business world is filled with situations that create, cultivate, and teach us fear of success. The new responsibilities that accompany an exalted position usher in new tensions, anxieties, and stress. No wonder many of us sabotage our efforts to become successful.

A young businessman was promoted to vice-president of his company at the age of thirty-five. Unexpectedly, this new position radically changed his life, not only at work but also at home. Things became more complex as he became more accountable to a greater number of people. For the first six months as a VP, he was out sick on four different occasions. His performance took a nose-dive, and he became increasingly unhappy. His family life became nonexistent, and his two children suffered from not seeing their father as much as they had before his successful climb up the corporate ladder. His "promotion commotion" took a toll. Within a year he resigned his position and left the company for a lower-paying, more relaxed job. He had learned to fear success.

Clearly, he wasn't aware of the "failure of success" syndrome. He is now terrified about the possibility of ever being a success and will probably sabotage any effort to succeed in the future.

To Choose or Not to Choose—Success

Most of us at one time or another resist knowing our potential. If your goals are realistic and attainable and if you are willing to persist with patience, successful outcomes are yours for the asking. Yet other considerations are also important. This exercise will help you see that success is a choice, and when you activate that personal power, you will always feel successful.

If you knew that you were quite good at something, you would feel compelled to act on it, or else feel guilty about not developing that potential. But maybe you would rather not act on it—after all, developing this aspect of yourself and living up (in your mind and others') to that standard may require hard work. Becoming totally committed to excellence in business and life often means taking time away from your family and friends. It's a decision that can have painful repercussions. As a result, you may choose a road that avoids success, with all its pressures; success becomes a frightening entity. But if you turn your back on your talent, you create another pain to contend with: You must grow old constantly wondering how good you could have been. Your many regrets that you did not act in your earlier, more formative time of life could prove to be an even greater burden than the difficulties attached to becoming successful. The choice is yours to make. Being cognizant of this choice may make it easier for you to determine what is more important. If you think you'll have regrets later, "go for it" now, while you are still capable. If not, don't get down on yourself for calling a halt before you succeed.

A client came to me confused, angry, and disappointed over the treatment he experienced from his friends. At the age of forty-eight, he had changed his life through healthy eating, exercise, and meditation. This forced his friends to examine their own lifestyles, and they seemed to feel threatened by this and excluded him from their social gatherings. Rather than conform to their lifestyle and put aside his new path, he decided to follow his dreams. This, of course, created harsh feelings. To help him with this, I suggested that he communicate his feelings directly to those involved. He did, telling them, "I sense some changes in our relationships—I feel ignored. My decision to change my lifestyle doesn't change my good feelings for you." They appreciated this tremendously. If people are true friends, they will support your successes in life. If they don't, can you still consider them friends?

Living the Tao in the Face of Success

Once you achieve success in business and life, you can help yourself ride the wave, without sabotaging it, by seeing your success as part of the larger process of life. Use your success as a feedback mechanism that indicates you are on the right track. Set new goals that will keep you on this path into the future. Remember that success is a wonderful journey and that real success is the quality of that journey. Understand that cycles of decline usually accompany cycles of success. Accept this balance and all that it has to offer.

Each day, practice ways that you can follow your bliss. At work or at home, do the things you love to do as often as you can. This will increase your feelings of being successful, regardless of the outcome of your efforts.

Try to remember not to take yourself so seriously. Flow with life's movement, and experience your transition. It's great to be alive! You are never as great as your successes, and never as bad as your failures.

SLUMPS

Coordinate your forces so that there is a
minimum conflict and maximum effect. One uses
four ounces to deflect four thousand pounds.

I CHING no. 61

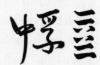

There are two kinds of athletes: those who have already experienced slumps, and those who will. Slumps are the common ground uniting all who compete in sport. Slumps, like people, come in all sizes and shapes—long ones, short ones, big ones, little ones, famous ones, and those you never hear about. You may remember the well-known Columbia University football team slump between 1984 and 1988, when they lost forty-four consecutive games before finally beating Princeton University. The New York Mets established records for winless streaks in the 1960s. One high school basketball team in Nebraska played sixty-four games without a victory.

One of the more famous recent, painful slumps occurred in women's long-distance running. In 1984, Lisa Weidenbach finished fourth in the Olympic trials marathon—only the top three go to the Olympics. In 1988, in her second attempt to make the team, she ran a wonderful race, but was denied again, once again finishing in fourth place. She expected the 1992 trials, held in Houston, Texas, to be her breakthrough. Although she ran a smart race with the lead pack and was in position to strike, she still fell short, finishing a frustrating fourth for the third consecutive time. Her slump lasted eight years.

During slumps, the skills we have mastered seem to desert us. A batter fails to hit safely in thirty-five attempts, a team loses twenty-one consecutive games, a tennis star's serve becomes ineffective, or a basketball player can't sink a foul shot. Whatever the game, slumps are inevitable, natural components. When their performance declines, most athletes try to force themselves to get back on track. In doing this, however, they often create more pressure, tension, and anxiety for themselves, thereby intensifying the slump, making it deeper and longer. When TaoAthletes yield, however, they place themselves in position to perform optimally. The power is subtle: "The most yielding parts of the world overtake the most rigid parts of the world." (*Tao Te Ching* no. 43)

TAOSPORT TRAINING FOR ATHLETICS

TaoAthletes break their slumps by paying attention to their energy flow and to the rhythms of their sport or practice, and going with them. Observe how a child skier handles a fall: rolling with the direction of the force, the child laughs, gets up, and continues down the slope. An adult skier, however, usually applies a counterforce by trying to fight the fall and resist it; he or she can end up needing a stretcher and emergency care. Think of your slump as a fall that was inevitable. Resisting it is counterproductive. Relax into it, and you will limit the damage it does to your mind, emotions, and overall performance.

Observe yourself calmly in your slump. Set up a schedule for meditating. At first, for two or three weeks, meditate to relax and quiet your mind and your body. Get back in touch with yourself, your natural rhythms. Go with the flow; don't try to fight your way through your slump. A good cyclist tucks behind another to avoid fighting the force of the wind. Good mountain climbers don't conquer a mountain; they align with its natural forces or contour. Japanese martial artists blend with the force of their opponent. In basketball, don't force your shots; get into a flow, and when you see an opening, fire away. In tennis, don't force your serve; relax and flow through the motions. In football, when a block or pass comes your way, blend into it: when you are pushed—pull.

I asked a professional football player how he could continually survive the vicious pounding he got from the opposition. He said that he works according to a game plan in which he takes the oncoming defensive player and diverts his force to the side rather than opposing it. Theoretically, the harder his opponent's attack, the easier it is for him to direct his force to the ground, away from the ball.

Visualization: Slumps

Professional basketball player Tim Hardaway of the Golden State Warriors knows what slumps are all about. Averaging twenty-five points a game, he suddenly went ice-cold, shooting 0 for 17 in one game, to set an NBA record for missed field goals. You could see his frustration as he began to force each shot, hoping he could break the ice and score a point. But it was not to be. In one game, realizing that things eventually do turn around, he relaxed and netted thirty-five points in one of his best-scoring performances ever. The key to his turnaround was his ability to laugh, relax, and yield to his slump. He stopped forcing shots that weren't there.

This visualization exercise will help you to hasten your recovery from the slump to your natural level of play.

> In your relaxed state, imagine looking at yourself on videotape and noticing how you play when in the slump. See the obvious mistakes that are contributing to your problem. Now, let that go. Watch your performance again, this time in slow motion. See every detail of your play exactly as if you were executing perfectly. Once you see the tremendous improvement, gradually speed up the videotape until you are now able to see yourself in perfect play at real-life speed. Play this tape over and over in your mind's eye. Feel the joy of being back on the road of success. Now that you have seen yourself perform, become that player. Imagine yourself in your body, playing at this corrected level. Following this exercise, go and actually perform the skills physically that you were practicing mentally.

Affirmations for Coming Out of Slumps

When you find yourself in a slump and realize you are trying to force your way out, use the following touchstones to get yourself back to the TaoSport approach to slumps.

- *"Go with the flow like H_2O."*
- *"Soft is strong."*
- *"I feel relaxed, loose, and flowing."*
- *"I do not need to force; all is evolving according to a plan."*
- *"Less is more."*
- *"No need to defend when I yield and blend."*
- *"When I give up control, I get on a roll and play with some soul."*

TAOSPORTS FOR BUSINESS AND LIFE

In their late thirties, some wonderful friends of mine were trying to become pregnant. (They were in a reproductive slump.) Feeling the time constraints of aging, they tried to force nature by using every option this technological society makes available, but in vain. Their anxiety and tension mounted as they tried and tried. As each month passed with no positive results, they became increasingly tense and irritable. They couldn't have enjoyed the process in such a mental state. Finally, they stopped pushing and decided to adopt a child rather than to wait any longer. They experienced bliss with their "new" baby. Within two months of the arrival of the adopted child, they became pregnant. When they stopped forcing and pressuring themselves, their bodies had relaxed and the natural processes of conception had no longer been impeded by the tension and anxiety they both felt.

Although you may be quite anxious to proceed with your plans . . . don't push. The situation will develop at its own pace. . . . The cycles in life cannot be hastened.

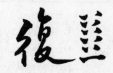

I CHING no 24

Guides for Getting Out of Slumps

The Tao teaches us that when we align our aims and goals to the natural flow of the cosmos, we create abundance with the attainment of our desires. And regardless of the outcome, your enjoyment of a process in a nonforceful manner will actually create what you are really in search of anyway—bottom-line joy, happiness, and peace. Use these TaoSport precepts, rather than control and force, to help get through a perceived "slump" or period of frustration:

- When you feel muscular tension and tightness, you may be trying to force or control a situation at hand. Be a positive influence on things while "taking your hands off the steering wheel." It helps to take a few deep breaths and affirm: "Soft is strong. My influence is enough to create the very best for all involved."

- When you are sick or injured, you need to relax. Trying to force a speedy recovery will only create tension and anxiety and thereby exacerbate the malady. Rest is indicated, so move only as fast as your body allows. Visualize yourself healing.

- Whenever you are riding a bike or driving a car, always yield to an opposing force—the oncoming cars. Automatically give others the right of way when they seem intent upon "pushing" you around.

- When you are entering a relationship, try to avoid forcing or hastening the process. Good friendships happen naturally—they take time to develop. When your social agenda slows down, rather than begin a "phone blitz" to fill the void, relax and enjoy the quiet time.

- When tension mounts between yourself and another person, try to find ways to back down rather than to force your opinion on him or her. Look for solutions, not fault. Ask yourself the question: Would you rather be happy or right? The latter requires that you control, force, or conquer an opponent. No one wins in that case.

Visualization: A Nonforce
Approach to Management

If you and your fellow workers are going through a bad time, if you are experiencing a work slump, rather than pushing or forcing your employees to be more productive, try being understanding, kind, and caring, and watch how things turn around. Everyone experiences slumps in productivity. And there's usually a legitimate reason for them, unrelated to the workers' ability.

A very successful and well-liked manager of a computer corporation in San Jose is very firm but quite fair with his employees. When an employee's productivity begins to slide, he doesn't hesitate to address the issue, and at the same time he listens to what is going on in the employee's life away from the job. He listens with understanding and kindness, reassuring the employee that, if possible, he will help him through the difficulty. This manager believes that this motivates employees to be more productive: "They like me, so they want to give their all. If I were harsh and detatched, they'd probably rebel like teenagers do with parents. They respect me too much to let me down, and that respect is what turns things around."

This visualization exercise will help you generate more respect from coworkers, children, and family. It emphasizes a nonforce approach to management.

> Begin this exercise in your state of relaxation by affirming: "I desire to create a relaxed, productive, and happy environment for all those under my guidance." Realize that excessive, continuous force will cost you the allegiance of those in your environment. See yourself treat others with kindness and fairness. You are firm and direct, yet you never attack or judge. Imagine the group process flowing freely and constructively—exactly as you would like it. See them wanting to go beyond what's required because you have created a safe, secure, healthy environment. Hear yourself asking them for ways to accomplish your goals rather than simply forcing your will to get the job done. Know that you are deeply respected and held in high esteem.

Affirmations for Nonforce Management

Consider putting cards with these or other affirmations in places where they will be readily visible and easily recited on a daily basis.

- *"I look for opportunities to direct others with kindness."*
- *"An office with fun is easy to run."*
- *"My care for the work is in my caring for the workers."*

FATIGUE

Nothing in the world,
Is as yielding as water;
Yet in attacking the firm and inflexible,
Nothing triumphs so well.

TAO TE CHING no. 78

It was the third mile of a grueling five-mile uphill race. My body was beginning to cramp up. The tightness and loss of fluidity were making me quite anxious. Thoughts of not finishing the race began to sabotage my efforts.

And then I remembered to "let go" and talk with this demon: "Hi, fatigue—it's you again. Perhaps you want to stay, but realize that I've got a job to complete here, and you'll have to wait until I finish." With that, a voice spoke out, "Okay, I'll wait." These words were uttered by a fellow runner who, without my knowing, was listening to what appeared to be a rather inane conversation. I managed to laugh, relax, and divert my attention from my unnecessary concern over my fatigue, and I finished the race tired, yet strong.

According to the Tao, nonresistance and a yielding attitude triumph against rigidity. In sport, fatigue is rigidity of the body. Your anxiety and tension greatly increase when you resist them, causing even greater fatigue. What you resist will persist.

Essentially, fatigue is a natural psychophysical response brought about by overexertion. Any athlete who pushes limits will experience a visit from this painful friend. Fatigue is simply your body's way of talking to you and telling you that you need more food or more rest, perhaps, or that you need to tune in to how your mind is holding and forcing your body.

During a performance, you can't take time to rest. But you may be able to cope more productively with the tension, anxiety, and stress created by the onset of fatigue. You can do this by yielding to your fatigue in the spirit of *wu wei*, which in Chinese means, among other things, "don't force." Fighting or becoming angry at fatigue will only frustrate or distract you, or make you lose your confidence, enthusiasm, and courage. This chapter will help you work with fatigue in a productive manner.

TAOSPORT TRAINING FOR ATHLETICS

Guides for Overcoming Fatigue

Fatigue is always a factor in sport. Treat it as a necessary element in your exploration of your potential. Give it life, and talk to it as I did in my race. Use these mental tips to help you blend with your fatigue rather than fight it:

- Focus on how close you are to the finish of the event. Don't think about the pain or hurt you're feeling and thereby emphasize it. See yourself with only one minute left in the race or game. Know that you're going to make it, and feel relieved that it's almost over. If there's a lot more time left, focus on small segments, not the entire remaining stretch. Tell yourself, for example, "I'll just get to the next mile," or "I'll play well for the next five minutes, then I'll see where things are and how I'm doing."

- Concentrate on the form, style, pacing, and other technical aspects of the performance rather than on the physical distractions. Imagine watching yourself from the side or above, and admire the way you play. Check on your form from outside yourself, and appreciate the beauty of your performance.

- Reinterpret your sensation of fatigue. If you change your beliefs about pain—look for other meanings it may have—you will change the pain. For example, you may want to interpret it simply as a feeling you get when your muscles are working hard. See it as a necessary step in the exploration of your potential. Contemplate how wonderful it will be to experience the significant breakthroughs that will result from pushing your limits.

- Talk yourself through the fatigue: "Everyone probably hurts—it's the price we pay for breaking our limits." Make fatigue your ally or companion on your journey. It's there because your effort is superb.

- Use visualization to see tight muscles "melting" like blocks of snow. Visualize your muscles hanging on your bones.

- Chant, sing, or think about something else. Dissociating from the fatigue in this way will bring temporary relief. For example, repeat to yourself often, "I feel great, I feel great, I feel great." One top professional volleyball player, when she gets tired, squeezes her thumb and index finger together until her attention is completely focused on the pain in her fingers. Then she lets go and feels a sense of relief. Her thoughts of fatigue vanish too.

- Bargain with your body by telling it that you will rest, nourish, and replenish it at the earliest possible time. Tell yourself that what you are doing is important and that it is worth tolerating the situation until you accomplish your goal.

Visualization: Fatigue Control

Since our bodies respond physiologically to the images our minds hold, choosing images of being relaxed, fluid, calm, and flowing will help lessen the fatigue brought on by anxiety and tension. Do the following exercise for five minutes a day for a minimum of seven days before a competition to help you gain greater control over the fatigue you think you might experience.

> In your relaxed state, mentally simulate a
> specific performance and imagine fatigue setting
> in. Feel its heaviness; notice how it distracts you

from the event and threatens your confidence. Now, see yourself respond to fatigue by befriending it, or thinking of a reward you will get or give yourself for enduring it. Discover what image works for you. Give yourself a trigger you can pull whenever you feel fatigue. Feel yourself becoming energized and smooth. Imagine the tight muscles as small blocks of snow quickly melting, becoming mere fluid. See yourself finishing the event in great spirits, tired yet exhilarated and strong.

TAOSPORTS FOR BUSINESS AND LIFE

Bill, a visionary manager at AT&T in Colorado, came to me with an open Beginner's Mind after one of my seminars, called "The Fatigue Intrigue." He asked me to visit him at his office to discuss his lack of energy over the previous two months. He ate a balanced, healthy diet, he told me, exercised daily, and got plenty of sleep each night. As we entered his work space, I noticed that his desk looked like a garbage dump, with numerous large stacks of folders and papers scattered everywhere. I felt fatigued just looking at the enormous amount of work to be done. I asked Bill which project needed immediate attention and told him to put that one on his desk and move all the remaining folders and papers into an empty file drawer. When he completed the task, I said, "Now, Bill, that's your workload. Just get that done—that's all you or anyone can do right now." His facial expression changed radically, and he seemed tremendously relieved. What Bill had learned was that much of his fatigue was mental, caused by the stress of seeing the enormity of the tasks on his desk he had to complete. Cleaning the desk enabled him to focus on a single project. Psychologically, he felt less tension and therefore an increased amount of energy.

Guides for Mitigating Fatigue

Fatigue is a pervasive problem in all of life's activities. When we fail to accept our weariness, and fight it or attempt to control it, we usually pay the price in reduced efficiency and in making mistakes. Remembering the following points may help you struggle less and yield to the Tao, to nature itself—the way it is meant to be.

- Pace yourself. Attempt to plan for potential fatigue-causing situations, and give yourself guideposts, markers, and halfway-point rewards. This will motivate you to go forward.

- Think in terms of small manageable segments of whatever job you are doing. To do otherwise is to become overwhelmed and exhausted. Mentally break up your tasks into pieces. Visualize each piece as a part of a beautiful mosaic that you are making.

- When you are driving, it is always wise to yield to fatigue. Stop in a safe place and rest until you are able to go on. I find that if I can relax for fifteen minutes and do the visualization below, I'm ready to begin driving once again.

- Search for the path that has the least number of obstacles. When you allow yourself to adapt to the flow of your work or home environment, you will have more energy than if you made an effort to control each situation. River water flows effortlessly because it yields to the contours and changes in the earth through which it runs. You will notice that at work, no matter how much you try to speed up the process, everyone's personal style dictates the pace at which things get done. There will always be obstacles that block your efforts. If you yield to this reality, your job will be smoother and easier. Notice the flow at work or at home, and blend with it to reduce tension and fatigue.

Visualization: Reenergizing

When you are fatigued during the middle of the day, fifteen minutes of relaxation, visualization, and meditation can reenergize your mental, physical, and emotional self. Here is a visualization that I find particularly helpful:

> Imagine someone you know who possesses lots
> of energy (an adult or a child). See a beautiful,
> bright-colored rainbow connecting each of you
> through your heads. Feel the wonderful energy
> flowing from this person to you through the

rainbow. See it come into your body and travel
through the arterial pathways to each muscle
group. Imagine it filling up your adrenal glands
with adrenaline. See this hormone being
secreted from the glands to all parts of the body.
Notice your energy level rising gradually until
you are fully restored with life's energy juice.
You feel relaxed and invigorated.

Whatever technique you use, remember that fatigue is a natural force that won't totally go away. You, however, refuse to add any more fuel to the fire. As you become absorbed in the TaoSport process of blending with fatigue, it will fade into the background. When it does, you may discover a new source of energy.

INJURIES

The superior man respectfully appreciates the
cycles of increase and decrease. . . . External ploys
will not put an end to the natural cycle of deterioration.
Time will. Nurture your mind and body. . . .
Look for wisdom in your acceptance of the times.

I CHING no. 23

Injury is a natural messenger crying out, "Attention—something is not right! Take a break and reevaluate what you are doing and what you need to be doing!"

U.S. professional cycling champion Davis Phinney was made aware of the powerful lessons that injury can teach. One day, while riding on wet pavement, his tires slipped and the bike was demolished by the team car following close behind him. Phinney himself rolled away, sustaining severe injuries to his legs and back. What would normally have been a devastating experience for any athlete became for him the opportunity of a lifetime.

When his injuries healed, he rejoined the race circuit. Despite weeks of no riding, he felt great, and he became a stage winner at the Tour Du Pont. The accident had forced him to reevaluate his training. He discovered that rest actually could help him improve his skills, giving him time to integrate training patterns physically and mentally. Decreased volume coupled with higher-quality workouts and rest is an ideal formula for success. Phinney now recovers from hard rides rather than from hard falls.

Cycles of progress and setback, advance and retreat, are constant. We cannot prevent them even if we fight against them. If you are injured or in a period of setback, the passage from the *I Ching* encourages you to accept it as a natural occurrence and take advantage of it as an opportunity for reflection on yourself and your life and your sport.

Aside from providing an opportunity to learn and make appropriate corrections in training, however, the agonizing crisis of injury seems to turn the typical athlete's world upside down. It creates not only physical loss but emotional turmoil, depression, anger, fear, tension, anxiety, and panic. These psychophysiological responses then create more stress, which exacerbates the already existing pain.

Injured athletes go through five stages of adjustment to the injury, which are common to everyone who experiences a loss. First, they experience denial. They say, "No, not me—there's no problem. It's not that serious." When reality hits as a result of their inability to perform optimally, or to perform at all, the next stage makes its abrupt appearance: Anger—"Why me, why now? Damn it!" This often ushers in panic, which intensifies their pain. Bargaining follows, with promises that "if I recover, I'll never————," in hopes that the pain will subside. They offer to rest as a gift for recovery. When this pleading proves futile, depression sets in. They realize that nothing can be done, that they will not be playing. They may withdraw and focus on self-pity. True healing usually occurs when acceptance arrives: "I'm injured, but I must get on with my life; besides, I could use the rest." Before they accept the reality of their loss, they alternate back and forth among the first four stages.

Some suggestions for dealing with injury follow.

TAOSPORT TRAINING FOR ATHLETICS

An athlete went to a physician for a prognosis of an untimely knee injury caused by a blind-side tackle in football. The doctor, in a very serious tone, announced that his injury was so severe that two out of five people who experience this injury never play ball again. Devastated by the gloomy report, the athlete sought another opinion. This doctor, looking on the brighter side of the matter, claimed that while the injury was severe, three out of five thoroughly heal and play again. This information, statistically equivalent to the first report, emphasized the positive side of things. The doctor also stated, "I want to work closely with you and do all I can to optimize your chances of being one of the three." This athlete felt a surge of hope and excitement that enabled him to focus totally on recovery. He believed he would play again—and he did.

Relieving Panic—Infusing Hope

When you are injured, you have many questions: "When will I play (participate) again? Is the injury more serious than it appears? How will I get by until I can resume? Where can I get help? How long will this last?" If these questions go unanswered, they create a solid foundation of frustration and stress.

Seek out appropriate professionals who can answer your questions—doctors and other health workers who will inject hope, the most essential ingredient for healing. Guard yourself against panic by gathering as much information as you can about your injury so that you have the means to strategize your recovery.

To control the panic response, focus on other positive things in your life. Notice how other athletes with the same condition healed and made comebacks. Quarterback Joe Montana of the San Francisco Forty-Niners, for example, came back from serious back surgery to lead his team to a Super Bowl championship. Distance runner Joan Benoit came back from knee surgery to make the Olympic team in 1984 and won the gold medal that year. Try to see the recovery as a challenge rather than a devastating blow.

Understand that as an injured athlete, you are in a crisis that brings with it a certain danger or warning that demands your complete attention. Also realize, however, that your injury presents you with an opportunity that you must consciously take advantage of. The injury allows you time to rest and catch up on other important aspects of life that you may have neglected because of your rigorous training program. Use the visualization on the next page to help you uncover the opportunities in your injury.

Recovery is a wonderful time to reevaluate athletic priorities and put life into perspective. Enjoy the absence of constant pressure to perform. When you begin to change your view of the "crisis," your emotions will change accordingly. With less stress and tension, the healing process will be facilitated.

Remember, injury is nature's way of telling you something is not right. If you resist injury, it will persist. Think *wu wei*—don't force; yield to the injury. Go with the flow. Act without forcing—move in accordance with what nature provides. The injury is reality. Observe and accept the situation. Your recovery will be hastened in the process.

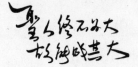

Evolved individuals, finally, take no great action,
And in that way the great is achieved.

TAO TE CHING no 63

Visualization: In Search of Opportunity

Injury and illness are nature's way of teaching us to reevaluate our lives. See the opportunities that are available as a result of your "down time." This visualization exercise will help you uncover the gifts inherent in your injury or illness.

In your state of relaxation, imagine your pain.
This suffering has come your way to enable you
to bring about positive change in your sport and
training program. This injury is a challenge, a
blessing in disguise. With this new way of
viewing the injury, you are ready to hear what
meaning it has in your life. Do not ask, "Why
does it hurt so much? Why did it happen to me?"
Rather, ask, "What is this pain telling me? Why is
it here at this time?" Take a minute to hear the
response. Imagine your mind slowly opening up;
it is empty and ready for new ideas and
possibilities. Your injury is nature's way of
reminding you that you deserve a rest. See it as
an opportunity to catch up on other important
aspects of life that you may have neglected. Feel
how relaxing it is to not have the constant
pressure to perform. Focus on your life, and put
your sport in perspective with everything else.

Yes, sport is important, yet you have many other
"points on your star" as well. As you relax,
imagine how rested you will be when you
return. Feel how hungry and excited you'll be
when the time arrives to begin again once you
are totally healed. Permit your body to relax and
rest and follow its natural healing process. See
yourself healing and whole, and carry this image
with you, bringing it up at least five times a day.

Visualization: Healing and Preventing Injury

Doctors and researchers are now demonstrating and documenting the incredible benefits of visualization in treatment programs for patients with serious injuries and life-threatening diseases. Images are so powerful, they sometimes prod the immunological system into destroying even the greatest malignancy. Research indicates a high correlation between positive treatment results and positive attitudes—or having a Beginner's Mind—in patients who use mental imagery in conjunction with other, more traditional therapeutic approaches.

Visualization works because it reduces the fears and anxieties of being injured that restrict blood circulation to an injured area and delay healing. By eliminating those destructive emotions, relaxation and visualization allow normal blood flow to resume and facilitate the healing process. Relaxation allows the body to function normally by decreasing stress; visualization sends powerful messages to the brain to stimulate the body in its healing.

Use this visualization to facilitate the healing process of your injury or illness.

In your relaxed state, see the area of concern.
Imagine white blood cells entering the infected
or injured area. Picture the color of the illness or
injury. Imagine it changing back to normal as
hundreds of tiny people massage the area,
"applying" a powerful healing ointment. Feel it
penetrate deeply into the area of concern. See
the hundreds of little hands in the healthy bone
or tissue join around and over the break or
injury, knitting it together. Then see it totally

> strong and better than it was before the injury
> occurred. Repeat the affirmation: "I am totally
> recovered, healthy, and well."

When you reduce your anxiety and tension, you will also subdue your pain. When you stop worrying and let go of the destructive emotions through relaxation and visualization, your blood pressure and your respiratory and immunological systems relax and begin to work more effectively in the facilitation of recovery.

Visualization is also a wonderful technique for preventing injury. If you are worried about accidents or injuries in your sport, get yourself into a relaxed state and go through the event in your mind. See yourself playing smoothly and efficiently; say, "Injury free—that's me." Repeat it often.

Affirmations for Health and Healing

- *"Every day, in every way, I get healthier and healthier."*
- *"Health is me—I'm injury free."*
- *"My limber, flexible self restores itself to health."*
- *"What I resist, will persist."*
- *"Let go as the healing juices flow."*
- *"My injury is an opportunity for me to learn what I need to do."*
- *"I am a strong, healthy, vibrant athlete."*
- *"Athletes who stay well, play well."*

TAOSPORTS FOR BUSINESS AND LIFE

Laughter Heals

Laughter is the best medicine. My grandmother was right—her beliefs have been validated by modern scientific studies. But even in earlier centuries, people believed that laughter produced a "feeling of health through the furtherance of the vital bodily processes," a statement from Immanuel Kant. Sigmund Freud found humor to be a useful way of coping with illness.

In Chinese writing, laughter is depicted by the picture language of a human with arms and legs flung wide apart, head up to the sky, vibrating with mirth like bamboo leaves in the wind. A close parallel is the familiar "Happy Buddha" posture, which is also the standing position of the breathing exercise called *qi gong* in China, now widely adapted and practiced internationally for healing cancer.

Norman Cousins, in *Anatomy of an Illness*, addresses the healing power of laughter in his own life. While he was hospitalized with a supposedly terminal illness, Cousins watched Laurel and Hardy, Abbott and Costello, the Three Stooges, and other comedies, accompanied by megadoses of vitamin C. He found that ten minutes of solid belly laughter would give him two hours of pain-free sleep. When he was in complete remission, his health restored, he continued taking large doses of comedy. Research now shows that not only laughter but all positive emotions cause the brain to secrete endorphins that relieve pain and tension. Happiness is one such emotion; like laughter, pleasant, happy thoughts relax the mind and lower stress. Happiness is a habit; if you cultivate it, it will help you prevent and treat injuries. The best way to develop this habit is to begin focusing on the positive aspects of injury or illness rather than the negative. Sit back, relax, and put the Marx Brothers on your VCR.

Swimmer Chrissy Ahmann-Leighton remembered when she was getting ready to race the 100-yard-butterfly relay at the NCAA championships. She said, "I started laughing." She also set a new American record.

Guides for Coping with Injury or Illness

Live the Tao in everyday life by adopting an attitude of acceptance toward inevitable cycles of crisis. Any loss—be it a job, friend, home, or love— requires a journey through the stages of denial, anger, bargaining, depression, and acceptance. Allow yourself time to be in each stage. You cannot bypass them or rush your healing process. To try to do so will only delay your journey. To help you pass through the stages of loss and pain and reach acceptance, search for the opportunities that such setbacks provide. These guides will help you to gain a Beginner's Mind—or TaoSport—perspective.

- When you are in crisis, *talk, talk, talk* with those who have had similar experiences. It helps to gain a broader perspective. Support from others will help you to relax.

- When you are mentally injured (burned out, feeling down), become quiet and calm, and avoid pushing forward professionally or socially. Take time to recover the passion.

- When you are physically injured with a cold or the flu, get plenty of sleep, eat nutritious foods, and take huge doses of C—comedy (as well as the vitamin).

- Setbacks through injury and illness are perfect times to step back and evaluate your situation. Try not to fight, resist, or force the pain. Embrace and yield to the pain. Try to understand what the pain is trying to tell you.

Visualization: Healing

Close your eyes, take five deep breaths, and enter a relaxed state:

> Look directly at the pain. Go over to it, sit by its side, and become partners on a journey to wellness. Ask it why it has come. What do you need to know at this time? Take a minute to enable it to respond. When it answers you, thank it for helping. Then imagine the pain stepping into a hot-air balloon, taking off, and flying high and far off into the distance. Wave good-bye to it as it sails out of sight.

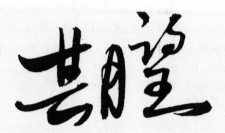

EXPECTATIONS

Thus, without expectation,
 One will always perceive the subtlety;
And, with expectation,
 One will always perceive the boundary.

TAO TE CHING no 1

The story is a familiar one: A basketball team expects to get by easily in the preliminary rounds of a tournament and looks forward to the semifinal games. Then they get knocked out of the preliminaries by a much weaker team because they were thinking beyond the task of the moment.

Consider the following story of disappointment. In 1980, I was living in Boulder, Colorado, home of twenty-five of the top hundred U.S. distance runners who were preparing for the Olympic games in Moscow. Naturally, people nationwide expected many of these hopefuls to make the team. You can imagine the pressure that people in their hometowns placed upon these athletes.

The U.S. Olympic Trials, held in Eugene, Oregon, that year, invited ten of the Boulder runners to compete against others from other parts of the United States. Representing the Boulder bunch was a group of national record-holders, including the first-, sixth-, ninth-, and fifteenth-ranked road racers in the world. Not one of the hopeful athletes made the team. These athletes were disappointed not to have fulfilled their own expectations as well as the expectations of friends and family in Boulder. (Ironically enough, no one from the United States went to the Olympics that year at all because of President Carter's decision to boycott the games.)

Expectations block your development and limit your horizons. (Expectations are different from goals, however, which we discuss in Part 4.) When you have an expectation, you are confident that something will turn out in a particular way. You may be looking forward to it, as if it were due to happen. Looking forward, however, distracts you from the moment—the task at hand. In the process, you become unfocused and uncentered, pressured and anxious, which interferes with your performance. When you do not tie yourself to expectations or preconceived notions, you begin to see and understand yourself and your world. You become open to endless possibilities, free to change and create enormous personal power. You, like a samurai warrior, expect nothing and become ready for anything.

> Evolved individuals act without expectation,
> Succeed without taking credit,
> And have no desire to display their excellence.

> TAO TE CHING no. 77

TAOSPORT TRAINING FOR ATHLETICS

When you put aside expectations, you accept that you can't control your future, only influence it. To help in this, focus on the direction in which your feet are pointed at each moment, and establish a strong preference instead of an expectation. A preference presupposes that you have less concern for the outcome, yet you still direct your efforts along the path of excellent performance. You keep yourself open to possibilities for greater expansion rather than limit yourself with defined expectations.

In 1972, the Pittsburgh Steelers of the National Football League knew better than to *expect* victory, with only twenty-two seconds remaining in a playoff game, trailing the Oakland Raiders 7 to 6 as they were. But, attempting to influence the outcome nonetheless, Steeler quarterback Terry Bradshaw took the ball on his own forty-yard line with fourth down and ten yards to go. With no expectations, he threw the ball in desperation, hoping the secondary receiver would catch it. But the receiver and defender collided, and the ball fell to within inches of the ground—into the hands of Steeler running back Franco Harris, who took it into the end zone. This unexpected play is well known as the Immaculate Reception.

Exercise: Changing Expectations to Preferences

This exercise will help you to expand your possibilities by getting rid of your limiting expectations.

1. List your expectations for an upcoming event or performance.

2. Upgrade each expectation and rewrite it as a preference, stating: "I definitely prefer ——— or something better." Notice that your preference is unlimited, open to possibilities.

3. Tell yourself, "I may or may not get what I prefer, yet I do not limit myself. The best will happen for the good of all."

4. If the outcome does not meet your preference, realize that your disappointment is less devastating than it might have been. You probably will perform at a higher level than you would have with expectations that could limit your play. We rarely go beyond what we expect.

5. See your preferences as guides whose job is to keep you on the path of excellence and success.

Affirmations for Unexpectedness

- *"I expect nothing yet am ready for anything."*
- *"Preferences direct, expectations destruct."*
- *"I infer what I prefer."*
- *"Being flexible with outcomes keeps me open to new possibilities."*

TAOSPORTS FOR BUSINESS AND LIFE

Many businesses and corporations that are involved in sales use quota systems as a means of motivating sales reps and managers to produce. These quotas often represent unrealistic expectations that create unnecessary anxiety and pressure—factors that, as we now realize, limit and block performance.

I recently worked with a bright, articulate, high-energy, talented sales manager for a Washington communications firm. For eight weeks, she had failed to meet the company's weekly expectation of 125 percent of quota. She began to take her failure personally, thinking that something was wrong with her. Her anxiety and stress levels were going off the charts as she feared not fulfilling that unrealistic expectation in the weeks to come. Her own fear interfered with her using a TaoSport approach. Then it occurred to her that if she thought of her performance in terms of a longer period of time, say one or two months, instead of each week, things would balance out and she would fulfill the demands of the company. To make this possible, she requested that her manager base her performance on monthly, not weekly, output. He agreed, and now that she was relaxed and focused with this new frame of mind, her output began to rise. Now she's working on convincing him of the benefits of lowering his expectations and establishing preferences instead, to reduce all the salespeople's stress level. Without pressure, the sales force may actually prove to be more productive than the company originally expected.

Expectations are setups for pressure, anxiety, and severe disappointment. They carry with them a heavy emotional "ego charge." But when you focus on having preferences, if things don't go your way, you understand that it's not you—things are simply beyond your control. Concentrate on how you may influence the direction you wish to go; then step back and let things unfold according to a natural plan.

Visualization: Releasing Expectations

One way of diverting your mind from expectation is to focus on the moment and ask: "What am I getting out of this activity now?" If the rewards are exciting and fun, see it as a worthwhile activity regardless of its outcome.

This visualization exercise will help you release your expectations and focus on the "here and now."

> Assign a word to each of your expectations—one that clearly identifies each of them. In your mind's eye, see the words with legs, walking over to a rocket ship, and climbing aboard. Watch the rocket take off into space never to return. Wave good-bye to those expectations.
>
> Immediately, welcome in your preferences—what you wish to experience in the present. See the words *calm, poised, relaxed, quick, champion, confident, courageous,* and others that indicate your present state of functioning. See yourself behaving in this moment according to these descriptions. Feel the excitement and joy at performing optimally in the present. Feel your influence as it affects others around you. The outcomes are influenced by your behavior and reflect the best for all involved. Know that the possibilities are greater without expectations.

Affirmations for Parents with Expectations

- *"I support and guide my children on their journey."*
- *"I simply model what I feel is healthy."*
- *"My basic preferences for my children are that they be happy and like who they are. With this, all is possible."*
- *"As long as they love what they do, I have no worries about results."*
- *"I refuse to limit my children's potential with my self-imposed expectations."*

Exercise: A Time of No Expectations

There was once a time in your life when you felt relatively free of the expectations of others. You were the new guy on the block, a neophyte at sport, or new on the job and totally oblivious to the "shoulds" and "have to's" of the world. Now, in your state of relaxation, re-create the feelings associated with those days—you were relaxed and free of pressure. Your performances reflected your love of and joy in the game or job. Transfer this feeling to your present situation, filled as it is with others' expectations. Say to yourself, "I refuse to give others permission to control me with their expectations. I am doing what I prefer to do to satisfy no one but myself. I enjoy the process and continue to focus on the joy I feel now."

SELF-CRITICISM

Those who cultivate Power,
Identify with Power.
Those who cultivate failure,
Identify with failure.

TAO TE CHING no. 23

With his team down 57-56 in an important league basketball game, Bill was fouled in the act of shooting with one second remaining. By making both free throws, he could secure a victory. One basket would tie the game. Chatter filled his mind. "Don't miss these. Don't choke. I could lose the game. I usually do." He stepped up to the line and threw and wasn't even close on either toss.

Practicing discipline over his thought patterns was the key to the consistent success of world tennis champion Bjorn Borg. In his epic Wimbledon match against the powerful John McEnroe, Borg truly thought he would lose after his drop-volley attempt failed in the fourth set tiebreaker, forcing a fifth set. When he lost the first two points of that final set, he switched his thought patterns from "I will lose" to "I must win." He took twenty-eight of his final twenty-nine service points to win a glorious victory—his fifth straight on British grass.

Borg could have easily gotten down on himself after he lost that crucial fourth set point. He might have said, "I'm a jerk, I don't deserve to win. What a loser." Instead, he silenced the criticism, cultivated positive self-talk, and won the match.

Harsh self-criticism is a setup for failure and misery. The mind constantly searches for ways to confirm negative self-talk and sabotage the chances for successful athletic performance. The words you choose to cultivate in yourself as an athlete will determine your identity and beliefs about yourself. Your self-image, in turn, dictates how you behave on and off the court.

Oftentimes, you learn skills in sport more slowly than you would like to. This might cause you to attack and tell yourself you're not good enough. Self-criticism is a negative force that creates disharmony with the Tao, the way of nature.

The cartoon character Pogo summed it up nicely: "We have met the enemy, and they is us." Through unacceptance and disapproval of self, we become our own judge, jury, and executioner. Unrelenting self-critical behavior patterns inhibit our courage, confidence, concentration, hope, motivation, and excitement, which are all necessary for extraordinary TaoSport performance.

When I encounter self-critical athletes (and many athletes are very self-critical), I ask them whether they would talk to their friends as critically as they talk to themselves. "Absolutely not!" they invariably reply. The anxiety, tension, and stress that such harsh criticism causes would hurt their friends too much and even destroy their friendships. I try to show them that they should be as friendly to themselves as they are to their friends in such situations. Your self-criticism has the same effects as criticism of others, because it makes you begin to abandon and distrust yourself; you lose confidence in your ability to perform. When you condemn, blame, censure, denounce, or reprehend yourself for a sub-par performance, your performance suffers further, or you begin to avoid athletic-related encounters at all.

These are some of the typical expressions of self-criticism used by athletes. Do you recognize any?

- "I don't have enough talent."

- "I'm just too slow, too short, too heavy."

- "I'm really out of shape."

- "I never win."

- "If only I were bigger, faster, stronger."

- "I'm over the hill."

- "There's no way I could do it."

- "I'm a failure."

- "I always choke in tough situations."

- "I'm just not meant to be [a golfer, a runner, a winner]."

- "I can't help it—I never could be number one."

- "I'm not good enough. I don't deserve to be a champion."

TAOSPORT TRAINING FOR ATHLETICS

You should exercise unrelenting discipline over
your thought patterns. Cultivate only productive
attitudes. . . . You are the product of everything
you put into your body and mind.

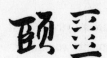

I CHING no. 27

Athletic performance mirrors your self-talk. When Paula, a client of mine, arrived at a ten-thousand-meter run, she looked around at her competition and immediately said, "There's no way I can win today. I'm just not good enough." Even so, when the race began, Paula took the lead. Comfortably in first place at mile four, she began to feel that she had made a mistake. Since she was awed by her competitors, she began to tell herself that they knew better than to go out as fast as she. They were, perhaps, smarter, waiting for the opportunity to catch up and race past her. "I'll probably pay for this mistake. I know I can't hold the lead. I don't deserve to be here. I don't have the talent." Listening to this negative self-talk, she actually began to get tense and fatigued and slowed her pace, finishing seventh. By her own admittance, her judgmental self-criticism led to her defeat.

Exercise: Feeling the Difference

When I use this exercise during my sports clinics on self-doubt and criticism, I ask an individual athlete to recite each of the following two scenarios as if they were true. The group then comments on the difference in the athlete's facial expression, body posture, and energy level between the recital of the negative self-criticism and the one of positive self-acceptance. Recite them aloud yourself, and determine which one gives you hope, motivation, courage, confidence, and excitement.

1. I am an over-the-hill, no-good, out-of-shape, pitiful loser who does not deserve to be here with all these athletes. I'm just not meant to be in sports.

2. I am a strong, vibrant, talented, physically fit winner who deserves the chance to be the best of all the athletes. I'm a perfect person to be in sports.

Affirmations for Self-Love

To create noncritical, nonjudgmental self-talk, list all the self-negative comments you have with regard to your level of play. Then proceed to change them to their opposite. For example, change

- *"I don't have enough talent"* to
  "I have an abundance of talent."
- *"I'm too slow, too short, too heavy"* to
  "I'm fast, tall enough, with the perfect weight."
- *"I'm a failure"* to
  "I'm a success."
- *"I always choke in tough situations"* to
  "I always get up for tough situations."
- *"I don't deserve to be here"* to
  "I deserve to be here."
- *"I'm not good enough"* to
  "I'm more than good enough."

When you recite the positive affirmations, be sure to create images of yourself that validate what you are saying. Actually see and feel yourself, for instance, getting up for a tough situation or having an abundance of talent.

TAOSPORTS FOR BUSINESS AND LIFE

When we plant a rosebush in the earth, it is not much more than a twig—but we do not criticize it. Instead, we give it the water and nourishment it requires, cover it in winter, and protect it with straw around its roots. When it begins to leaf, we don't condemn it as immature and underdeveloped; nor do we criticize the buds for not being open when they appear. Instead, we pick off the insects that attack it and feed it to strengthen it against its natural foes. We stand in wonder at the process taking place, and we give the plant the care it needs at each stage of its development. Within the rose, at all times, is its whole potential. It is constantly in the process of change; yet at each state, at each moment, it is perfectly all right as it is.

Like the Tao, you are a natural process: You grow, blossom, unfold, and perform according to the same principles as the rose. Nurture yourself with encouragement and love, and weed your garden of self-improvement by avoiding the negative self-criticism that kills the spirit. Replace it with affirmations of self-worth. The cultivated human, in Confucian ethics, is the person who daily reassesses his own actions, learning to be more human. It is an act of willingness to improve and change, to be more in tune with the Tao. The open, meditative ways of self-criticism can be extremely productive if we learn to appreciate the power of continual transformation, from being to becoming, in our daily life.

Exercise: Noticing Your Positive Qualities

You have more positive qualities and attributes than you realize, but you rarely notice them or give yourself credit for them. You may have a difficult time saying good things about yourself out of fear of appearing conceited. False humility traps you into believing you are less than you are.

Write down five personal attributes or qualities that define you as they pertain to each of the following five areas of life (a total of twenty-five attributes). If you need help discovering your greatness, ask others for input. Take some time to complete this if necessary. ("Strong," "thoughtful," "compassionate," "competent," "stable," "dependable," "fun-loving," "cheery," "fast," "giving," "loving" are examples of the descriptions you will be writing.)

Physical: _____

Spiritual: _____

Professional: _____

Emotional: _____

Social: _____

Next, turn each attribute into a positive affirmation to be recited by you daily. This exercise will help you to get in touch with the real you; it will help you to silence the harmful self-critical talk.

Guides for Self-Support and Nurturance

Many years ago, just out of college, I applied for my first job as a high school English teacher. It was July 1964, and I received a message to call the school principal immediately. I was working my part-time summer job as a playground supervisor and called the principal on my lunch break. He told me that they liked my resume and needed to fill the position before the week was out. He asked me to come over to the school after I got off work that day. I was unprepared mentally and physically—I was dirty and sweaty, dressed in shorts, T-shirt, and sneakers—hardly an impressive candidate. I didn't have time to go home, shower, and change, and I told him so when I arrived in his office, my self-confidence as wilted as my clothes. The principal quickly responded, "Jerry, clothes don't make the man. We like the person we see. That's what we value." With reinforced confidence, I was offered the job on the spot. He said I had great depth and integrity as a person. I have never forgotten the impact of his words, and to this day, when I'm being self-critical, I remind myself that the man inside has great depth. I *am* good enough.

- When you hear yourself using a particular "self-love-reducing" word, change it immediately to a "self-love-producing" word. For example, you just hit your thumb with a hammer and say, "You idiot!" Catch yourself and replace that phrase with, "I'm no idiot, but that hurt like . . . crazy."

- To help you reduce the frequency of your self-critical behavior, try to be less critical of others. If you give them a break, more than likely you'll do the same for yourself.

- Flood your mind with the numerous affirmations that you have created from the above exercises. I write mine on three-by-five-inch index cards and read them during the day, when I get the chance. These will gradually replace your old tapes of self-criticism.

- When you receive a compliment, take it in by saying, "Thank you, I appreciate that." To demur on a compliment is to put yourself down.

- Record every negative self-critical statement you make for one week in a notebook. When you have a good number (five to one hundred), challenge the rationality and validity of each one. Such awareness is crucial to change. Replace each one with its opposite self-supportive statement.

- Look for ways to pamper yourself—to create more personal abundance on a daily basis. Take yourself to a movie, for example, or dinner, or both. Treat yourself to some new clothes. Take the afternoon off, and go for a walk, run, or bike ride. Cook a good dinner to share with a friend.

PERFECTIONISM

The receptive triumphs over the inflexible;
The yielding triumphs over the rigid.

TAO TE CHING no 78

Perfectionism can often result in personal catastrophe. Some athletes even endanger their lives in their efforts to achieve a perfect body or performance, or they become self-destructive in the face of their failure to achieve this impossibility.

A talented woman who was an NCAA national champion distance runner was a perfectionist in all aspects of her life; she was a star athlete, an excellent student, and head of her class. She was almost unnaturally thin. During one important race, she was running in fourth place. Suddenly she dropped out of the race, ran to a nearby bridge, and jumped off. Today, she is paralyzed from her waist down. One wonders if this was the result of intense inner pressure to be perfect.

John Wooden, former coach of the UCLA Bruin basketball dynasty, knows something about perfection. His teams dominated the NCAA basketball scene for fifteen years, winning numerous national championships. Yet he never harped on maintaining perfect records, even during an undefeated season. He realized that each season has its share of problems and challenges, and that anxiety about remaining undefeated would have bred more anxiety in his athletes.

When one Olympic gymnast failed to get the perfect ten on her routine, the tone of voice of a television sports analyst indicated that she had totally blown it. Another athlete who did score the "big ten" was still disgruntled by what she personally thought was a sub-ten performance. Some athletes miss the perfect score and are severely disappointed; others achieve it but it's not good enough. Either way, you are in a no-win situation.

The *Tao Te Ching* explains that efforts to be perfect are actually limits that we put on ourselves. Athletes who strive for perfection constantly fail because perfection is unattainable. Rigid adherence to the desire for perfect outcomes is a setup for setback because you always come down hard on yourself for never attaining the goal.

Watch out for the "red-light" indications of a tendency toward perfectionism: an obsession with external rewards; satisfaction only by external measurements, such as others' opinions; rigid, unattainable goals; intolerance of failure; dwelling on negative outcomes; self-worth equated with end results; a constant fear of failure; procrastination or a play-it-safe attitude; indecision and pessimism; tunnel vision and harsh self-judgment coupled with constant frustration.

The search for perfection is an inflexible attitude, an attempt to force what can't be. The Tao teaches you to let go of futile behavior. Try to strive for excellence instead. Shoot for the sun. If you fall short, you'll still be one of the stars. That which is yielding has no limits and ultimately will achieve victory. This yielding approach does enable you to set high standards. If you don't attain these standards, however, you can still win by yielding to your setbacks as lessons that will ultimately enable you to rise to greater heights.

Refuse to beat up on yourself for not being perfect. Don't place all of your eggs of satisfaction in the basket of outcomes. By releasing the need to be one hundred percent perfect, you reduce the anxiety, stress, and tension caused by this quest and, consequently, your performance improves. You begin to experience more joy and fulfillment from your sport as you recapture your passion for the process of the game.

Striving for excellence requires a strong internal reward system that focuses on the pursuit of satisfaction, pride, peace, joy, and fun. In the pursuit of excellence, you set realistic, flexible goals that act as road markers on your path. An average performance, although not welcomed by a Tao-Athlete, is understood to be part of competing in sport. You have a sense of self-worth just from participating and pursuing excellence; you don't equate your self-worth with the game's outcome. Instead of constantly fearing failure, you feel the joy of being in the arena and you feel fortunate to have the talents and abilities you do have in order to compete, regardless of results. TaoAthletes do not internalize failure as a statement of their athletic self-worth.

According to the Tao, nature balances extremes. Things come and go; you're up, then you're down. Improvement in sport is a series of errors, mistakes, and setbacks, and when they are corrected, you begin to approach your potential. Every athlete and coach needs to remember the roller-coaster rhythms of performance. Remember that you live in a world where even the greatest athletes are imperfect.

In the words of psychologist Carl Jung, "Perfection belongs to the gods; the most that we can hope for is excellence."

TAOSPORT TRAINING FOR ATHLETICS

A collegiate volleyball player came to me at the request of her astute coach, who realized that she was sabotaging her potential by being a perfectionist. If this player wasn't thoroughly achieving and successful in every aspect of the game, she'd sulk and be negative with the entire team. Her perfectionistic goals were entirely irrational and unrealistic, causing her much stress. She even wanted to quit the team because playing had become no longer fun.

I realized that these patterns of perfectionism had developed early on in her life and that it would take some time to get beyond them. What she needed was support and encouragement from her coach and parents that they would still love her regardless of her performance. Then, to help her to believe that it was acceptable to be less than perfect, we used "cognitive restructuring." This technique teaches you that what you feel is the result of how you view a situation; if you change your view, the feelings (tension and anxiety) will change as well. We explored the fact that success is a roller coaster. It is impossible to be "right on" every day. We have to expect ups and downs. No one escapes setbacks. I told her that mistakes can be teachers and are natural aspects of the growth process. She began to understand that her perfectionism was irrational and that, like all performers and achievers, she would continue to experience fluctuations on the road to excellence. With the help of her coach, she embraced the setbacks of her performance as springboards for improvement. Her letting go of perfection culminated in her being awarded all-American status in her senior year.

Exercise: Profit and Loss

Notice those times when you tend to be perfectionistic in sport. In two side-by-side columns, list the pros and cons of such behavior. What do you gain by being a perfectionist? What do you lose? On the "pro" side, for example, you place yourself on the path of excellence and feel good about your conscientiousness about the work or project. On the "con" side, however, your self-worth is determined by the outcome, so you experience much tension and anxiety, which interfere with the outcome. Frustration is pervasive. Remember that, by definition, perfectionism is not simply a matter of wanting to do the best—we all want that. It's the process of getting down on yourself when you fail to do or get the best. This leads to other negative behaviors such as procrastination and indecision (and the "red lights" on page 145).

Perfectionists often procrastinate because it is difficult to start anything if you believe that the outcome will not be in your favor. For the perfectionist, this undesirable outcome will lead to self-criticism and abuse. We pay a heavy price for following our self-destructive paths.

Affirmations for Going Beyond the Perfectionism Trap

- *"Performance is never perfect—just get into the game as a process."*
- *"Perfection is an illusion."*
- *"I may not be perfect, but I perform like a champion."*
- *"Mistakes are lessons, not comments on my self-worth."*
- *"With a sense of humor, I enjoy my sport."*
- *"I accept and like myself regardless of the results."*

TAOSPORTS FOR BUSINESS AND LIFE

A top-level corporate executive client of mine was having much difficulty with her staff. She was an "impossible to please" perfectionist, always trying to exert control over them. The more perfection she demanded, the more they rebelled by producing inferior work. The anxiety, tension, and fear that she created became obstacles standing in the way of productivity. Everyone was miserable.

When she asked me if she needed to hire new people, I told her that the real culprit might be the controlling, perfectionistic environment she was creating. "Is anyone having any fun or enjoying their work? What do they find satisfying about the job?" I asked. After some introspective sessions, she began to see that she was losing perspective on her own job and that she was pushing and forcing her limiting opinions and views upon the rest of the staff. She already had talented people working for her, and she needed to tap into them by giving them room to grow and produce.

She decided to hold a meeting of all workers to discuss a new direction, a new focus, one that emphasized joy, pleasure, and cooperation, with a minimum of perfection and control. She asked them to write up their suggestions on how to improve the work environment and what they needed from her to help them perform more effectively. At first, they were shocked by her change of heart. But she took their suggestions seriously and initiated radical changes. Everyone experienced a rebirth of enthusiasm and a resurgence in performance. Their office theme became one of "excellence with joy and satisfaction." She reports that these changes in her attitudes about perfection have helped her in her home as well.

This was not an easy transformation process, but once she saw how she could make work easier and more fulfilling she became motivated to make the switch to a TaoSport approach.

Visualization: Letting Go of Perfectionism

This visualization exercise will help you experience excellence in your business and life and let go of the obstacle of perfection.

> In your state of relaxation, imagine yourself
> getting ready to take on a specific important task

at work or at home. See, in your mind's eye, how you intend to go about doing this project. Begin the project, and notice how proud you feel for doing an excellent job. However, you have just made a mistake. This setback begins to annoy you. Feel the let-down. Before you begin to judge yourself say, "Stop." Validate your self-worth by saying, "I am an effective, competent, and excellent worker." Learn from the setback, correct it, and forge ahead to completion. Feel the satisfaction of doing an excellent job, knowing that mistakes are part of the learning process. Perfection is an impossible state. Your excellent work stands on its own, regardless of errors or setbacks. Feel relaxed, calm, and energized. You are now capable of much more because you're not controlled by the perfectionist trap.

Guides for Side-stepping Perfectionism

- Understand that basically, life is a roller coaster, where ups and downs, ons and offs, and victory and defeat are natural. By accepting this, you defuse the heavy emotional attachment to outcomes and results.

- Choose realistic, flexible goals that have greater possibilities for attainment. This will help you to procrastinate less and become more decisive.

- It is totally irrational to believe that you can be thoroughly competent and achieving at all times. Instead, focus on the joy, satisfaction, and fun of the process rather than the importance of the product (outcome). In this way, you'll experience less anxiety, and your performance will improve.

- Gandhi, Jesus, Martin Luther King, and Mother Teresa were not perfect. You are in good company by not being perfect.

- Perfection is a dead end; it places you in a losing "catch-22" battle. If people recognize your great work, you'll worry about meeting their high expectations next time around. If you fail in their eyes, you'll be devastated. Either way, you'll be anxious and tense. It's the "perfect" no-win situation, and that's about as close as you'll get to perfection!

心境

MORE TAOSPORT MINDSETS
FOR EXTRAORDINARY PERFORMANCE

In this part of the journey, you will be constructing new mental frames of reference on which to develop higher levels of performance. These psychological postures will help you more easily implement the TaoSport strategies for extraordinary performance in the later parts of the book. These TaoSport mental states are confidence, assertiveness, courageousness, detachment, egolessness, selflessness, and conscientiousness.

CONFIDENCE

信心

Those who cultivate the Tao
Identify with the Tao.
Those who cultivate Power,
Identify with Power.

TAO TE CHING no. 23

In Taoist terms, our power is the influence we have over daily living. In TaoSports, power is an athlete's inner balance and confidence. Feeling confident is a state of being, an inner spiritual feeling about who you are and how you are capable of performing. A TaoAthlete's confidence is not tied to victory or outcome. It is an inner knowing that you will play up to your capability—physically, mentally, and emotionally. It is a positive attitude, an essential state of being in the moment.

Western approaches to athletics teach athletes that confidence is a transient state of mind. Some athletes regard confidence as a sometime thing, something they can pump up at will by boasting and bragging and acting larger than life to experience power over others. They are taught that this blustering confidence will put the outcome of a game under their control. Although it is possible to be truly confident in this kind of role-playing, most such confidence is false and unrealistic and can be deflated as easily and suddenly as it is pumped up. Because they do realize at bottom

153

that their confidence is false, many excellent athletes are vulnerable to losing confidence in their ability to perform when competitors use psych-out techniques or when they suffer inevitable losses or setbacks.

Joe Namath, former quarterback for the New York Jets, was one of the few players who could feel confident about controlling the outcome of a game. Prior to Super Bowl III, in 1969, "Broadway" Joe told a group of reporters that the Jets were a better team than the Baltimore Colts and guaranteed that New York would win the championship. On January 12, 1969, the Jets defeated the Colts 16 to 7, in what is still considered one of the biggest upsets in all professional sports.

Obviously, Joe's confidence was informed by both a true inner state of self-confidence as well as by our culture's inclination to braggadocio. Bragging to psych up yourself or your team, however, can easily backfire into a psych-out by the opposing team. Rather than following the cultural tendency to try to psych-out your opponent with false self-confidence, work at developing real inner confidence. You may never feel like Broadway Joe, but you can build your confidence by focusing on your ability to play well, your mental and emotional readiness, your personal goals, your excellent practice sessions, and your past success.

TAOSPORT TRAINING FOR ATHLETICS

Susan, an extremely gifted high school tennis athlete, had played number-two singles as a freshman and number-one the following year. Now a junior, she expected—as did everyone else—that she would win the league championship. She came to me to find the confidence to do so. I told her that such confidence comes in tiny green tablets that cost a dollar each. Susan laughed and said, "I'll take two dozen." She got the point. You don't develop "winning" confidence instantly. Even with all her prior successes, she still had trouble conjuring up that feeling of total confidence. However, you can discover or create an innate confidence in your own ability to play well and use that as your source of strength.

I suggested to Susan that she concentrate on her mental and physical strengths and affirm that she was as ready as ever to "go for it." We invited her coach in for a session, and he validated her ability to play championship tennis even if she didn't win this one. He said to her, "Be confident that you will have fun out there. I want you simply to enjoy the opportunity. Then you'll play well enough to win."

With the help of this talk and some visualization and affirmations, Susan breezed to victory in the championship match. She had simply realized that she already was a TaoAthlete and had the confidence to play well and have fun. Once she saw that, she played like a champion.

Guides for Developing Confidence

In the 1980 Winter Olympics in Lake Placid, the U.S. bobsled team made the mistake of observing and dwelling upon the awesome presence of the East German team and their intimidating black helmets with the national insignia emblazoned on the front. This destructive mental pattern shattered the American team's confidence.

If competitors have this effect on you, consider avoiding situations where you'll be forced to see them: look away, show up at the last moment, meditate by yourself. Building athletes' confidence is a process of diverting their energy away from winning and into developing a sense of their inner self, of focusing on their personal capabilities and readiness. The following guides will help you develop and maintain real inner confidence:

- Repeat each day, over and over, the affirmation: "Calm and confident, I play like a true champion." This affirmation reinforces your confidence in your self-ability rather than in whether you will win.

- Nothing builds confidence like success. Develop short-term, realistic, attainable goals for daily practice and competition. This way, you will increase the chances of receiving immediate positive feedback, thus reinforcing the thought, "I am a person who is successful—I get what I want."

- Past successes are wonderful confidence-builders and -reinforcers. Recall past competitions where you experienced success in your performance. Get in touch with the feelings of pride and exhilaration that you felt. Notice how you played and executed your moves with total confidence.

Visualization: Confidence

Constantly, on a daily basis, visualize yourself being extremely confident about your ability to perform up to your capability and beyond. This visualization exercise will help you develop confidence.

In your relaxed state, recall a time when you felt confident of your ability to perform. This may have been in a practice session or during the "heat" of competition. Feel a sense of oneness with your sport; your play is a natural extension of the greatness within you. Feel the exhilaration and satisfaction of perfect execution. Take this feeling and pair it with an anchor, such as the circle formed by pressing your index finger and thumb together. This is your reference point for the feeling of confident play. Use it during moments when your confidence wanes. Now, with anchor in place, imagine yourself just prior to an upcoming performance. See yourself calm and confident. Enter the arena of play, and perform exactly the way you know you can. This is the state of being truly confident in your ability to perform well—under any circumstances.

Affirmations for True Confidence

- *"Calm and confident, I play well."*
- *"Regardless of the score, I am much more."*
- *"My practice performance indicates a readiness to excel."*
- *"I may not win, but I play like a fearless warrior."*
- *"I possess all that I need to perform like a tireless champion."*
- *"I am ready, willing, and able to exhibit my power as an athlete."*

TAOSPORTS FOR BUSINESS AND LIFE

Living a trained, true TaoSport confidence based on inner self-knowledge will enable you to exert greater influence over any performance situation in your life, be it a job interview, an exam, a presentation at work, or a musical recital. This confidence focuses on the process of performance rather than on winning. To establish any influence over winning or over the outcome of any situation, you need to influence the process—especially the confidence in how you perform. Allow the outcome to evolve accordingly. Eight years after I graduated from college, I recall, I felt quite uneasy about applying to a doctoral graduate program. After all, I had been only a marginal student in college. I sought out two reliable confidants for their input and support. Both agreed that I was older, more mature, and wiser now than I had been in college. Their validation encouraged me to go forward with my dream. I observed people who had been through a program similar to the one in which I was interested. They seemed neither smarter nor more capable than I. I observed graduate classes at the university, and it became quite clear that my self-doubt was irrational and unfounded. My confidence level increased exponentially. I was accepted into the graduate program for that fall quarter.

Guides for Confidence

These guides will help you to the TaoSport state of confidence, an inner sense of calm about performance.

- When you feel a lack of confidence as you embark on something new, ask your friends for support and feedback. Also, observe others with abilities similar to yours, and see that their success is telling you that you, too, can make it.

- Affirm: "Plan the work, work the plan." By doing your homework, you enable yourself to prepare thoroughly and focus on the excellent performance that you are capable of achieving. Capitalize on little success experiences by using them as reinforcers for true confidence.

- A true indication of a lack of confidence is the use of bragging and boasting to psych oneself up. Such behavior detracts from performance since it creates pressure, anxiety, and tension to succeed. Align yourself with TaoSport precepts, and "low key" your prowess and abilities.

Create no false expectations, and focus on exerting your powerful influence instead. This will enable you to feel less stress.

Visualization: Confidence in Pressure Situations

Situations such as negotiating a business deal, interviewing for a new position, and making an important sales pitch or presentation require a state of confidence. This visualization will help you get in touch with your confidence during those pressured moments.

> Using the "anchor" you developed in the section on athletics, above, as a reference point, imagine yourself calmly approaching a difficult task. See yourself performing exactly the way you can when everything goes your way. Feel confidence penetrate all parts of your body via the arterial pathways: to the head, shoulders, abdomen, back, arms, hands, legs, and feet. Affirm: "I am now in position to strike and perform as I'd like. I perform like the excellent professional that I am."

ASSERTIVENESS

Produce but do not possess.
Advance without dominating.
These are called the Subtle Powers.

TAO TE CHING no 10

It seemed like an innocuous comment to the winning team but not to the team that was down 8–0 in the preliminary round of the 1987 Jose Cuervo Pro Beach Volleyball tournament in Santa Cruz, California. Following an errant serve by the losing team, one of the members of the opposing team shouted across the net, "Hey, nice serve." The losing team didn't appreciate the remark and responded to the ridicule by reeling off ten straight points and closing out the match and eventually qualifying for the prize money rounds.

Aggression produces a corresponding counteraggression, according to the Tao. Such negative cycles are self-perpetuating. When you align with the Tao, you can transcend these recurrent negative cycles. You can learn to shape the course of events not with force, but with direct, assertive behavior.

In sport, you achieve greater levels of performance when you simply assert yourself and your power. Asserting your power is quite different from the traditional Western aggressiveness, which aims to dominate an opponent. This aggressiveness includes a sense of ruthlessness, cruelty, or pitilessness toward the competitor. This negative, external orientation focuses your energy outward onto the opponent rather than concentrating your inner

159

energy on your own performance. This external focus generates extreme tension, fatigue, and distraction and ultimately hinders your and your teammates' performances.

The case of an all-American tennis star from the University of California at Santa Cruz illustrates the futility in the aggressive approach. At a recent championship match, he proudly said, he had tried to dominate his opponent. His intimidation tactics had worked—for one set. After that, he had experienced a swift decline and defeat. He sought me out to discover how he could keep the aggression going—he didn't quite understand that his tactics had backfired, creating aggression in his opponent while depleting his own energy supply, physically and mentally. I suggested that he focus, instead, on asserting his strengths. Asserting his talents would strongly influence the progression of the match in his favor. Rather than show concern for the opponent by "dominating" him, he should demonstrate confidence in his own abilities and skill levels. He took the suggestion and began to play beyond expectation because he was putting less energy into aggressive behavior and into dealing with the accompanying tension and stress.

Remember that harsh, aggressive behavior on your part suggests to an aware opponent that you are uncertain about your abilities. Even if your aggression brings you short-term success, it could fail in the long run by setting you up for aggression from your competition in the future.

Aggressive movements toward one's goal ultimately have no lasting effect. The TaoAthlete realizes that "heated confrontation" does not yield benefits in the long run and is too difficult to sustain. Assertion is a more relaxed mindset toward performance. Assertiveness is the way of the Tao-Athlete. The assertive TaoAthlete exhibits determination, with clarity of intent. Assertiveness can be employed with greater consistency than aggressiveness; it is subtler and therefore more effective. TaoSports subtle efforts, subtle powers yield the best results, shaping outcomes in a positive way. Assertiveness is not an attack technique—it will not feed an opponent's negative behavior or energy.

Not destructive, it is more powerful in enabling you to achieve the original objective of your aggression—your influence over the process and an excellent performance. Your inner strength is demonstrated in your refusal to attack your opponent's advantages or assail his or her integrity. This simple switch in attitude enables TaoAthletes to master their environment by mastering themselves.

Webster's dictionary defines *assertion* as a behavior that emphasizes self-confidence and persistent determination to express oneself in a positive way. Because you do not seek your opponent's annihilation, you can achieve success and avoid counterreactions.

好言不争

The Tao of Nature
is to serve without spoiling.
The Tao of evolved individuals
is to act without contending.

TAO TE CHING no. 81

TAOSPORT TRAINING FOR ATHLETICS

Many athletes and teams fail to realize that their aggressive acts toward an opponent, such as taunting, ridicule, and provocative comments, create in the opponent passion and drive to retaliate. Following a touchdown, for example, football players have been known to mock an opponent by doing a suggestive dance in the end zone, as if to say, "We're so terrific, you guys can't even come close to us." Often the ridiculed team comes right back with one or more immediate scores of its own. Coach Mike Ditka of the Chicago Bears said in a television interview that those who show off after a score lack class. The real pros, those who are winners, do what's required to score, then immediately hand the ball to the referee. It's a subtle act of assertion, not aggression.

Cross-bay rivals Stanford University and Cal Berkeley annually clash in what has become known as The Big Game. This contest is considered so important that to win it is to have a winning season, regardless of the team's overall record. In 1991, Berkeley was having a stellar season, with a major Bowl bid in the bag. The week prior to the annual showdown, athletes from Cal made claims about their prowess and boasted that the outcome of the game was a foregone conclusion. They intimated that Stanford was wasting its time even showing up. As the Stanford players took the field, it was obvious to everyone that their adrenaline was overflowing—they were fired up. Refusing to be intimidated by Cal's aggressive jeering, Stanford proceeded to tear apart the Cal defense in one of the most lopsided routs in the history of the rivalry, winning 38 to 21.

Affirmations for Assertiveness

These affirmations will enable you to keep aligned with the Tao by exhibiting powerful inner strength and directing the flow of a performance.

- *"Direct the flow with an assertive show."*
- *"Focus energy within to increase the chances of a win."*
- *"I don't dominate—I demonstrate."*
- *"Assertion is the only way I make my powerful presence felt."*
- *"I act without contending."*
- *"I refuse to waste valuable energy on dominating my opponent."*
- *"Aggression indicates weakness in my opponent."*

Visualization: Identifying with the Asserter

Many athletes identify with aggressors, accepting without question the need for a dominating posture to achieve success. This visualization exercise will help you change your attitude to accept and exhibit the stronger, more powerful, assertive TaoSport approach.

Before you begin, think of an animal or person that exemplifies the concept of assertiveness for you. It could be a dolphin, a whale, a deer—or a famous person or friend who exhibits qualities of strength, confidence, and power through assertion.

In your relaxed state, imagine your animal or person. Notice all the qualities that make this animal or person strong and powerful, physically and mentally. They may be courageous, focused, self-assured, confident. See this model act assertively in various situations. Discover these same traits within yourself. If you can identify certain traits in others, you probably have them within yourself, even if they are dormant. Feel the same power within as you face your

opponent. Know that you need not dominate.
Simply asserting your tremendous athletic being
is enough to perform optimally. Feel more
focused, more centered, and more capable of
influencing the flow of the event. Experience the
joy playing according to this image. Affirm: "I
am an assertive competitor, capable of anything
I wish."

TAOSPORTS FOR BUSINESS AND LIFE

In an act of aggression, an irate manager shouted to one of his staff supervisors in a stern, parental voice, "Never, never take it upon yourself to go ahead with the project until you get my permission! You're not in charge here—I am!" The supervisor just listened without saying a word. His superior said, "Did you hear me?" To this the man replied, "I heard you, and you're absolutely right. I don't appreciate the way you said it, though."

The manager's aggressive style diminished the respect his fellow workers had for him. Had he asserted his feelings rather than tried to dominate, he would have created a positive change in the supervisor's behavior. For instance, he could have said, "I'm confused about something. I'm wondering why you decided on your own to move ahead with the project. I thought this was a team effort." By being assertive in this way, he would have improved his chances of shaping the course of events in the future. By being aggressive, he lost his real power and influence.

Guides for Assertiveness

All aggressive behaviors in life are counterproductive. Just as athletic performance suffers when you focus on the killer instinct, aggressive action keeps you vulnerable to aggression in other situations. Neutralizing these negative cycles is possible when you live the Tao. Develop an assertive approach to problems that allows you to exhibit your inner integrity and a strong sense of self. As a business person, you have been told that aggressiveness is essential to success. But such dominating behavior alienates others by creating negative environments of ruthlessness and cruelty. Resentment and harsh feelings develop among those treated in this way, and tension, anxiety, and stress

increase as performance declines. Being assertive, on the other hand, creates a "worker-centered" environment where you can achieve your objectives more effectively, with greater cooperation and respect.

Here are some suggestions for the TaoSport approach to assertion.

- When you are disappointed, angry, or frustrated with another person, rather than aggressively blame and find fault, say how *you* feel rather than how they caused you to feel. People will open up when they are not judged or ridiculed. They will take responsibility for their behavior if you're assertive rather than aggressive. Be sure to maintain eye contact while you are being assertive. In this way you exert your presence and establish your integrity. Others will listen to you and take you more seriously.

- If you don't agree with another person's political, religious, or social philosophy, rather than attack or try to prove them wrong, you can simply state, "That's interesting. I see it differently, however. What I believe is . . ." By so doing, you assert your opinion without waging war or, even worse, denying your own feelings.

- Practice being assertive by asking for what you need, want, or deserve—usually you will get it. Resentment builds up when you feel cheated at not getting what you deserve. Not asking for what you want could lead to future aggressive behavior. By asking, you circumvent that possibility.

- In business, it is more effective and powerful to suggest what needs to be done rather than aggressively forcing your demands on others. Rather than say, "Do this!" try saying, "I suggest that we find a more effective way of doing this." Then you can encourage the offering of solutions to the problem.

- The affirmation: "*Wu wei* is the only way" will help you avoid aggressive acts. (*Wu wei*, as we have seen, means nonforced, nonviolent flow. It implies action with a sense of yielding.) Write this statement on a large card and place it where it will be visible to all who work or live in your environment.

丧可分诤
石道牟己

Fulfill your purpose without violence.
Bravado when strong hastens decay;
This is contrary to the Tao.
What is contrary to the Tao comes to an early end.

TAO TE CHING no. 30

Exercise: Coping Assertively with Aggressive People

1. Choose a person you know who reacts aggressively in most situations.

2. Create a mental scenario where you feel attacked or put down. Close your eyes, and imagine how that feels. You are tense, frightened, and anxious.

3. Take one deep breath and affirm to yourself: "I am at one with the Tao; I choose not to play these games." Feel yourself calm, poised, and strong.

4. Now, continue the interaction and express how you feel to this person. Refrain from judgments, accusations, or name-calling. Assert your rights: "I do not deserve to be treated like this. No one does." Take another deep breath, relax, and wait for a response.

5. See your aggressor back off, apologize, and treat you as you deserve to be treated.

Practice this often, and make it relevant to your particular situation. The important thing is to feel your power as you assert yourself. Creating positive images about how to handle aggressive situations will enable you to behave more appropriately when you are taken off-guard.

Much is being said today about sexual harassment in the workplace, a common aggression situation, particularly for women. If you are a woman dealing with unwanted sexual advances, add the following steps to the above exercise:

1. Look your aggressor in the eye. Assert yourself by stepping into his space, to show him you will not accept his invasion of your space. Keep your eyes on his at all times. If he is bigger than you are, point your finger up at him to show you are not intimidated and will not accept his negative energy.

2. Tell him that his comments and behavior make you uncomfortable and that you will not accept them: "So *stop* it." If he protests and says, "What do you mean?" say, "You *know* what I mean, and you will stop it."

3. Stand your ground, and he will step back and leave. This usually works for public harassers (aggressive men on buses or elevators) too.

Affirmations for Assertiveness

- "*I accept and practice a more peaceful way.*"
- "*I am one with the Tao.*"
- "*Wu wei keeps hostility at bay.*"
- "*Softness overcomes hardness.*"
- "*I resolve aggression with assertion.*"

COURAGEOUSNESS

Frequent encounters with danger are a part
of life . . . making you inwardly strong . . .
instilling in you a profound awareness of life . . .
bringing new meaning, and richness.

I CHING no. 29

Taking risks is part of being alive. It is a natural stepping-stone to a more richly rewarding existence. The *I Ching* uses the word *danger*, although *risking* would be a congruent substitute.

In sports you risk losing games or failing to reach goals. Some athletic events even involve an element of danger to one's physical well-being; in a few sports, death is a possibility. For the purposes of this discussion, however, let's focus on taking risks that could lead to significant breakthroughs in your sport.

Most successful athletes, when asked how they improve, say that their secret is to take calculated risks along the way. They possess a high tolerance for loss, setback, and failure and know that taking risks and learning from them is the only way to enhance their sports performance. All admit to experiencing thousands of mistakes and errors in their careers. Babe Ruth hit many home runs during his years, yet he struck out 1,333 times in the process of swinging for the fences.

When you fail, step back, embrace the failure, learn from it, and if necessary change your direction. Don't fight this failure; see it as a natural experience that must occur. The empty space created by loss or failure is always filled. When you feel most devastated from taking a risk and suffering a setback, you can be sure that you are about to learn from the experience in some way that will help you improve. If you overlook this lesson of the Tao, or resist learning it, you create new limitations that will impede your performance.

TAOSPORT TRAINING FOR ATHLETICS

Running marathons presented me with plenty of opportunities to test my courage. When I was running with the lead pack at mile ten in the Summit Marathon in California, I decided to put it on the line and surged into the front, eventually winning the race. This was risky, however, because a surge so early in a twenty-six-mile event could cause muscle cramping, oxygen debt, too quick a burnup of glycogen fuel, and a host of other potential physiological problems. Yet by doing it, I established myself as a front-runner and psychologically demoralized my competitors. Taking this tactical risk helped me in every race I've run subsequently, by enabling me to raise my competitive courage as well as improve my performance.

Exercise: Courage to Take the Risk

The purpose of this exercise is twofold: to create the courage to take risks, then to overcome feeling like a failure if the risk is unsuccessful. Follow the steps in order.

1. Will taking the risk possibly improve your performance? If your answer is yes, go on to the next question.

2. What is your worst-case scenario for the risk? If you can accept the down side, go for it. If not, put it on hold. Consider the options: To take repeated sojourns into *terra incognita* without proper assessment of the possible outcomes is sheer foolishness. You set yourself up for

failure if the stakes are too high. If you asked me to dive off a boat into forty-nine-degree water at midnight and swim two miles to shore in the rough sea, I'd decline. But if it meant saving my child from drowning, I would take the risk without hesitation.

3. What is your plan? If you decide to take the risk, fastidious planning ahead of time will help prevent an inferior performance. Obtain instructions and information that will facilitate success. If you fail to plan, you plan to fail. Having done this, listen to your Beginner's Mind, your intuitive self. If you have any hesitancy, don't be afraid to change your mind. There will be another time.

4. When are congratulations in order? Immediately! Praise yourself and feel proud for having the courage to take the risk, knowing that, in time, taking repeated risks will ultimately lead to success. Without taking the risk, you will definitely not succeed. Courage is the willingness to take the risk regardless of the possibility of failure.

5. What if you suffer a setback? Use the Beginner's Mind to go beyond the obstacle. See the failure as the dues you pay to be vibrantly alive and able to participate in your sport. Look for the lessons it offers. You are already successful just for having taken the risk—the bonus is what you've learned from the setback. Such tolerance at this point is essential to reinforcing the TaoSport process, enabling you to try again. Negative criticism will extinguish the flames of courage.

Affirmations for Risk Taking

- *"Risks are a natural way to be alive in sport."*
- *"The athlete I most admire takes the risks that sport requires."*
- *"Risks are the dues I pay for breakthroughs."*
- *"I am rich because I can risk."*
- *"I risk temporary loss for the chance for permanent improvement."*
- *"I possess a high tolerance for setbacks due to risks."*
- *"I am a courageous, risk-taking warrior."*

TAOSPORTS FOR BUSINESS AND LIFE

In the play *No Exit* by Jean-Paul Sartre, three people are trapped in a metaphysical, self-imposed hell—one room, no windows, crowded together, and not able to leave. After they had spent much time in hell, a door opened and they were free to go. But they stayed because the unknown was too risky. They had become comfortable with their horrendous lives and chose suffering over the possibility of freedom.

How many of us are trapped and lack the courage to take the risk to create positive change? Changing professions, moving our home, going back to school, improving our lifestyles are possibilities staring many of us in the face.

These touching words of wisdom were expressed by a participant in a courage and risk-taking workshop that I regularly conduct.

> I had always tended to be somewhat cautious and
> conservative in my approach to life. I never took risks
> or chances . . . always played it close to the chest.
> When I turned thirty-five, my safe world received a
> tremendous jolt: I was told I had a malignancy and
> was given less than a year to live. Then, a miracle
> happened. A mistake had been made in the diagnosis,
> giving me a new lease on life. I had learned that life is
> a tenuous, chance proposition. From that moment, I
> truly began to live and search for opportunities to take
> lots of good, healthy risks. It's the only way to live.

Risk taking in daily living can be fulfilling and rewarding. Yes, it does raise fears, yet with proper training and planning you can control your anxiety and increase the probability of a positive outcome. An effective way to plan properly is to follow the "Courage to Risk" exercise.

Guides for Risk Taking

A life of risk contributes to a life of depth and breadth. Know that a full, enjoyable life, one where you push the limits of your creative, emotional, spiritual, and personal potential, will necessarily include thousands of risks and many setbacks. The pain of taking a risk must be weighed against the pain of not taking the risk, which could be a life of deep regret or remorse. Although I initially resist taking big risks, I usually end up taking them for their hidden opportunities. For the most part, my life can be seen as a series of constant, well-calculated risks. These thoughts and strategies help me go for it.

- According to philosopher and author André Gide, "Man cannot discover new oceans unless he has the courage to lose sight of the shore." Courage indicates a willingness to take risks.

- If you take the risk and experience a setback, think of the impact this setback will have on your life in five years. This helps put it into perspective. In most cases, you'll see that the setback is meaningless aside from the wonderful lessons it can teach.

- When you take the time to choose realistic, short-term, challenging goals, you minimize the risk factors. When you select a direction of personal passion, you fortify your courage to take the risk.

Exercise: Courage to Risk

If the truth were known, you probably are a successful risk-taker—you just need to become aware of it. To encourage yourself to move forward, go back to a time when you had a successful experience with risks.

1. Write down a risk you took in business or life that worked out positively.

2. What was your initial fear prior to the risk?

3. Did the fear materialize? Was it rational?

4. How did you feel after taking the risk?

5. How did this action affect your life then? Now?

Now you can see patterns to taking risks. You may always have a certain fear that proves to be unfounded. But usually, taking the risk pays off.

Visualization:
On-the-Job Risk Taking

Create a scenario related to taking a risk at work. Giving a difficult presentation, trying a new way to manage the group or make a sales pitch, or being radically different in your approach to product development are a few of the ways we take risks at work. Besides making sure you have thoroughly planned your actions, try the following visualization to prepare yourself for the future.

Envision yourself about to take a risk, doing something that is very new for you. Perhaps it's a way of approaching your boss for a raise or a new position. Or maybe you want to try a new way of doing the same boring tasks. Feel your nervousness, tension, and anxiety. Really get in touch with these feelings by creating images associated with the risk. Affirm the words: "Taking this risk makes me courageous and alive. I can only gain professionally as I learn from this experience."

See yourself performing this task, and feel the exhilaration as it turns out well. Hear those close by give you praise for taking the risk. Feel the deep sense of satisfaction for having taken the risk. See risks in the future as opportunities to come alive and feel vibrant.

Remember that success is already yours for having the courage to take the risk at all. After all, the most damaging or painful risk could very well be *not* taking the risk to improve your life. Don't ask, "Will this risk create failure?" Better to ask, "Will this risk put me in position for major breakthroughs and growth?" The only real failure is the unfulfillment or remorse created by avoiding taking risks.

Courageousness in Chinese is two symbols, courage and daring. The symbol of *Kan*, in *I Ching* no. 29, is the abyss, the deep of the water, danger and risk we must encounter when we have the courage to sink deep into our psychic consciousness. In Chinese mythology, the Monkey King dived deep into the bottom of the ocean to battle the ruler of the underwater, and earned his most treasured weapon, the magical golden staff.

As the English essayist Francis Bacon once said, "There's no comparison between what's lost by not trying and what's lost by not succeeding."

DETACHMENT

The stronger the attachments,
  The greater the cost.
The more that is hoarded,
  The deeper the loss.
Know what is enough;
  Be without disgrace.

TAO TE CHING no. 44

Patrice had devoted three wonderful years of diligent training, hoping to earn the right to run in the 1992 women's marathon trials in Houston, Texas. Prior to her last chance at qualifying, I asked how she would feel if she didn't make the 2-hour 45-minute cut-off time. She responded as a true TaoSport athlete: "I'll give it my best. I realize that I've had three terrific years getting ready for this race. I really care about it, but it won't kill me if I don't make it. I've already come out on top by having so much fun training." Relaxed, fit, and enthusiastic, Patti ran the race of her dreams, qualifying in 2:41:18.

Detachment quiets the ego and opens the heart to extraordinary levels of energy, awareness, joy, and power. Let go of your attachment to winning and achievement, and they will come your way. Athletes often claim to have let go during an event and have felt injected with reserves they didn't know they had, as a result.

174

The TaoAthlete understands that by limiting desire for possessions, praise, and other external attachments, one creates enormous personal power. Athletes who are overly attached to winning medals and trophies, prize money, sponsorships, and accolades are at a great disadvantage because such ephemeral desires create much tension and pressure, which interfere with the joy, fun, and fulfillment of performance. Detaching from these external desires reduces tension and improves performance.

Detachment doesn't mean that you cease to care about a sporting event. You care immensely about how you play—the process itself is important as a vehicle for growth and discovery about what you can and can't do. The outcome is a gauge that measures your level of improvement—accept it for what it truly is. Detachment means detaching from all the ego ramifications that we attribute to success. A loss—or a victory, for that matter—is never a measure of your self-worth as an athlete or a person. By practicing detachment, your perspective on your sport is healthier. You can love it with passion, yet see it as only a microcosmic event in a universe of activity.

R. L. Wing states poignantly in *The Tao of Power*, "Strong desires that are dependent on outside events . . . lead individuals away from the cultivation of personal power." As a TaoAthlete lets go of desire, he experiences more joy and success, an increase in personal freedom that enables him to take more risks in sport without the fear of putting anything on the line. Such freedom allows him to dance the game completely uninhibited, the way it was meant to be.

The author of *Zorba the Greek*, Nikos Kazantzakis, wrote his own epitaph, which clearly depicts the essence of this freedom:

> I do not hope for anything
> I do not fear for anything
> I am free.

TAOSPORT TRAINING FOR ATHLETICS

When I talk with athletes who struggle with their performances, I ask them to recall how often they have fun when they are playing. Most cannot remember the last time they enjoyed the game, which is ironic since fun was the initial attraction to their sport. I surmise that the reason they can't remember is that they cannot detach from themselves, the game, and its outcome. Their emotional involvement reduces the level of joy they can experience in their sport. They lose awareness of the dance of the game, which interferes, paradoxically, with the outcome. When you become attached to playing better and winning more, you push, force, or try harder. This creates anxiety, tension, and pressure; the result is less fun, joy, and fulfillment, coupled with sub-par performance.

A cyclist client of mine felt as if each ride with his buddies was a vast ego check. They all attempted to prove their prowess by constantly trying to "drop" one another on the climbs (first one to the top of the hill is the king of the mountain). My client had been dueling it out with one other rider for weeks with no success. He became disgruntled, dissatisfied, and burned-out. Gone was the joy in cycling, the fun of the experience. He was attached only to results.

As his performance declined, he gave excuses for not showing up for scheduled workouts. His distaste for the others' trying always to prove themselves and for the pressure to join in this craziness was too great. I asked him what he originally liked about riding. His answer—the incredible exhilaration of the workouts, and the "rush" from the speed. I suggested that he go on a ride with these friends and detach from results by focusing on the joy of being able to exercise while experiencing wonderful health and fitness.

He followed the suggestions, and now he rides more relaxed with less pressure—he recently outclimbed the group for the first time ever. Although he has not repeated this feat, he feels he performs with greater consistency at a higher level and experiences a lot less pain in the process. He learned much about himself.

So can you if you begin to attach less value to how you perform. Ask yourself the question, "What do I love about my sport?" Then, focus on your passion.

Affirmations for Detachment from Results

- *"When I'm detached, my play can't be matched."*
- *"The stronger the attachment, the greater the cost."*
- *"When I detach from results, things begin to go my way."*

- *"When in the moment I stay, I improve my play."*

Visualization: Seeing Yourself Detached

In your state of relaxation, imagine yourself playing your sport with incredible calm. You are at one with the game, your body floating instinctively with every move. You are "dancing" with such ease, effortlessness, and lightness that you are unaware of your own body. You are playing "out of body," responding naturally to the flow of the game. Feel the ecstasy and the joy that accompany an excellent process, even though the outcome may or may not be in your favor. See the event coming to conclusion; even though you did not win, you feel excited and complete about the way you performed. You excelled beyond your dreams, and you are now ready to learn from this "losing outcome" and be a better athlete as a result. See yourself as the TaoAthlete you are, detached from results by focusing on the fun and improvement. Know that your level of play is higher when you refocus on the process of your sport.

TAOSPORTS FOR BUSINESS AND LIFE

Whether an outcome seems positive or negative, your emotional attachment to it is a setup for disappointment and pain. In a classic Taoist story, a wise father helps his son reduce his attachment to appearances. The story goes like this.

A very old Chinese man and his young son lived during a period of much civil strife. They were considered rich by the villagers because they owned a horse. One morning, the son awoke to find his horse had run away. Running to his father, he informed him of this tragedy, saying this was the worst thing that could have happened. His father, in all his wisdom, replied, "Is that so? How do you know what it means?" The next day, as the boy was working in the barn, he heard the sound of horses galloping in the distance. When he looked up, he saw his horse leading a herd of wild ponies toward him. Seeing this, he ran to the house shouting, "The horse has come back leading a herd. This is the greatest thing that's ever happened!" In all his wisdom, the old man replied once again: "Is that so? How do you know what it means?" That afternoon, the boy decided to tame one of the ponies. As he proudly sat atop the new-found gift, the horse bucked, throwing the boy to the ground, causing a broken collarbone and a fractured arm. As he was placed in his bed by his father, he said, "All those horses coming—that's the worst thing that could have happened." Once again, the old man spoke: "Is that so? How do you know what it means?" The next day, father and son were abruptly awakened by the sound of militia knocking on their door. They were here to take the boy to fight in the civil war. The old man said, "There he is, take him." The captain took one look and said, "He's useless to us," and left. The boy said, "This is the best luck I've ever had." And the old man, in his wisdom replied, "Is that so? How do you know what it means?"

How do any of us know the real meaning of outcomes in business and life? The Tao teaches us to stay in the "now," to be with what is happening, and to detach from judging outcomes. Attachment creates tension, anxiety, and fear. When you let go, you experience a freedom, a sense of relief.

Exercise: Seven Steps to Detachment

This exercise will help you to identify your attachments and get beyond them.

1. Tell yourself that you are willing and able to be perfectly honest with yourself. Pretend that you have swallowed a truth serum to complete this exercise.

2. Make a list of your attachments.

3. Annotate this list: Mark the good things about each attachment and the drawbacks of each. (For example: A beautiful home gives comfort and quiet. It also brings a high mortgage and a need to meet monthly payments by being employed in a job you may not like.)

4. Make a list of the attachments from which you wish to detach.

5. After a careful reading of each attachment, answer the question,

"Why do I wish to detach?" You may actually value these items quite highly. You can't detach and attach at the same time—this conflict will set you up for unhappiness. Maybe you are attached to what they represent. A relationship may fill a void you do not want to face, for example, or owning a certain car may make you feel rich or important.

6. Decide what you can truly let go of. It is imperative that the benefits of detaching from a certain thing be greater than the benefits of holding on. (For example, I value the freedom and happiness I got from selling my expensive car and having money for other things and for the future much more than I valued feeling rich.)

7. Once you define the value in detachment, you are ready to let go and affirm: "I love the freedom and happiness that comes with shedding." Attachments are fun and even helpful, yet they are not essential. When I detach, life goes on in a much more freeing, fearless way.

Visualization: Personal Freedom

In your relaxed state, affirm: "I would rather be free and happy than be attached and tense, stressed, and fearful." Imagine those things that hold you emotionally captive: a stain on a favorite shirt, a scratch on a new car, kids dirtying the walls or floors. Feel your tension rise as you experience your attachments. You are tight, rigid, and angry. Now, shout out the word *"Stop"* in your mind, and redirect your view of the situation. Feel yourself being healthier and more free as you "let go." Take two deep breaths, and as you exhale, imagine your attachments exiting through your mouth into a balloon and flying away with the wind until they get so small, they are no longer visible. Notice the calm and peace that follow. Affirm: "I'm free again, free at last. I am no longer controlled by my attachments."

How to Catch Butterflies

A young boy received a butterfly net for his birthday. On a hot, humid summer day, he ran wild trying to catch one of these elusive aviators. After much tension and anxiety from many futile attempts, he fell to the ground in exhaustion. While quietly resting in the grass, he detached from his quest, and the butterfly landed on his nose.

EGOLESSNESS

They do not display themselves;
  Therefore they are illuminated.
They do not define themselves;
  Therefore they are distinguished.
They do not make claims;
  Therefore they are credited.
They do not boast;
  Therefore they advance.

TAO TE CHING no. 22

In his classic work, *Zen in the Art of Archery,* Eugene Herrigel comments on how a student swordsman may approach the level of master or greatness: "The more he tries to make the brilliance of his swordplay dependent on his own reflection . . . the more he inhibits the free working of the heart. . . . How does sovereign control of technique turn into master swordplay? Only by the pupil's becoming purposeless and egoless. He must be taught to be detached not only from his opponent but from himself."

Some incredibly talented athletes possess all the skills to make it big, yet they fall short. Often, their ego involvement becomes an obstacle, causing friction between them and other athletes. Much energy is wasted in defending their "greatness," physically and emotionally. They don't support, cooperate,

181

or encourage their athletic colleagues, and they get none in return because they alienate their teammates by the harshness of their egocentric posture.

The TaoSport way to inner power and recognition is to detach from the need for such power. The less you focus upon your greatness in relation to others, on how well you play compared with your teammates or competitors, the more effective and appreciated you will become. In the preceding chapter, you learned to detach from external forces. In this chapter, you can learn to detach from the negative force of egocentricity.

> You can achieve your aims through the encouragement
> of others. Encouragement is one of the great
> powers. . . . Kindness and gentleness in your relations
> brings allegiance, co-operation and, ultimately, success.
>
> *I CHING* no. 58

Egocentricity is a hindrance to performance. The constant need to live up to self-centered illusions creates unnecessary and inhibiting anxiety and tension. The athlete who needs to boast and impress others is usually doing so out of feelings of deep insecurity and uncertainty and is wasting a lot of energy.

Egoless TaoAthletes understand that the less they focus on themselves, the more effective they are. Championship teams conceal their advantages and downplay their previous excellent performances, thereby diminishing the chance of a counterforce emerging. They appear reserved and humble. They are quiet. Seeming to be almost weak, or at least nonthreatening, has helped many teams overcome apparently stronger teams that actually squander their energies in displays of false dominance.

TAOSPORT TRAINING FOR ATHLETICS

I recently visited with a close running and cycling buddy in Colorado, Bob Anderson. When I arrived at his home, I was introduced to a friend of his named Bill. He was obviously well built and looked strong. Bill began to tell me how he enjoyed my books; he asked me questions about myself, my life, my family, and my interests. Time passed quickly, and I never got the chance to know Bill. Upon his departure, I asked Bob if Bill worked out. "Work out? A little. Between 1956 and 1971, he won the title Mr. Universe four times."

I was in the company of the Joe Montana, Michael Jordan, and Wayne Gretzky of body-building. Bill Pearl, at the age of sixty, still pumps iron two and a half hours a day.

Visualization: Egolessness

This visualization exercise (adapted from *Healing Visualizations: Creative Health Through Imagery* by Gerald Epstein, M.D.) will help you to let go of egocentric tendencies in order to feel less pressure and, as a result, improve your performance. Like most of the visualizations in this book, this exercise is performed entirely in the mind.

> In your state of relaxation, identify all egocentric traits that you tend to exhibit periodically in your sport. See yourself writing these on a sheet of red paper. (Red is, according to the *I Ching*, the color of fire or transformation.) Fold the sheet, and carry it to a place in the wilderness. There, burn the paper, collect its ashes, and bury them in a deep hole. Cover up the hole, walk over to the lake nearby, and jump in. Cleanse yourself of any residual egocentric traits. Exit the water, and allow yourself to dry off in the warmth of the sun. Get dressed in clean athletic wear, and walk away feeling strong, soft, and egoless. Imagine yourself behaving in this manner in situations in your sport where your ego would normally dominate others.

Affirmations for Egolessness

Use any of these affirmations, or others you may create, in order to let go of egocentric tendencies as they appear.

- *"The less I talk about me, the more other athletes will see."*
- *"Humility is always rewarded in athletics."*
- *"Let go of E-go."*

- *"Conceal my advantages to become more effective in sport."*

TAOSPORTS FOR BUSINESS AND LIFE

Visualization: Egolessness

To help you display egoless qualities at work or at home, use this visualization exercise.

> Imagine an environment where you are standing with another person. You make a conscious choice to focus on his needs and wants. Hear yourself listening to his troubles and reflecting his feelings. See yourself showing compassion and concern. Point out what you appreciate about him and how happy you are to have him available in your life. Imagine him complimenting you, as you simply respond, "Thank you." You are so secure within that there's no need to become absorbed by what you've done. Notice how wonderful you feel giving to another person in this way. And notice that this person still holds you in high esteem. Use this feeling of strength as a touchstone when you wish to demonstrate egolessness with others.

Guides for Egolessness

Your real power as a person comes when you relate to others from your heart rather than your head. These thoughts will help you to focus your approach toward others with less egocentricity.

- When you meet people, rather than focus on the impression you're creating on them, concentrate on trying to discover the greatness within them. What traits do they possess that you admire?

- Ask yourself how you can be more kind and gentle. This is true strength and power, as the Tao teaches: "Soft is strong."

- Look for opportunities when you can sincerely affirm others as professionals and friends. Tell them how much you appreciate and respect them. Ask them questions about things they love in life.

- Before you divulge your accomplishments, advantages, or achievements to people, ask yourself what your purpose is and what good it will do for others to hear of these. A legitimate, non–ego-related purpose would be to help them see that they, too, can achieve—that they are as good as you. If others ask you about yourself, remember that a fine line exists between boasting and reporting.

SELFLESSNESS

Evolved Individuals put themselves last,
and yet they are first.
Put themselves outside, and yet they remain.
Is it not because they are without self-interest
That their interests succeed?

TAO TE CHING no. 7

In an ancient Eastern story, heaven and hell are exactly alike: Each is an enormous banquet where the most incredible, delectable dishes are placed on huge tables. Those who partake in the feast are given chopsticks *five feet long.* In the banquet in hell, people give up struggling to feed themselves with these awkward utensils and remain ravenously unfulfilled. In heaven, everyone selflessly feeds the person across the table.

According to the Tao, those who are in the background will eventually be brought forward. Even in the Judeo-Christian tradition, the meek—the truly humble, unboastful, selfless people—will be recognized as worthy. Lao-tzu encourages action without self-interest; selflessness ultimately brings personal fulfillment.

Whereas egolessness is a passive process of holding back, of not forcing yourself on others, selflessness is an active process of devotion to others' welfare and interests—even sometimes at the expense of your own. Giving to your teammates enhances your own performance as they look for ways to reciprocate. Bring out another's best, give him praise, help him to improve, to score, to get free, to be in position, and the same will be provided for you over and over. What you give, you get back.

A professional athlete who epitomizes selflessness is basketball great Larry Bird of the Boston Celtics. I have seen him pass the ball to a trailing player during a fast break when he could have easily taken the layup himself. He takes a sincere interest in helping the younger players on the team improve. Because of this, players throughout the NBA have the utmost respect for Bird. He gives so much, yet he gets back a hundredfold from the admiration of his peers and certainly his fans.

Selflessness is personal power. Taoists call it *tz'u*, which means "caring" or "compassion." In TaoSports, it is caring for others' performances, individually and as a team. The more you give to others, the more you possess. Teams with selfish athletes experience much friction and anxiety that detract from team unity and performance, but it's difficult to be at odds with those who give. Selflessness creates peace and conserves energy, which allows for higher levels of play.

TAOSPORT TRAINING FOR ATHLETICS

Perhaps one of the most spectacular demonstrations of selflessness in athletics comes to us from the 1976 Summer Olympics in Montreal. Japan's bid for a gold medal in gymnastics was in jeopardy when their star specialist in the rings could not compete due to an incapacitating injury. The only other team member who could possibly do the routine was twenty-six-year-old Shun Fujimoto, who had a severely broken bone in his right leg—an injury sustained in his floor exercise. Despite the fact that the required dismount jump from the rings at the conclusion of the event would subject him to enormous pain and possibly more broken bones, he selflessly put his country first and took on the burden. A plastic cast was prepared for Fujimoto, which he wore during the performance. Following a triple-somersault and twist, he nailed his dismount long enough to clinch the gold for Japan. Seconds later, his leg gave way under excruciating pain. "Pain shot through me like a knife," he remarked later. "It brought tears to my eyes." Sixteen years later he continued to give to his country as Japan's national women's gymnastics head coach going into the Summer Olympics in Barcelona, Spain.

A very talented yet selfish collegiate tennis champion at the University of California at Santa Cruz couldn't have cared less about his team and its athletes, and his play was erratic. He was the source of much friction with his peers, and his behavior threatened the team's chances at the nationals. The coach told him that he might not play if his selfishness persisted. Members of the team individually told him to shape up or quit the team. When he realized how alone and isolated he was, he began to give his position some thought. Even his father got on his case and threatened to withdraw financial support if he didn't come around. Eventually, he began to change with the coach's help, by realizing that his true individual victory, his real challenge, was to support the team effort at the nationals. He played and lost the singles championships, but he cheered his buddies on as they enjoyed a wonderful team triumph. He was disappointed by his own poor showing, but admitted to feeling terrific as part of an NCAA championship team.

Visualization: Selfless Play

In a quiet place, with your eyes closed, take five deep breaths and relax. Imagine yourself as part of a team in which you are well liked and respected. See yourself giving praise to various team members for the good work they do. Feel the joy in being involved in this way. See yourself taking someone aside and giving her pointers on improving her performance. Hear her extend appreciation, thanking you for your time and expertise. See yourself in a situation where you help bring out the best in another. Feel the joy of contributing in this powerful way. As you play, notice that other team members seem to give so much to you. Feel the pats on the back. Hear their encouraging words, see them assisting you in your superb performance. Affirm: "My devotion to others on the team causes them to reciprocate, and as a result, my own performance improves."

Affirmations for Selflessness

These affirmations will help you solidify your commitment to selflessness in sport. Use them as touchstones to remember during those self-indulgent moments.

- *"I am a selfless athlete who creates opportunities for success through giving."*
- *"I am a caring champion who puts the interests of the team above my own."*
- *"Every day, in every way, I give more and more."*
- *"When I selflessly play, I ensure that I stay."*
- *"Helping others find their way gives me the chance for better play."*

TAOSPORTS FOR BUSINESS AND LIFE

When my wife, Jan, was pregnant with our third child, I decided to de-emphasize my professional self-interest and focus entirely on selfless giving during this nine-month period. This was a radical switch in attitude from our first two children's births—much tension and anxiety had brewed as the pending arrivals conflicted with what I considered important work. I wanted this birth to be stressless and smooth. Taking a back seat was a struggle, yet I began to see that this birth was more important than anything else I could do. This awareness allowed me to relax and let go of selfish needs. The birth of Brennan Michael was a transformational experience beyond words. Para-doxically, the more I gave to my son's birthing process, the more I experienced a birthing process of my own, professionally. The quality and quantity of my work expanded tremendously. When I gave, I received.

It is well known that managers, supervisors, and leaders who are most effective and successful within the work environment tend to be compassionate, caring, giving, and selfless in their approach to employees. When they give in this way, workers usually reciprocate.

A client of mine was talking about the one saving grace at work, the reason why he continues to stay with his underpaying job: "Jerry, my manager is terrific. I've never met a woman like her. Somehow, she makes us all feel as though we truly count, that our efforts are appreciated. It makes us want to give a thousand percent. We'd do anything for her. I guess what goes around, comes around."

Guides for Making a Difference

To live the Tao, to create more fulfillment and joy, consider nature's law of reciprocity: What you give, you'll get back a hundredfold. The real payoff, however, is not what you receive directly from others. It is the joy you experience knowing you made a difference in another's life. These strategies will help you to refocus your energies on selflessness in daily life:

- Blend with the flow of the group—family, friends, co-workers—rather than trying to exert your own powerful influence. Notice that this is a source of inner power as well.

- When you meet new people, take the initiative and give to them by showing interest in their lives. Listening is the key to caring.

- Find ways to praise and compliment others sincerely for how they look, how they work, how they do things well, or how much you appreciate how they are as friends.

- When you are with people who are in distress, ask yourself, "How can I help?" and proceed to carry out the answer.

- To form successful patterns of selflessness, practice giving unconditionally to children. Their reactions are pure and emotionally uncontaminated; rarely will they take advantage of your kindness.

Forgiving—For Giving Selflessly

Forgiveness is perhaps the ultimate in giving. It is an act of the heart rather than the head. To hold grudges or ill feelings toward another person creates inner strife and anxiety for all involved.

Forgiving does not mean you must love the person in question, although love may be recaptured or ignited once forgiveness takes place and you experience inner peace. But it's not a necessary component of the process.

Forgiveness is the releasing of the past and the letting go of your fear of the future. It is an action that blends perfectly well with the Tao. Nature is forgiving. By forgiving, you give to others as well as yourself calm, peace, and happiness.

Observe a child when he is upset with you. With no concept of the past or future, he quickly forgives and shares his love; holding on to an emotion is not yet part of his behavior. Children sustain enormous happiness for themselves by releasing such tension and anxiety.

The key to forgiveness is to stop focusing on yourself and to realize that, deep inside, we all have the same basic heart of the child. If we can see ourselves in this way, forgiveness becomes a possibility. We all are humans and by definition make mistakes. We need to understand that our forgiveness of others' mistakes is really the forgiveness of our own when we behave in similar ways. I forgive you because, on some level, I am capable of doing the same thing for myself. We are all basically children who need acceptance and love through forgiveness.

CONSCIENTIOUSNESS

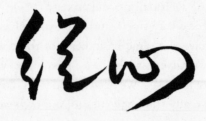

Be as conscientious as possible in your dealings
with the outside world. . . . Self-control and attention
to detail are character traits that will allow you
to accomplish your aims . . . do not overlook anything.

I CHING no 62

Conscientiousness is the process of acting in accordance with what you know is right. If you are conscientious, you cover all your bases and are in harmony with the Tao, which encourages you not to overlook anything.

Athletes generally know what makes for excellent performance, yet they often ignore their own knowledge. But you are being conscientious as an athlete if you show care for your diet, for instance, and obtain adequate periods of rest following hard workouts, as you know you should. Attentive, diligent athletes and coaches care for their team members, seeing to it that all are treated fairly and have a role in the squad's mission.

When you pay attention to detail, you are being conscientious. For the TaoAthlete, this means teaching and learning the fundamentals, the basics of the sport. When you build strong foundations, you can create castles in the sky. Conscientious athletes manage their time and resources effectively. Waste is anathema for attentive optimal performers, and in this way, they are aligned with the Tao.

Affirmations for Conscientiousness

- *"I cover all bases."*
- *"I attend to detail."*
- *"I know what is right—I do it!"*
- *"I overlook nothing."*
- *"I am complete!"*
- *"I am a diligent, mindful person, manager, athlete, student."*

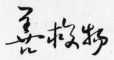

They are always good at saving things;
Hence nothing is wasted.

TAO TE CHING no. 27

Through TaoSports you can learn a conscientious self-control. You do not need to become a Spartan, yet you need to enact some form of restraint—social, nutritional, and professional. Self-control and conscientiousness in the training program will contribute to more joy, excellence, and fulfillment.

The conscientious TaoAthlete needs to establish a well-thought-out, holistic program of personal development in sport. Nothing that enhances optimal performance can be overlooked.

TAOSPORT TRAINING FOR ATHLETICS

An athlete I know epitomizes conscientiousness. He leaves nothing to chance. Prior to every training run and afterward he stretches his body and mind by visualizing terrific workouts and races. The first time we ran together in the mountains of Winter Park, Colorado, he completed the run just ahead of me, and I saw him duck into the bushes. Figuring that he was attending to nature's call, I patiently waited for him to finish. After ten long minutes I called to him, "Rick, are you finished yet?" There was no answer. I looked closely through the foliage. He was lying on the ground, and his eyes were shut. Had he fallen asleep? Should I wake him? Fifteen minutes had passed, and as if nothing had happened, Rick suddenly walked out of the bushes with a smile on his face. "That was a great race I just had," he said. He had been visualizing an upcoming event the following week and had actually dozed off for a few minutes.

Conscientious athletes do need to guard against becoming obsessive or perfectionistic. Being conscientious about cleanliness means showering once a day, but when you clean yourself so much that it interferes with your daily tasks, the behavior is obsessive. Conscientiousness means doing all that you can to promote excellence. If you fall short and you then get down on yourself for not being complete in all details, you are being perfectionistic.

The key to conscientiousness is to be flexible and go with the flow, bending in the face of any obstacles or changes.

Checklist for Conscientiousness

If you wish to optimize your athletic potential, this list will help you to focus on the top ten factors for improvement.

- Physical training: quality workout program designed by experts

- Mental training: fifteen minutes of visualization each day you work out physically

- Nutritional training: a diet that is conducive to your performance

- Emotional training: attending to your personal emotional issues in order to focus effectively

- Weight training: complementing the quality workouts, for strength

- Wait training: developing patience and persistence, which takes time

- Environment: one relatively free of stress and anxiety

- Rest: plenty of rest to recover from difficult workouts

- Social life: in moderation, social activities enhance athletic lifestyles

- Time management: a realistic time frame for each day

Visualization: Conscientiousness

Affirm to yourself: "I am a caring athlete who does what's right. I overlook nothing on my path to being the TaoAthlete." Imagine a typical day in your life as an athlete, from the time you awaken to bedtime. See yourself beginning with a visualization, mentally preparing for play. Imagine eating healthy, nourishing foods that enhance your performance. Feel the exhilaration of "pumping iron," followed by a good workout with your sport. Take time to rest between each. Feel yourself calm and peaceful and getting along well with your family and friends. You are filled with tremendous energy and strength. There is the sense of being complete. All is covered.

TAOSPORTS FOR BUSINESS AND LIFE

To live a more conscientious life and do what you know is right, construct a monthly chart to help you keep in touch with the important things you need to do on a daily basis.

Take a large sheet of paper. Write the numbers one to thirty-one across the top. These represent the number of days in most months. Down the left-hand side of the page, list all the activities that you feel you need to do on a daily basis—activities that you know are right. These may include: exercise, floss teeth, read, meditate, visualize, eat healthily, socialize, work, lift weights, help others in need, rest, consume water (eight twelve-ounce glasses minimum a day), and others depending upon your evaluation of what's important. Then draw graph lines down and across, creating many boxes that you can check upon the completion of that activity for that day.

Photocopy this blank sheet so that you'll have a supply. Tape this month's sheet in a visible place, and check off the box when you complete an activity. Watch for patterns. Why do you avoid some things and not others? Notice how you feel about such conscientious living after one month of recording data.

You can create a similar chart for the workplace. Many activities, if accomplished, make you a more conscientious worker or manager. This task-oriented approach will help you to become more productive. Those around you may even follow your lead.

Guides for Conscientious Behavior

- Consider being more conscientious about your environment. Recycle glass, aluminum cans, paper, and other reusable items. Clean up your garbage wherever it may be. If you see empty cans, bottles, or boxes in the street, throw them in the trash.

- Notice how pleased and thankful others are when you are conscientious about your commitments. You, too, will feel internally reward for keeping your word.

- Be conscientious about your own health. Adopt a holistic approach wellness by creating healthy physical, mental, emotional, and n tional environments. Pay attention to what you do and how you Live as if you loved yourself.

V

THE
INNER STRUCTURE

TAOSPORT STRATEGIES AND TECHNIQUES

Now that you have practiced Beginner's Mind
and other TaoSport mindsets, you can develop
and use advanced strategies and techniques
for extraordinary performances, both on and
off the field. By redefining concepts such as
competition, winning, motivation, and goal
setting, you will be able to plan strategies and
gain success, regardless of the outcome. This
part of the book gives you specific tools and
techniques for self-improvement and gaining
the advantage. These proven, time-honored
psychological tactics will help you hone your
TaoSport skills. Whether you're a coach, manager, teacher, or parent, you will learn specific
ways to facilitate positive change with people
who are under your influence, using the principles of TaoSports.

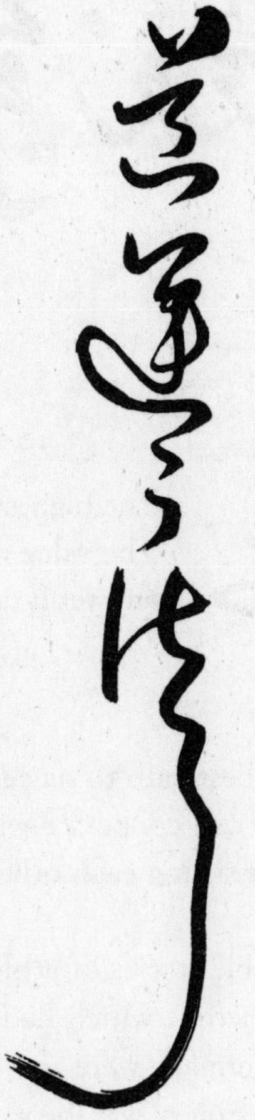

COMPETITION

The highest value is like water.
The value in water benefits all things,
and yet it does not contend.

TAO TE CHING no. 8

The killer instinct is not the best path to success. True strength, like water, blends with other forces. We can cooperate with our competitors in a way that makes us like partners, assisting each other on the road to heightened performance.

One of the most memorable stories of athletes as partners comes to us from the 1936 Olympics in Berlin, which had been orchestrated by Adolf Hitler to "prove" that the Germans were the master race. Jesse Owens, a black athlete from the United States, was the world record holder in the long jump. After fouling in his first two attempts, Owens was on the verge of being eliminated. Then Germany's top jumper, Lutz Long, rushed to his side and made a crucial tactical suggestion. Owens followed his advice and qualified for the finals. Both athletes continued to push each other, and Owens, in his last jump, set an Olympic record. Overjoyed, Lutz held Owens's hand high in front of thousands of cheering spectators; both walked out of the stadium arm-in-arm, Owens with four gold medals. This is the true meaning of TaoSport competition, two elite athletes working as partners toward optimal performance.

Contrast this story with that of Olympian runner Billy Mills in the movie *Running Brave*. Mills slows down at the finish line well ahead of his nearest competitor. On the sideline, his coach screams, "Crush your opponent . . . take him for everything . . . own him!"

In his book *The Ultimate Athlete*, George Leonard claims that "every aikidoist faces the problem of finding a good partner who will attack with real intent. The greatest gift he can receive from his opponent is clean, true attack, the blow that, unless blocked or avoided, will strike home with real effect." Working together is clearly encouraged by the *I Ching*:

You and the object of your inquiry are dependent
upon each other. Working together, the
interaction of your spheres of influence can achieve
significant deeds. Synergistic interaction will
provide surplus energy for continued growth.

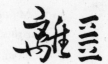

I CHING no. 30

TAOSPORT TRAINING FOR ATHLETICS

Be thankful for your opponents. They are gifts that enable you to experience the process of sport, great teachers who push you to heights you might not attain without them.

A competitive distance runner for many years, I learned firsthand how our competitors can teach us. One of my fellow runners was always out to annihilate me; he would make it known to everyone at each race that "today's the day I crush Lynch." Because he would run all-out at each race, he made me focus and try my best. He pushed me so well that I ran superb races against him, never losing once in twenty-five tries. Finally, however, one day, he ran the race of his life—which he had to in order to beat me. Afterward he was jumping all around, celebrating his win by announcing it over and over to everyone. He caught my attention and, in his usual obnoxious manner, proceeded to say, "I gotcha! I did you in! I've been trying for so long to beat you, and now I've done it." Hoping I could open his heart a little, I replied, "I feel so wonderful to be able to create such joy for you. And thanks for being here—because of you I ran better today than I thought possible." He looked confused; I don't think he knew what I was talking about. But I maintained my composure and inner balance by not meeting his bragging with my own.

If you compete like a TaoAthlete, you will remain always successful on the journey of extraordinary performance.

Affirmations for Competition Partnership

These affirmations will help you view your competitors as partners for excellence.

- *"I don't contend—I blend."*
- *"Working together, we achieve so much more."*
- *"My opponent is a gift that pushes me to greater heights."*
- *"Competition is the key to fruition."*
- *"I join with my opponent and play my best in the moment."*

Visualization: A New View of Competition

> In your state of relaxation, affirm: "We are together today to help each other push the limitless boundaries of our potential." Imagine greeting your opponent in person or with eye contact and mentally embracing him for being present. Feel thankful that he agrees to bring out your best. Notice his pleasure in knowing that you will provide the same opportunity for him. You both will do all that it takes to keep the other "honest." You both want to win. See the competitive event unfold. Feel the exhilaration of being challenged and rising to the occasion. The contest is over. Thank your competitor, and show appreciation by focusing on the level of play, not who won or lost.

TAOSPORTS FOR BUSINESS AND LIFE

U.S. Olympic biathlete Dick Taylor talks about the fullness of healthy competition: "It is a ritual, a highly compacted human experience situation. . . . It is the measure of our curiosity about optimum human possibility . . . the sustenance coming from a shared sense that all are relatively more alive from having 'died' a little as well. The experience of expanded personal potential and relativity with other humans is both profound and rare . . . a deeper sense of belonging, to oneself and to a community. Self-confirmation happens simultaneously with a community venture . . . ultimately making a winner of everybody."

In business, coming out on top is important when negotiating, signing a contract, competing for the bid, interviewing for a job, making an important sales pitch, or enhancing productivity. Keep in mind, however, that you should recognize your rivals, opponents, and competitors for their role in enabling you to succeed. Don't overlook their contribution to your efforts because you are too busy basking in your own glory. Avoid the tendency to "put down" the competition or make them seem less than they are in the eyes of others.

In the race to get to the moon in the 1960s, two superpowers, the United States and the Soviet Union, competed against each other, spending enormous amounts of money to get there first. A cooperative effort, a coming together of great minds, would have succeeded faster and cheaper. Thirty years later, both countries now realize the power of cooperative competition and partnership.

Guides for Healthy Competition

• When you are working for a corporation or a university, creative, reliable, and productive co-workers can often seem threatening to you. You may fear that you will be judged as somehow less than they. Turn your fear into a positive opportunity by trying to learn from these peers effective strategies and techniques to raise your own competency level. Others are often catalytic agents for personal growth.

• Blame is a way of competing. Finding fault with another person can give you the illusion that you are better. Rather than find fault, try to encourage cooperation and find a solution. Attempt to create situations where others can cooperatively work together from the beginning to accomplish something more easily, quickly, and effectively.

- "Keep up with the Joneses" is a familiar expression of competition with neighbors and friends. Buying bigger and better houses and expensive cars, going to fashionable restaurants—it's all part of the game. Rather than going broke trying to keep up, consider making a more cooperative effort of pooling your resources to bring about more with less. Start a group for co-housing, for example, to eventually purchase large parcels of land together and keep down the costs of real estate and other expensive items such as cars, machinery, washers, and dryers. If this is too much to think about now, try having potluck dinners together, cooperative efforts to keep the cost of meals down.

- A general rule of thumb: In situations in business and life where you have to compete and try to win, use the excellent play of your opposition as a key to self-improvement. Because of your opponent, you are in position to extend your personal boundaries of excellence. If you truly do not need to compete, collaborate in efforts that are greater than the sum of each individual contribution.

Visualization: Function Without Conflict

In your state of relaxation, see yourself in the midst of conflict and fighting, be it at work, with friends, or with family. Feel peaceful, calm, and centered. See yourself functioning without conflict, searching for solutions to the problem. Now, create a signal (finger on nose, thumb pressing against index finger, a full fist). Tell yourself that when you use this signal, it will remind you of how to function in this state for the benefit of all involved.

WINNING

Evolved individuals produce but do not possess,
Succeed without taking credit.
Since they take no credit, it remains with them.

TAO TE CHING no. 2

Former world tennis champion Billie Jean King has stated that "winning isn't that big a deal. The real joy comes from the very thing that involves people in the first place . . . the fun of execution, the fun of playing." The above passage from the Tao, too, reminds you simply to be all you can be in the process of living, and success will be yours. You are a winner if your journey is one of quality.

In an interview with *Sports Illustrated,* coach Ken O'Keefe of the Allegheny College NCAA Division III football team was quoted as saying to his team prior to the 1990 championship game: "Play like champions; four quarters total team effort. Relax and have fun. The results will take care of themselves." And they did in a 21-to-14 win over their archrival, Lycoming. Never once did O'Keefe emphasize "winning" as the objective, choosing instead to focus on "the moment" and the inner gratification of each player.

After a number of losing seasons, the Stanford University football team finally received an invitation to a postseason Bowl game. When Jack Elway, the Cardinal head coach, was interviewed by the press, he was asked how it felt to now be a winner. His reply was that the team had been winners for years—it just didn't show on the scoreboard.

If winning is unimportant, then, why keep score? To the TaoAthlete the outcome of any event is important—but not as an end in itself. Keeping score enables you to measure your performance level throughout the event and get an indication of how you are progressing over a period of time. And it's fun to win.

But being free of the *need* to win results in greater personal power and performance. Let the possibility of winning keep you alert and sharp. If you win, terrific; if not, feel the joy and satisfaction of having participated. Focus on how well you are mastering specific skills. Notice how the event provided you with an opportunity to display your skills against challenging competition. Win or lose, you have to dig down inside and discover other aspects of your essence. Prizes and victories are transitory, while outstanding performances, regardless of the outcome, are tremendously rewarding. Focusing on the moment-by-moment joy and elation of the event will usually be reflected in winning outcomes.

This healthier approach to playing and winning is aligned with the TaoSport concept of "letting go." Let go of the obsessive desire to produce or possess, and focus on the joy, the dance, the flow. Be in the moment, and feel victories now, as you play. According to Fred Rohé, author of the classic book *The Zen of Running*:

> There are no standards and no possible victories
> > except the joy you are living while dancing your run.
> In any life joy is only known in the moment—now!
>
> So feel the flow of your dance and know
> > you are not running for some future reward—
> The real reward is NOW!

TAOSPORT TRAINING FOR ATHLETICS

As a member of the U.S. speed-skating hall of fame and former North American speed-skating champion, Jim Campbell subscribes to the belief that winning is overrated. He related his experience of competing in an important national event:

With a quarter of a mile to go, the leader Jack
Disney burst away from the field, and as I took chase,
the crowd responded to the pursuit. With each
succeeding stroke I inched closer, and even I became
excited as the crowd cheered us on. As we came out of
the last corner, I was at his shoulder, and as we sped
across the finish line, we were as one. But I knew he
had won and I had lost, no matter by how little. As I
stood up out of the skating position, I was exhilarated.
Not at the defeat, certainly, but at the chase, the
competition, the union between winner and loser. I
thought to myself that it doesn't get better than this.
There *is* a dignity in losing. Especially when you have
done your very best. And I had!

Affirmations for Winners

Use these affirmations for creating a TaoSport "winner's attitude," regardless of outcome.

- *"Winning is an attitude."*
- *"I am a winner, regardless of the outcome."*
- *"Winning is a rewarding voyage, not a
  destination."*
- *"The joy of sport is in the fun of execution."*
- *"When I do my best, there's dignity even in
  losing."*
- *"Victory is transitory, while outstanding
  performances are not."*
- *"I focus on the process, and the product takes
  care of itself."*
- *"Act like a winner, and I am a winner."*
- *"I might not control the outcome, but I can
  control my level of play. I play like a winner."*

Visualization: Acting "As If"
You're a Winner

You know what it takes to be a winner. This visualization will help you to act as if you are one, now.

> In your state of relaxation, see yourself
> participating in your sport. How does it feel to
> play like a winner? See the way you walk, the way
> you stand, the confident expression on your face.
> Exhibit excellence in all aspects of your play.
> Focus on the moment-by-moment exhilaration of
> competing. You're happy and fortunate to be able
> to demonstrate such a high level of excellence.
> Know that the ultimate outcome will be
> influenced by such a demonstration. Affirm: "I
> am a winner in every sense of the word."
> Regardless of the outcome, focus on the
> satisfaction of having played so well.

TAOSPORTS FOR BUSINESS AND LIFE

When you focus on the process of execution in business and life, rather than on winning, you bring about desirable outcomes or a personal redefinition of what winning really is. My six-year-old son, Daniel, for example, was at the age where the prospect of winning games was the only reason to play them. Sitting in an adjacent room, I overheard him say to his mother during a card game called Go Fish, "Mom, it's not fair—you always win. I never do." To which she replied in her gentle way, "You're right, Dan. I do, but not because I end up with more cards than you. I always win because I have so much fun playing with this wonderful boy whom I love so much." Stunned by her response, he ceased his complaining and began to laugh much more. Dan became an instant winner.

Four days later I was playing basketball with Dan and became rather frustrated and angered at my inability to sink a shot. He looked me in the face and said, "But, Dad, aren't you enjoying playing with me?" He helped me to put things into perspective, and I made the next four baskets.

Guides for a Winning Attitude

A TaoSport winning attitude, or caring about how you play the game, can carry over into business and life.

A well-known winner is Senator Bill Bradley from New Jersey. While he was at Princeton University, he led his basketball team to high national rankings, exhibiting the qualities of a winner. Following a Rhodes scholarship, he returned to lead his New York Knicks to two professional basketball championships. He applied his winning attitude to politics after his retirement from sports and was elected to the U.S. Senate. Winners like Bill Bradley and other champion athletes have characteristics that you can use as TaoSport guides to "winning" in business and life.

- Whatever you are involved with, be sure to act in such a way that will enable you to feel proud. Ask yourself: "How will I feel about my efforts when this is completed? What will enable me to feel a stronger sense of pride?" The answers to these queries will direct your behavior.

- Feel good about yourself and how you work or act. Respect yourself for caring about how you perform, even if it's not up to your standards.

- Focus your output on bringing out your best, not on what others may be capable of doing. What is the top range of your capabilities in performing this task? Are you giving as much as you possibly can under the circumstances? For example, if you are ill and your performance is off, you are still a winner if you accept the fact that you can't possibly do better.

- Concentrate on ways to improve your performance. Rather than focus upon outcomes, rely on improving as a result of having tried. Ask others to help you to see where you failed and how to correct it.

- Conversations and arguments tend to be about winning. Avoid getting into debates over who's right or who's wrong. Instead, choose to be happy rather than right by not entering the battle. This is the only way to win.

- The next time you are sensing the need to be one up on your competitor, think "one down," and notice how the buildup of tension, anxiety, and pressure gets released. In this state of mind you are more effective and peaceful. It's your conscious choice and, therefore, no victory for your opponent. If you don't compete, he can't win. And you will probably see how to accomplish what you need to because you will be thinking and planning in a more relaxed way.

PSYCHOLOGICAL TACTICS

The yielding can triumph over the inflexible;
The weak can triumph over the strong.
Fish should not be taken from deep waters;
Nor should organizations make obvious their advantages.

TAO TE CHING no 36

The Tao suggests two basic strategies to gain psychological advantage over an opponent and enhance one's position: First, conceal any advantages, so as not to create any resistance or counterforce, and second, yield to overcome those who are inflexible.

The immortal work of Sun-tzu, *The Art of War*, is a classic book about psychological tactics whose primary lesson is that one can achieve triumph through tactical strategy without resorting to conflict. TaoSport strategies work without effort, naturally following the path of least resistance.

One national-class cyclist makes good use of the techniques of Sun-tzu. He always sets up a ride to be, on the surface, nonthreatening. Concealing his advantages relaxes his competitors, placing him in position to act. He then creates the illusion of being vulnerable, presenting a false sense of weakness. He'll say, "I'm tired, I've had no rest," or "I haven't been on the bike in a week," or "My back is sore." This strategy protects him because his competitors expect him to have an "off ride"; if he happens to ride well— then wow! And he always praises others, builds them up, while at the same time minimizing his own strengths. His low profile tends to catch others off-guard. He gives the appearance of being nonconfrontational, then strikes with lightning speed, "dropping" everyone behind in the process.

These tactics can help create an advantage in most athletic events. You can apply the Tao to any sports situation and develop other natural maneuvers to give you a competitive advantage.

TAOSPORT TRAINING FOR ATHLETICS

The Taoist law of polarity will provide you with insight into what's happening throughout a contest. What goes up must come down; getting ahead in a match or game is often followed by losing the lead. An athlete who looks beyond the moment sees polarity or paradox—while staying in the moment—and understands the probable direction of change.

The Law of Polarity

Understanding these paradoxes can help you gain the advantage and enhance your psychological position over an opponent.

- When you let go of the obsessive need to win, you decrease your tension, stress, and anxiety and increase your probability of winning.

- When you want to run faster or be stronger, don't force it—relax instead.

- When you let go of the desire to be a star, you will become one.

- When you want greater results, don't use power plays. Relax, and they will come.

- Insecure athletes and teams promote themselves: They attempt to appear strong, when in reality they're not.

- Trying to quicken your rise to the top sets you back. Evolve slowly as an athlete.

- When you meet with rigidity, become flexible.

- When you want to achieve in sport, you must give—time, effort, and yourself.

- Give the appearance of vulnerability, and you'll be stronger.

- Conceal your advantages to catch others off-guard.

The greatest space has no corners;
The greatest talents are slowly mastered;
The greatest music has the rarest sound;
The Great Image has no form.

TAO TE CHING no. 41

Exercise: Don't Work Harder—Work Smarter

This exercise demonstrates that you can obtain better results when you apply less effort. It's better to be smart and relax.

Get into a position to do pushups on the floor. Try harder by tensing the muscles of your arms, then do two pushups.

Now relax your arms, keeping them firm, and do two more pushups. You should notice a marked difference in the second set, which is easier and more fluid.

Whether you are lifting weights, running hills, or batting a ball, improve your performance by relaxing your muscles. Yield to force, and become less rigid.

The most yielding parts of the world
        Overtake the most rigid parts of the world.
            The insubstantial can penetrate continually.
    Therefore I know that without action there
        is advantage.

TAO TE CHING no. 43

Visualization: Seeking the Paradox

For most of us, the psych-out tactics we've practiced in school and other sports are usually counterproductive. But if you can see and practice the law of polarity, you will improve your performance without the negative effects of most belligerent psych-out techniques.

This visualization will help you become more aware of how you can triumph through the use of the psychological strategy of minimum conflict:

PART 1

See yourself approach your event with a dire
need to perform like a star and a strong drive to
win. How do you feel? Hear others asking you,
"Are you ready?" and your responding by
emoting all the good results you've had in
training and saying that you've never been in
such good shape. You appear to everyone to be
strong and invincible. During the contest, you
get behind. Feel yourself pushing hard to catch
up. You are feeling tense and anxious about
living up to the hype and prior billing as the
likely victor. This pressure is counterproductive.
You are tight, less fluid, and fatigued.

PART 2

Now, stop this scenario. Tell yourself that to gain
the true advantage, you will reverse the above
tendencies, take the polarity position, and
paradoxically create more power. Imagine
"letting go" of the obsessive need to win and
simply focus on playing like a champion.

Conceal any advantages. When asked how you are, hear yourself downplaying your strengths. Hear yourself take the focus away from you and build up the opposition. No one expects anything from you, and you are in position to take others off-guard. You fall behind in the contest. Feel calm, relaxed, yet firm in your attempt to catch up. Remember that "what goes up must come down." Imagine your opponent experiencing a "cold spell" as you surge forward. Feel your strength as a result of your relaxation and your freedom from pressure to live up to the expectations from self and others. Say to yourself, "When I go contrary to normal tendencies, I follow a more natural way and gain the advantage."

TAOSPORTS FOR BUSINESS AND LIFE

A talented author and speaker was scheduled to give a presentation at a conference in Portland, Oregon, but he felt insecure among the many other "big name" presenters. These headliners had biographies that read like a "who's who" in their fields. He was a dynamic speaker with fine credentials, but the program bulletin didn't reflect those assets. He began to feel less than they, and he came to me looking for ways to help him measure up to these stars.

I told him that he had all that he needed now to be terrific. We did a fifteen-minute visualization to help him see that. I asked him to consider his low-key biography as a blessing in disguise, one that would keep the pressure off. By concealing his advantage, others would be delighted when they experienced what he had to offer. I encouraged him to "let go" of the need to be one of the stars and quietly to exert his influence through good work.

As it turned out, the conference evaluations indicated that many of those in attendance had been disappointed in the presentations. His seminar, however, received great reviews. People came to him individually to express their appreciation for his excellent contribution. He's been invited back for next year.

Guides for Psychological Tactics

Gaining the advantage through psychological tactics in sport can work equally well in most of life's contests and competitive circumstances. These TaoSport guides will help you gain the advantage when you need or deserve it.

- If you are in a managerial or supervisory position at work, avoid tendencies to govern egocentrically by demanding to have things your way all the time. Paradoxically, when you manage from a selfless position, you obtain more cooperation, and the group becomes more effective and productive. Being selfless means including others in the decision-making process and the creation of company policy. Give workers a chance to control their destinies on the job. Individualize tasks when possible, tailoring the jobs to each of the worker's strengths.

- When you, as a manager, feel that you must exert power and intercede harshly, the workers may listen to you, but you will ultimately lose their loyalty and cooperation. Rather than use force to get what you want, try telling a person how you feel and ask them to help you solve the problem. For instance: "Sam, I'm confused and upset by your tardiness. There must be some way we could work together to make it easier for you to get here on time." This approach usually works. You may have to be more direct and give him a choice between two options, both of which would accomplish your goal. Either way, the results will be more lasting than the results of, "Sam, you get here by eight or else!" Soft tactics help you acquire the advantage.

- When you are in a discussion with inflexible, opinionated, ignorant people, they will continually try to get the advantage by attempting to make themselves appear better than they are. As a psychological tactic, refuse to take part in the discussion. Yield by smiling and nodding. By being soft, you exhibit strength.

- When you find yourself in an argument where someone is shouting and blaming you for an injustice, try to find a small bit of truth in their accusations and immediately accept responsibility for it. Say, "You know, Fred, you are right about my being late at times. I'm sorry for that." You will notice a significant change in your opponent's attitude as you defuse the feelings and gain control.

- Whenever you are meeting an individual or group for the first time, downplay your background so as not to create high expectations. Let people slowly find out about your wonderful qualities, assets, experiences, and attributes. Self-promotion often cues others that you are insecure.

- Notice that anything good that has come your way in life usually took longer to arrive than you would have liked. When you tried to accelerate the process, you experienced setbacks. Don't try hard to get results. They come in time with good, consistent, patient efforts. Remembering this paradox will give you an advantage.

- When you want someone's attention, try the following strategy. If the person is busy looking around to see who else is at the lunch or party and not paying attention to you, apply the same behavior and outperform him until he realizes that he should be focusing on your conversation. If you are dealing with a loud, angry employee, you might choose to get very quiet and reasonable rather than act angry and match that behavior. Your quiet will probably bring down his anger because he will hear himself overreacting.

Affirmations for Gaining the Advantage

- *"When my advantages are concealed, I have no trouble leading the field."*
- *"I am in position to strike and get what I like."*
- *"When I yield, I triumph."*
- *"Being humble means being exalted."*
- *"Appear weak when I'm strong to get the advantage all along."*

MOTIVATION

The enlighted person knows
the Secret Source and moves
with the Divine Force without delay.

I CHING (Great Appendix)

Athletes often ask, "How can I get motivated?" Neophytes wonder how they can remain on the path of fitness and maintain their new-found enthusiasm for working out. There is no magic involved. To become motivated, you simply need to follow the advice of proverb: Identify all that you love and fill your life with that. Your excitement and enthusiasm will flow uncontrollably. If you love to be fit and strongly value health, find a sport or exercise you love, and the rest will be easy. The rituals of your workout, the small joys of taking each stroke, step, or motion, will become rewarding in themselves, as will the healthy afterglow.

Even if you loathe exercise, you can learn to love it and the benefits it affords. If this love connection never takes place, you will always struggle with exercise as "work." Motivation is a result of love for what you're doing. Without that love, exercise, working out—any participation at all—is difficult.

TAOSPORT TRAINING FOR ATHLETICS

Carol was a high school basketball athlete who never quite lived up to her capabilities. She wasn't nearly as good as most of her other team members, and she didn't have the enthusiasm to do what was required of her to improve. She was actually more suited for sports with less team emphasis, for track or gymnastics. In her senior year, she decided to use her natural speed and joined the cross-country team. She loved her new-found sport and won herself not only a league championship but a four-year track scholarship to a wonderful college. By integrating her values with what she did, she discovered what true motivation was all about.

To find your own motivation and love for athletic activity, follow the advice of TaoSports: *Notice!* Ask yourself, "What do I want, and how do I want it?"

Do you like solitude? Perhaps walking or running would suit you. Do you enjoy speed and quiet? Then cycling would be a good choice. If you enjoy the feel and sound of water, swimming would be a good choice. If you value companionship and working out strategies with others, team sports might excite you. If you love the outdoors and a prescribed course, golf may become your passion.

To facilitate identifying your passion in sport, answer the following questions:

1. What five things do you really value about sport? (Your values might include fitness and health, the challenges, camaraderie, excitement, speed, self-worth, opportunity for inner growth, travel to various competitive sites, and pure fun.) List your values, and see if there is a pattern interwoven throughout them that a particular sport could satisfy. When you narrow the gap between what you value and what you do in sport (and business and life too) you follow the Tao and create the process called "integrative living."

2. What sport would you choose if it were guaranteed that you would be somewhat successful at it? Looking at it this way silences the critical self that influences our choices in life. Your answer indicates a sport that you love. If you're not involved in that sport, why not? Since you love it, chances are you'll do well in it if you try. Perhaps there's a good reason for not doing that particular sport. If so, what other sport offers similar rewards and is in line with your values? There's always

more than one path to a destination. The key is to know where you're going—to that which you love and value—and the path will become obvious.

Guides for Maintaining Motivation

Once you find your passion, keep vigilant to assure that your fires of motivation reignite during the lull times. These strategies will help you maintain your motivation.

- Do not become rigid in your sports schedule. Your motivation has its seasons, and you will experience occasional down time. Take time to "go with the flow of the low" periods of motivation. The Tao teaches that it's natural to lose it and that with patience, it will return.

- Your level of motivation is directly proportional to the pleasure you receive from participation in your sport. Motivation and enthusiasm evaporate rapidly if the sport brings no pleasure. Lack of interest and boredom are the greatest obstacles to consistent training. Too many athletic programs are "work only"—serious, joyless, anhedonic regimens. In his classic book *The Zen of Running*, Fred Rohé captures the essence of this problem:

  > If the dance of the run isn't fun then discover another
  > dance, because without fun the good of the run is undone, and
  > a suffering runner always quits, sooner or later.

  The fun factor can be facilitated by changing your routine, giving yourself certain rewards, and including others in your program.

- Whether you are pumping iron, pounding the roads, doing laps, or hitting the ball, remember that there is a point of diminishing return. Excessive activity or practice is harmful when it causes burnout.
  A forty-year-old man, after only six months of running, took to the roads twice a day to get his mileage up. He did his second workout at night, running on the side of a road in front of the lights of a friend's car, which lit up his way. After a few months of this routine, he suddenly quit and did not run a step for the next eight months. After his long hiatus, he resumed running, but only four times a week. He is

very excited—he was fortunate that he had learned from his radical running behavior, rather than give it up altogether.

Regardless of how much you love a sport, you need a break. Establish moderation in your routine. According to the Tao, less is more. Excess creates turmoil, mentally and physically. Moderation fuels motivation over a long period of time.

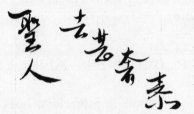

Evolved individuals
Avoid extremes,
Avoid extravagance,
Avoid excess.

TAO TE CHING no 29

- If you invest too much ego in your sport, if you measure your self-worth by the results, your activity can become a dangerous mechanism for ego-deflation. Given a string of defeats, you will begin to avoid such situations, and your motivation will drop drastically. TaoSports, as you recall, teaches that failure and mistakes are lessons. Blend with these natural forces, and understand that excellence is the result of improving upon error. Loss simply tells you how to reach greater heights.

- Repetition with variation helps you maintain pleasure and contributes to your motivation. The Tao teaches *balance* in all things. Variety is the spice of sport. Seek out opportunities to change where and how you train. This will create excitement and rejuvenate your enthusiasm.

- Finally, keep your perspective. If you have a tendency to take yourself too seriously, lighten up. Remember the pleasure of your sport that led you to take it up in the first place. Have fun. It's only a game, and tomorrow's a new day.

Visualization: Motivation

Once you have identified your values and love in your sport, this visualization will help to raise your level of motivation. If you are truly burned out, take a break and do this exercise at a time when you're about ready to get back into it.

> In a quiet place, with your eyes closed, take five
> deep breaths and relax. Focus entirely on the
> aspects of your sport that you love. See yourself
> performing according to those passions. Feel the
> joy, excitement, and fun upon the perfect
> execution of your performance. Affirm: "I feel
> terrific when I participate on this level. I play this
> way each day." Imagine your sport consistently
> being this pleasurable.

TAOSPORTS FOR BUSINESS AND LIFE

Immediately after I received my doctorate in psychology, I did what was expected of me; I landed a position as a psychologist at a mental health center in Denver, Colorado. After three months of dealing with bureaucratic frustration and unprofessional conduct on the part of my peers, I could no longer face going to work. I regretted my professional choice and resigned the position.

Disappointed, angry, and fearful, I took time out to evaluate where to go professionally. I thought I'd have an answer in a month, but I realized that I had serious reservations about my field. I didn't love the work. I flashed on the words of a musician friend of mine who once said, "Imagine getting paid for doing something you'd be doing anyway."

Two years later, and after many hours of thinking, it came to me—I could create a marriage between my avocation and my vocation. I value sports, Eastern philosophies, writing, and speaking. I have aligned these with my Western psychology background and now earn a living helping athletes, corporations, and private individuals create a world where extraordinary performance is possible.

If you wish to be motivated in work or in love but you're not, focus on what you really care about. Lack of motivation for doing something you love may indicate burnout, the result of too much of an activity. Take a break for a week or ten days, or for however long it takes to recharge your enthusiasm.

To help you to focus on what you value, answer these questions.

1. What are your three greatest personal achievements? Notice that your achievements are aligned with certain of your personal values. You achieved because you loved what you were doing. You cared about those activities. To become motivated now, search for work or

activities that are similar to your accomplishments. Try to repeat the activities you cared about so much. Find ways to bring this love back into your life.

2. What three words, qualities, or attributes would you like to have identified with your name? These are probably aligned with your values. What are you doing in your life now to assure yourself of such recognition? This will help you to integrate what you value with what you do. Motivation is the by-product.

Visualization: Choosing Options You Value

This visualization will help you identify what activity you need in your life, what energy you would like to contact or reconnect with.

> Relax and get in touch with the various options available to you in your world. Imagine yourself involved with each one, one at a time. How do you feel as you participate? Which one seems to "fit"? Which seems natural? Which is more fun? Now, contact and ask your adviser, your inner spiritual guide, "What is the best choice for me?" "What direction do I need to take?" The answer should show immediately. If not, thank him and ask him to return later with the answer.

Guides for Creating Motivation

• When you are trying to get motivated to perform in any area, identify what your *motive* is—what your goal is—for doing a certain task or activity in the first place. In this way you will identify the benefits of going ahead. Now think of any obstacles to accomplishing your goal, such as extreme fatigue or personal doubt. Money may be a factor, or your timing may not be right, due to responsibilities at work or at home. Obstacles may delay your goals, but focusing on your motive will help you find ways to get beyond the obstacles.

• Often you may have to motivate yourself to do something that you really don't want to do—unpleasant tasks at work or for the family. First, break the task down into small, manageable segments. When a job seems easier to do, when you believe it's possible, motivation is more available. Next, set up a system of rewards. Give yourself a payoff for achieving each segment. For example, buy something nice, watch a favorite program, or eat a special food, when you complete a segment.

I recently had to take one of my children to the dentist, and I motivated him to go by promising to take him out for breakfast—one of our favorite things to do together. He was excited upon waking up that morning and couldn't wait to get going.

- Affiliation with a group can strengthen your commitment, and love and caring for the group can raise your level of motivation. It's easier to run on a given morning knowing you're committed to the group of runners.

- If you are tired of your daily routine, change it slightly to make a new routine. Change is a great motivator and source of energy. Change the layout of your office; change the time of day and place you run; change the foods you eat for dinner; go out to new places; change your usual approach to solving problems.

- Create a new challenge that is realistic and fun. Enthusiasm is intricately woven into the fabric of challenge. For example, take a class on new management styles, then try to institute them at your office. At home, purchase a piano and take lessons, or take a cooking class and treat your family to something exciting.

- There's nothing like a good vacation, away from mundane realities, to rekindle the love of life, the enthusiasm of the child. A weekend trip to a place near your home can open your mind and clear your head. Try a sports weekend, or a tennis, volleyball, or basketball camp or clinic. Try a yoga or dance class, a drumming group—something to get you out of your set routine, even if the activity seems slightly odd for you.

GOAL SETTING

Within the Self, there is a central force of character
that unifies thoughts and actions. When you are not
in accord with your goals, you may feel indecision,
conflict, or malaise; when you are, a sense of self-
confidence and well-being will surround you.

I CHING no. 45

According to the *I Ching*, we each have a "central force of character" that
can be interpreted as our strong, deep-rooted desires or goals. This central
force "unifies thoughts and actions"—our dreams and visions are unified
with our actions and behavior through the process of setting challenging,
realistic goals. Goals are dreams or mental images toward which you choose
to work.

A man once sought enlightenment from a Taoist master who practiced
pottery making. After the student had been with the master for some time,
he began to feel that he was close to enlightenment. One day, he picked up
one of the master's pots to admire it, then dropped it. He felt a tremendous
sense of loss as the pot shattered. But the master said, "You don't need to be
remorseful. It's still there."

This wise old sage realized that the pot was the goal that enabled him to
experience the wonderful process of making it. It kept him on the track of joy
and fulfillment each and every moment.

Goals are the beacons that keep the TaoAthlete on a successful, excit-ing, and fulfilling journey. You need them as markers or as encouragement toward optimal performance, but you don't become attached to them. Trying to accomplish goals for the sake of achievement alone creates tension and pressure for many athletes. Such an approach separates you from the true meaning of the sport. It makes it impossible for you to become fully im-mersed in the moment. Once you achieve goals you've set for yourself, you then should establish newer, more challenging ones to keep alive in the process and quest for self-understanding.

Dr. Damon Burton, a sports research scientist, has said, "The most successful athletes all have one thing in common. They set specific goals and strive to reach them."

The Big Sur coast of California offers many athletic challenges. One day I contemplated a run to the summit of a multilayered mountain. I was pretty tense and anxious about it. I decided to take it one step at a time by running only to the first level. There I found a field of wildflowers, and I "danced" with a deer that suddenly appeared and led me up the rocky terrain. I was ecstatic, euphoric; the views were breathtaking.

Filled with excitement and endless energy, I continued to chase this beautiful deer until suddenly it disappeared into a grove of trees. At that moment I realized I had reached the pinnacle with little effort and a lot of fun. While my goal had been to get to the top, I had enjoyed the moment-by-moment process much more than my arrival.

Goals, for the TaoAthlete, are part of an internal, spiritual quest—one of fulfillment and excellence in the here and now. The key to goal realization is to choose challenging destinations that will enable you to create joy during the journey.

TAOSPORT TRAINING FOR ATHLETICS

When creating your direction in sport, you need to set both short-term and long-term goals. Short-term goals, if they are realistic and attainable, will build confidence, keep you motivated and enthusiastic, and lessen your fear of the overwhelming long-term goals. On his journey around the world in a wheelchair, world champion Rick Hansen told himself, "Don't look down the road—you might scare yourself. Just wheel one session at a time, three hours or twenty-three miles per session, three sessions per day. Don't think about 24,901 miles—think about twenty-three." To keep yourself going, you have to establish goals-within-goals, carrots dangling out there in front of you to break the ordeal into mental and physical segments, as Hansen did. Hopefully, each segment will provide you with the inner satisfaction and motivation to challenge the next segment.

Among the elite marathoners at the U.S. Olympic Training Center in Colorado, each athlete clearly divides his training program into three distinct segments—stamina, strength, and speed. Stamina can be achieved by running for miles and miles—you might decide to run seventy-five miles per week for six to eight weeks. Strength can be developed by adding hill workouts. Speed can be increased by cutting back on mileage and doing quality track and racing workouts. Each type of training program has a specific purpose; gear your goal for that purpose. Each week of each phase requires setting a short-term goal directed toward your final long-term objective, whatever it may be. Establish your own individual hierarchy of segmented goals that will keep you on track, with pleasure and satisfaction, toward the long-range goal.

Sprint cyclist Connie Paraskevin-Young cross-trains in numerous other activities, including roller-blading, running, and weights. She has participated in two different sports in three different Olympics: speed skating in 1980 and 1984, and cycling in 1988—the sport's first year in the Olympics—when she medaled in bronze. "I'm methodical about conditioning," she has said. "I have to have a game plan. If I work hard and stick to the blueprint, then I will be the best I can be on that particular day."

Visualization: Goals

Think about the goals that you would like to achieve in sport. Choose directions that will enable you to experience your sport as joyful. My own goals for marathoning always assured me that I'd live the three months leading up to the race eating well, and feeling fit, and satisfied with life in general. The marathon was the beacon that kept me on the track of overall wellness.

> In your state of relaxation, articulate an athletic
> goal. Now, imagine the process—what you'll
> have to do to get there. What's involved? Feel the
> joy, the excitement. See the changes your body
> goes through. Feel fit, healthy, and strong. Feel

satisfied with your life as a result of your choice to go this route. See yourself just before the realization of your goal. You are ready to display the results of all your challenging, joyful work. You attain the goal, celebrate, and now it's time to direct yourself once again.

Affirmations for Goal Setting

- *"Goals are nature's gifts that create 'in the moment' joy and satisfaction."*
- *"The arrival is nothing compared with the journey."*
- *"The internal, spiritual quest is the best. Follow the beacon."*
- *"A goal is the toll for creating what I deserve now."*
- *"I set challenging, attainable goals, and focus on the process involved in achieving them."*

TAOSPORTS FOR BUSINESS AND LIFE

Exercise: Setting Goals

For each of the following five categories, write a short paragraph describing your ideal life's goals and your journey toward them. Act "as if" all is possible, and let your imagination run wild. Choose a script that creates passion, love, joy, and excitement on the journey.

1. Work/career/professional:

2. Educational:

3. Financial:

4. Spiritual:

5. Emotional:

Once you have completed the scripts, follow these guidelines to create specific short-term goals.

- List the overall top-ten most important goals from the five scenarios. They could all be from one category, or spread out from different ones.

- From these, make a list of goals to be achieved in five years, such as "owning a home on five acres of land."

- List five or six one-year goals that will put you in position to achieve your five-year plan, such as "purchase an inexpensive starter home this year."

- List your intermediate six-month goals, such as "look for property within six months."

- Record your one-month, one-week, and one-day goals, all in conjunction with the preceding ones. For this month, "contact a realtor" would be one; for this week, "ask various friends for names of agents." Today: "think of friends who could help."

The key to successful goal setting and goal attainment is to be sure that the short-term objectives—day, week, month—provide a strong sense of satisfaction and fulfillment.

Visualization: The Process

Once you have your lists from the "Goal Setting" exercise, you can use this visualization to help you on your journey.

> Starting with your shortest-term goal, imagine the feeling of joy and satisfaction you will receive from the process of working toward it. When you achieve the goal, affirm: "I get what I want with much pleasure." Go to the next level, and feel the exhilaration from the work you're doing. These are the rewards you receive from the goals you have set. Take the entire journey, and experience the fullness of what it has to offer. See yourself arriving at the ultimate goal. Look back over the process, and feel the joy you had and your sadness at its completion. It's like finishing a good book. Feel proud of what you've accomplished. Use this exercise as often as you need to stay motivated and in touch with your real purpose.

SELF-IMPROVEMENT

To know that you do not know is best.
To not know of knowing is a disease.

TAO TE CHING no. 71

No matter how much you know or how good you are, you can always improve. Lao-tzu believed that it is important to strive to become aware of one's own ignorance and shortcomings. The Beginner's Mind can help you become like an empty cup ready to be filled with new things.

In 1977 at a Boston Marathon clinic, a panel of elite, favored runners were having their brains picked by an enthusiastic crowd of participants looking for the secrets of successful marathoning. The inevitable question of diet came up: What do the elite eat? The marathoners' responses would have shocked most nutritional experts in today's athletic world. They were completely at odds even with many commonsensical dietary guidelines. Some runners believed that candy bars and soda were excellent fuel for running, even though they have been proven to cause energy sinks. Others praised beer and coffee as performance enhancers, even though both are diuretics and contribute to dehydration. These elite were presented with healthy alternatives, yet they rejected them. They were not open to change. They felt that as world-class runners, they must be nutritional experts as well. Of course, the audience didn't hesitate to digest these magical potions as if they had found the missing link to successful marathoning.

As an athlete, you are a vortex of potential. If you believe you have all the answers, you impose a false limit on yourself. Self-improvement in any sport may happen in an infinite number of ways—be open to them. See yourself constantly as a beginner, and you'll always be protected against thinking you know it all. Examine the attitudes and behavior that you think are right— you may see that you've been in error. Then look for options that will help you improve.

You develop personal mastery, paradoxically, when you recognize that you have yet to experience the entire, ever-evolving universe of information. Refuse to remain ignorant of the illusion created by triumph. Oliver Wendell Holmes once said, "The greatest thing in this world is not so much where we are, but in what direction we are moving." When you see yourself as empty and ready to receive, you will be able to become full of that which you need for continual mastery and self-improvement as an athlete, as a person.

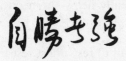 Those who master themselves have strength.

TAO TE CHING no. 33

TAOSPORT TRAINING FOR ATHLETICS

I once had the fortunate experience of talking with an Olympic caliber archer. Trying to understand what attracted her to her unusual sport, I asked if she could elaborate on her passion. She explained that "hitting the mark" was an ecstatic, euphoric process, one that required an ongoing, continuous willingness to being open to change. "I'm always searching for ways to subtly improve the physical, mental, nutritional, emotional, and environmental aspect of my sport. To evaluate and consider each variable and then hit the bull's-eye is an unbelievable feeling of mastery—mastery over all the variables at the same time. To do this, without any mistakes or miscalculation, reveals a high degree of excellence and beauty in sport. I feel I'll always be able to improve, and that's why I do it."

Her last comment is crucial. Because she believes she'll always be able to improve, she will search for the ways, and naturally, she will find them. We use only a small percentage of our physical and mental potential; improvement is always possible.

Guides for Continual Self-Improvement

The recipe for self-improvement contains many important ingredients. These ten crucial, essential principles should not be overlooked, particularly when you seek improvement in your forties and fifties and beyond.

- *Coaching.* Align yourself with someone who understands the direction you wish to go and can help you to get there. Coaches are usually willing to work with anyone who wants to improve.

- *Hydration.* Most athletes fail to drink a sufficient amount of water throughout the day. If you wait until you're thirsty, you're not drinking enough. "Drink fluid to keep fluid" is an affirmation I say to keep me going every day, in every way. Water will help you to stay fresh, limber, and less sore and fatigued. A minimum of two quarts per day is advised.

- *Stress.* To experience breakthroughs, you need to extend a bit beyond your normal comfort zones. But you don't want to stress your body or push it too hard. This is where coaching really helps—someone to evaluate how far you should go.

- *Rest.* Many athletes are quick to stress but fail to rest. Most research from reputable sports physiologists indicates that sufficient rest after stressful workouts facilitates improvement. Without rest, you risk severe burnout, injury, or illness.

- *Stretch.* When you stretch, you enable your muscles to reach their full range of motion. Failure to stretch creates stiffness, soreness, and tightness, and leads to injury. This becomes even more crucial as we age.

- *Fuel.* Too many of us see food in terms of weight gain. If you want to improve as an athlete, see food as the fuel your body requires to sustain energy. Complex carbohydrates (vegetables, grains, fruits, pasta) store themselves as glycogen in your muscles, ready to be used at a moment's notice.

- *Equipment.* Improvement will come much faster and more easily if you purchase decent equipment. You do not need to be fashionable and buy hundred-dollar running shoes, but you should avoid the ten-dollar clunkers. Be sure that whatever you buy is comfortable.

- *Consistency.* Improvement in anything is a direct result of how consistently you engage in the activity. It's better to work out for thirty minutes four times a week than to spend two hours each Saturday to cram it all in.

- *Gradualness.* The journey to continual self-improvement is a slow one. Significant gain takes time. Be patient and persistent, and celebrate small strides.

- *Emptiness.* Establish an attitude of openness to new and better ways. When you think you have all the answers, you won't see other ways. See yourself as an empty vase, ready and willing to take in all that may help you to improve.

Affirmations for Self-Improvement

- *"I am never too complete to continue to improve."*
- *"I am only as strong as my weakest link. Strengthen it, and I will improve."*
- *"When I see myself as a beginner, I'm more likely to become a winner."*
- *"When I'm open to improve, I keep on the move."*
- *"Every day is a new opportunity to improve in another way."*
- *"I'm never too old to discover the gold."*

TAOSPORTS FOR BUSINESS AND LIFE

A project manager for a small California-based computer software firm was approached by a team member who questioned certain company policies and sought to improve them. When he asked why things were the way they were, the manager replied, "We've always done it that way. That's the way it is. Why fool with success?"

About two weeks later at a project staff meeting, this same manager innocently asked why nothing had been placed in the suggestion box for work improvement. "It's so empty because you're so full," responded a coworker. Everyone felt that the manager was closed to new ideas for improvement and change.

Guides for Self-Improvement

If you consider, in the grand scheme of things, that you are truly a beginner, you will be in position to see numerous options and directions in all your endeavors. You may find this difficult to do all the time, to be sure. You can easily fall into the trap of defending what you know as if it were the only truth. Such rigidity becomes an obstacle for self-improvement. Keep your TaoSport Beginner's Mind open to improvement by putting any of these guides into practice.

- At work, create a suggestion box and encourage ideas for improvement. You need to read and discuss the suggestions with everyone involved. It's not necessary to adopt everything suggested. The key to keep the ideas flowing is an attitude of openness to change.

- For your own self-improvement, read a book on a topic that is completely foreign to your general scope of knowledge yet in an area of personal interest. Consider taking a class to learn a new skill or improve upon one you already have. Learn a martial art, or how to dance, cook, or paint. Yoga and drumming are interesting alternatives for self-improvement.

- Notice those aspects of your life at work or at home where weak points exist. Make a list, and prioritize them according to how much you feel they are holding you back. Then take steps to strengthen those weaknesses. For example, communication skills can be learned from a class or a good book. Perhaps you wish to improve your skills negotiating or writing. Maybe you'd enjoy fixing your own car. Whatever your area of concern, there are avenues to help you on your journey.

- When you argue the loudest, it's probably because you are wrong, unsure of what you're saying, afraid to hear the truth, or all of the above. By so doing, you prevent positive growth and change in yourself from occurring. Stop, and open up to what people are saying to you. You may improve things in your life by listening.

- Self-improvement is most rapid if you consciously seek out constructive feedback from your peers and friends with regard to your professional, personal, and physical lives. You'll receive much respect, for example, if you say, "I'm struggling with ———— in my job/life. Can you give me some suggestions to help?" Or, "How would you handle ————?" Listen closely as they offer you worthwhile and creative options to help you with your concerns.

Visualization: Self-Improvement

Mentally explore fantasies and dreams about a new career, lifestyle, or improved ways to be in your world. This visualization will help you to see possibilities for improvement:

> Think of one way that you could improve yourself
> in your athletic, professional, social, nutritional,
> spiritual, or family life. Imagine the changes
> taking place one by one. Feel the joy and
> satisfaction that accompanies each improvement.
> See yourself in this totally new way. Affirm: "Every
> day in every way, I get better and better."

Exercise: Leadership Self-Improvement

This exercise is for anyone in a leadership position—manager, supervisor, teacher, parent, officer—who would like to know how to improve their performance.

Ask the following two questions of all those who are under your guidance, whether at work, in the classroom, or at home. Their names should be withheld to protect their anonymity. It is crucial for the responses to be specific, concrete, and detailed.

1. If a good friend of yours were to take this class (or take this job, or come to live in this house), what important things would you tell him about your teacher (or manager, or parents)?

2. If you were to take this class (or this job, or this home environment) again, what things would you change? Why? What would you keep? Why?

The answers to both questions will reflect both the good and the bad characteristics. Keep the good aspects, and find ways to change the bad, if they are valid. Pay close attention to comments that are mentioned frequently and consistently.

Exercise: Daily Self-Improvement

Fill in the blanks, affirm, and act for daily improvement.

> Today, I improve my home environment by————.
> Today, I improve my work environment by————.

SYNERGY

It is of great importance that the need for
creating unity is recognized. The human spirit
is nourished by a sense of connectedness.

I CHING no. 8

In sport, too, the human spirit is empowered through the efforts of working together. Synergy or cooperative action is an essential ingredient for team success in athletics. The impact of unity and teamwork is best portrayed by Alan Morehead as he describes the synergistic experience on the Burke-Wills expedition across South America: "They were now committed together. . . . Any weakness in one man weakened them all and each little triumph was a shared accomplishment. One was best with a rifle, another at cooking, a third with his physical strength. Everything depended upon their liking and respecting one another."

How could they not succeed with such synergistic power? They worked together so that the whole team was able to accomplish much more than the sum of the members' collected talents. Synergy is the key to team success in all sports. Olympic volleyball player Lori Endicott has said, "There are six people on the volleyball court. We all have different strengths, weaknesses, personalities. It creates a dynamic that's more exhilarating than an individual sport." The slightest hint of dissension or disharmony can lead to chaos, loss of enthusiasm, focus, and commitment in any team. According to the *I Ching*:

Cultures strive for spiritual togetherness in order to break up
dissension and reunite the hearts and minds of the people.

I CHING no 59

A powerful synergistic experience occurred in 1989 at the University of
California in Santa Cruz. Coach Bob Hansen's varsity tennis team was
ranked number two nationally and had all it would take to become NCAA
champions—except harmony. There were a number of personality clashes
between key players, and the dissension could potentially fracture the focus,
enthusiasm, and mental energy of the entire team. Just prior to their
departure to Michigan, the coach called a team meeting where, for two
hours, the athletes engaged in a powerful team-building "Circle of Recognition" exercise (see page 239). All residual conflicts were resolved by getting
feelings of misunderstanding out into the open. Afterward, the interper-
sonal love emanating from that group had each player walking on air. From
the moment of their arrival in Michigan, their sense of synergy and togetherness was felt by the opposition. The team affirmation, "Straight line in '89,"
became a reality as they won the NCAA Division III Tennis Championship.
All strongly agreed that the crucial ingredient had been their unifying efforts
prior to departure.

The ancient Taoist and war strategist Sun-tzu believed that the key to
triumph in battle is unity of purpose and mind. If team spirit and cohesiveness are lost, the team ultimately fails.

TAOSPORT TRAINING FOR ATHLETICS

In Lake Placid during the 1980 Winter Olympics, a scrappy but unified
bunch of underdogs known as Team U.S.A. took on the powerful Soviet
hockey team in the preliminary round. With a 4-to-3 lead, the U.S. goalie,
Jim Craig, held the opposition scoreless for the final ten minutes of play. The
team synergy was electrifying, the crowd went berserk, and the players rolled
around on the ice in a big pile of hugging humans. They went on to beat
Finland for the gold. No team could have beaten that group of pumped-up,
synergized athletes after their Soviet triumph.

Sports history is filled with similarly dramatic examples of the power of
cohesiveness in team athletics. Clearly, it is a phenomenal advantage capa-

ble of helping its beneficiaries overcome many natural obstacles on the path of victory.

Exercise: Circle of Recognition

This very powerful exercise gives each team member the opportunity to exhibit caring, compassion, love, and recognition to the other athletes on the team. Team synergy, unity, spirit, and confidence are greatly enhanced as well.

> Prior to an important event, the team sits in a circle and gives positive recognition and appreciation to each other. It is important that all comments be specific and pertinent. Avoid statements like, "I think you're great"; better to say, "It's great the way you give your time to the new players," or "I love your sense of humor—it really relaxes me." Be sure to look directly at the person that you are addressing so that they feel the power of your statement. Each athlete turns to the person on his left and expresses what he feels are wonderful contributions, qualities, skills, and attributes of that person. Continue around the circle, with each member getting a turn, then reverse the direction. When this is completed have each member take a turn expressing to the coach appreciation and recognition about his work and contributions. To conclude the exercise, the athletes hold hands while in the circle, and with their eyes closed, they visualize having unity, confidence, and team spirit.

Guides for Fueling the Fires of Spirit

Synergy or team spirit is the responsibility of the coach as well as the individual team members. These guides will help you to contribute to your team's synergy as one of its players:

- *Spirit slogans.* Positive affirmationlike statements will help team members to focus on goals, directives, what the team represents to each other, or any other intimate concept that serves to bring all together for a common cause. For example: "We're number one because we have fun," "Straight line in '89," "We are Penn State," "Lion proud," and "Inseparable, we're unbeatable" are expressions that bring athletes together, working as a unit, as one.

- *Social unity.* The team that plays together, stays together—the key is the word *together*. Whenever you unify your efforts, your bond becomes stronger. Team parties, picnics, and outings during an off-season are excellent ways to encourage togetherness. Social gatherings create opportunities to get to understand and accept the different personalities, essential to team synergy. Consider using positive nicknames to spur on spirit. These lighthearted, affectionate titles give each member a specialness and sense of belonging. Make sure everyone is comfortable with his or her nickname.

- *Positive encouragement.* Each team member eventually experiences discouragement and disappointment from poor performance. To keep team spirit alive, give the dejected athlete sincere words of praise and encouragement. Let him know his part of the machine, and do all you can to help him through this tough time. Be sure to check up on his progress daily.

Visualization: Synergy

This visualization exercise is to be done by the entire team simultaneously. It will help to strengthen the bonds that already exist among its members.

> Mentally scan the room looking at your
> teammates dressed in uniform. Imagine them
> milling around, stopping to talk to each other.
> They are shaking hands, smiling, and hugging
> each other. Go over to each member and express
> your appreciation for his contribution to the
> team and how fortunate you feel being a part of
> this group. When everyone has done this, you
> are now ready, as a team, to go about your

performance. See yourself and the team playing
against the opponent. Notice how "together" you
are, how each is contributing to the other's great
performance. The team is unstoppable and as
fluid as a well-oiled machine. See the
performance being the model of team harmony
and execution. Feel the exhilaration as you all
play together to secure victory.

TAOSPORTS FOR BUSINESS AND LIFE

Visualization: Synergy

Unite with each aspect of yourself. Through self-knowledge and "inner
exploration," begin to create a "total you" that bonds synergistically as you
cooperate, accept, and love all aspects of who you are. Use this visualization
to accomplish this.

Be open to seeing your entire self. See your good
points as well as your shortcomings. Be honest
with the picture you create, and accept it as the
real you. When you are "dialed into" this total
picture, you function at a higher level, free of
pretense, without the need to cover up. This
releases an enormous amount of energy for you
to put into everything else in your life. You are
imperfect, make errors and mistakes, and
occasionally "blow it." But you are human and
unique. Feel the unity of body, mind, and spirit.
When all aspects of yourself work together, you
become so much more than any one part. See
and feel the warm smile of self-acceptance.

Guides for Synergy

When we fight each other, the alienation we create obstructs the flow of life.
So much more is possible, both individually and as a group, when we work
together. Here are some ways to realize synergy in your life.

- Create a spiritual renewal with your family or group at work. Take time out to notice why you are together and what makes you feel good about each other. Vacations, outings, and picnics enable the group members to see each other apart from daily mundane realities. It gives everyone a chance to laugh, play, sing, and dance together. Work together within the group or family to build cooperation and teamwork for getting the chores or work projects done with fun.

- Join a cooperative group with homogeneous goals: a local food co-op, perhaps, or a preschool co-op, a Greenpeace group, or a neighborhood environmental group. Create local unity by having block parties and neighborhood watches against crime. Get personally aligned with your environment by learning about the plants and wildlife indigenous to your geographical area.

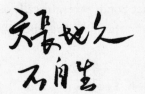

Heaven is eternal, the Earth everlasting.
They can be eternal and everlasting
Because they do not exist for themselves.
For that reason they can exist eternally.

TAO TE CHING no. 7

Affirmations for Synergy

If these affirmations are placed on cards and posted throughout the work environment, they will help all members to focus on team unity.

- *"I am a team player contributing to the mission of my group."*
- *"With our hearts and minds together, our work is as light as a feather."*
- *"When we work together, we achieve so much more."*
- *"The team is the dream. Keep it alive!"*
- *"The whole is greater than the sum of its parts. Unite!"*
- *"The greatest rewards come from unity of purpose."*
- *"Act like a team, think like a team, be a team!"*

LEADERSHIP

Superior leaders are those whose existence
is merely known;
The next best are loved and honored;
The next are respected; and the next
are ridiculed.

TAO TE CHING no. 17

Leadership is the art of leading softly, from afar, while extending trust and respect to those who would be led. Firmness, through gently worded directives and commands, gives people a sense of self-worth and results in greater quantity and quality of output.

In sport, team members are more productive and play more optimally when their coaches and team captains guide them rather than rule them. Leaders need to set the example by treating others as they themselves would like to be treated. The question a leader should ask is, "How can I best help you to perform in this sport?" When the players experience a sense of self-government, the leaders become more powerful. According to the Tao, all leaders must notice how their restrictions and interferences divide the group. Force creates counterforce according to the Tao; too many controls and prohibitions and harsh interventions lead to aggressive counterforces that defeat the purpose.

Western coaches tend to use force on athletes routinely. In such circumstances, athletes revolt against their coaches, and ultimately, force alienates the team. John Heider notes in *The Tao of Leadership* that "even if they succeed brilliantly, there is no cause for celebration. There has been injury. . . . Later on, the person who has been violated may well become less open. . . . There will be resistance and possibly resentment. . . . They may do what you [the coach] tell them to do but will cringe inwardly . . . plotting revenge." Notice in your own life that the more others disrespect, control, or manipulate you, the more you reject them.

> Do not disrespect their position;
> Do not reject their lives.
> Since, indeed, they are not rejected,
> They do not reject.

TAO TE CHING no. 72

The Associated Press recently disclosed that two major university athletic programs had replaced their head basketball coaches after players boycotted practice, complaining that the coaches were too harsh. Another coach resigned because the athletes accused him of verbal abuse. Unfortunately, such incidents are probably common, although they go unreported. I will always remember the following story:

I had been working with a number of athletes from different sports at a major university. One athlete in particular was a world-class distance runner whose stellar performance at a major track meet qualified him for the NCAA championships in the 10,000-meter run. This was quite an achievement, the pinnacle of excellence for this sport. His diligent physical and mental efforts were rewarded with great success.

He ran one more race prior to the nationals and, with no incentive to run well, used it simply as a good workout, leading up to the "big one." His time was below his best, and his coach was furious. Rather than trying to understand that the athlete had just wanted a workout, the coach jumped all over him and prohibited his star from going to the championships lest he embarrass the program. The young man admitted to me that he was devastated by this severe emotional abuse. He never got the chance to go to the nationals, and to this day he must feel the terrible loss caused by the insensitive, self-indulgent, ego-filled coach.

But a revolution seems to be brewing in athletics throughout the country, precipitated by a demand for humanistic treatment. Athletes are revolting against exploitation and standing up for their rights. They are raising the consciousness of their leaders by claiming they have a mutual need to understand and respect one another. After all, athletes need coaches for guidance, and coaches need athletes to serve or they'd have no job. Now, instead of winning being the most important thing, enlightened coaches believe that if you treat athletes humanely, with respect and compassion, you enhance their chances of winning.

> Friendliness, kindness toward others will create
> a spirit unparalleled in loyalty. Followers will take
> upon themselves . . . hardship and sacrifice
> toward the attainment of goals. . . . It is necessary
> that the leader have firmness and correctness
> within, and an encouraging attitude toward others.
>
> *I CHING* no 58

Perhaps one of the most important components of championship team play is the designation of a leader, a team captain, who can create a powerful, positive influence among the other team members. This leader may or may not be the most talented athlete; but the chosen leader must have the respect and trust of others and be able to create the team unity and cohesiveness essential to winning efforts.

Major collegiate athletic programs are always searching for strong leaders to provide stability for talented teams. Such a player can get the team through challenging situations. In December 1965, at Madison Square Garden in New York City, the Holiday Festival Basketball Tournament was in high gear. The final four teams were playing to decide which would go on to the championship game. The first matchup, which proved to be one of the most exciting games in the history of the Garden, was between Princeton University and the University of Michigan, the latter led by all-American Cazzie Russell. The Tigers of Princeton had an all-American leader of their own, Bill Bradley, whose presence on the court kept the underdog Ivy Leaguers in the thick of things against the powerful Wolverines. The Tigers relied on Diamond Bill's leadership to set plays, score points, block shots, and help his peers play their individual bests.

With two minutes to go, Princeton led by a comfortable margin of twelve points, and a trip to the finals was a virtual certainty. People flooded out of the Garden with the game "iced"; I was one of them. While I was reading the paper the next morning, my eye caught the headline, WOLVERINES

SHOCK TIGERS. After scoring forty-one points, Bill Bradley fouled out, and Michigan took advantage of a "leaderless" team.

Players in sports like football, soccer, volleyball, baseball, and rugby also rally around their "court stabilizer" for strength, confidence, and inspiration. The leader, in every case, is the hub of the wheel around which all things revolve.

What are the most noteworthy characteristics of a team captain? Traditional team leaders are outgoing, forceful, and center stage—in the spotlight, or in a word, in control. Yet to control is to force, and according to the *Tao Te Ching*, force creates a counterforce—followers rebel against force. In sport, this means team dissension.

TaoSport team leaders refrain from forceful control and run the show without necessarily having to get their way. Team members will not tolerate egocentric athletes, preferring instead leaders who direct from the heart. A team leader needs to give unselfish support and respect to peers, listen when they have something to say, and know when to direct and when to withdraw.

TaoSport team leaders realize that their power continues to grow and flow only when it is passed to others—team members need to feel this power. Basically, leaders who follow the Tao will influence others by example. They will place the well-being of their athletes above the well-being of themselves.

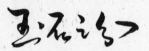

Attain honor without being honored.
Do not desire to shine like jade.

TAO TE CHING no. 39

Too many leaders forget this precept and get lost in their own self-importance. Such selfishness creates animosity and an imbalance among co-athletes. The less credit you take as a team captain, the more you will get.

Your leadership abilities start within. You must be centered and have your life in order before you can affect others. Your influence begins inside and ripples outward.

With an attitude of unassuring modesty you pose no
threat to those around you and they, therefore, loyally align
themselves to your authority. . . . With gentleness and
goodness you will win their hearts. . . . Through compassion
—you move them to loyalty and gain their obedience.

I CHING no. 14

治古國若亨小鮮

TAOSPORT TRAINING FOR ATHLETICS

The quintessential model of a powerful team leader is none other than the former Los Angeles Laker, Magic Johnson. Sports aficionados agree that his greatest contribution as a player was his team leadership on and off the court. Because of his ability to bring a group of individual stars together as a harmonious unit, the Lakers were the most consistent winners for a decade. When Magic spoke, everyone listened. He was the favorite interviewee of reporters, handling that task with great aplomb. From the opening tap of the game, all eyes were on Magic, the originator of the famous "showtime"; because of his leadership, the Lakers always put on a good show before the stage-conscious L.A. crowd. He led not only his team but the fans as well. Magic Johnson was admired, looked up to, and respected by each team player. When he retired, it became clear that people who knew him throughout the world shared similar feelings about this true TaoSport leader.

A highly evolved coach representing the professional basketball sector is Phil Jackson of the Chicago Bulls. Egalitarian by nature, Jackson exhibits a tender touch with his players, insisting upon treating them as people in a partnership for excellence. The players have enormous respect for their teacher and coach, who has been known to give them books to read on road trips, often opting for a bus rather than a plane so they can relax and enjoy the beautiful landscapes. In an industry that still believes that "winning is the only thing," Jackson has been able to keep his humanitarian, TaoSport approach on the road to the Bulls' NBA championship in 1991, their first in the history of the franchise.

Guides for Conscious Leadership

The wise coach creates an environment that is trusting, open, and harmonious. If you respect, understand, and listen to your athletes, you won't lose power or control—you'll gain it. They will mirror your behavior.

An attitude of servitude demonstrated by the leader
toward the people encourages them to approach him for
advice and guidance. In this way the leader can
direct others into areas of greater development and order.

I CHING no. 31

These guides will help you to be a conscious TaoSport leader and direct athletes into places of improved development and performance.

- As a coach or team leader, you need to understand that your position is only as strong and secure as you make your athletes feel. The players can make you or break you. The key is to treat everyone exactly the way you'd like to be treated in every circumstance.

- Make a sincere effort to know each member of the team personally. This can best be done away from the playing field. It is important for you to communicate to them their individual importance to the overall team effort. Specifically define their function on the squad and what you expect them to contribute. An athlete needs to know, "I count—I make a difference."

- Create an open, positive environment where all feel accepted and respected and able to grow as individuals. Be fair, and show no favoritism to the "stars." For example, all athletes on the team should work equally hard. With regard to the guidelines for team conduct, be firm and consistent. Team members appreciate behavior boundaries. They foster a sense of security. But within that structure, be sure to give them the freedom to develop and be themselves.

- Before you criticize athletes, look for ways to give them credit. Be sure to provide concrete, specific data for your critique. Avoid gross generalizations such as "you always" or "you never." Search for ways that you, together with the athlete, can address the problem. Suggestions coming from the athlete will hold more weight, and compliance will come more easily. When feasible, don't criticize during a performance. Your comments will be more effective if you wait and introduce them before the next practice session.

- Be open to listening to criticism from the athletes, particularly if it comes from a majority of the team. Show them your openness to feedback by asking them periodically (especially during times of tension and disharmony) to respond in writing to the question: "If you were the coach or captain and had complete freedom to handle things your way, what would you do and how would you do it?" They should do this anonymously. They will respect and admire you for this, especially if you initiate positive change based on their suggestions and criticisms.

- Formulate team goals and directions during a preseason team meeting by encouraging and accepting input from all members in a mutually respectful way. When athletes have input on these matters, their motivation to carry them out will be extremely high. Once goals have been defined, create team affirmations to make these directions firm. For example, a goal of winning the championship can be written as: "We're number one," or, "We are the 1992 Surf City Champs."

TAOSPORTS FOR BUSINESS AND LIFE

A division manager from one of the most innovative personal computer manufacturers in Silicon Valley was struggling with his job requirements. He had trouble giving and taking directions. He told me that growing up in the era of Vietnam and Watergate had jaded his respect for people in positions of authority. He wasn't comfortable as an authority figure, either, telling people what to do or how to do it. Still, he wasn't ready to walk away from a well-paying position with terrific benefits. He was very open to new creative options for effective management and expressed interest in the TaoSport approach for corporate clients.

Excited about the possibilities, I encouraged him to make a personal study of his effectiveness through daily physical exercise and meditation-visualization. Both these techniques enabled him to be more relaxed, focused, and alert while he was on the job. Feeling physically and mentally strong enabled him to meet the daily challenges and stresses of the job with greater ease.

Next, I tailored the Guides for Conscious Leadership (see page 249) to his needs for conscious management. He immediately put these guides to use by seeing his workers as players in the game of business. This approach enabled him to see his position of authority as an opportunity to create work environments that make sense, based on social consciousness, peace, non-violence, and awareness of human rights and strong ethical values.

Within six months, he had gained a reputation as *the* boss to work with. Many employees were trying to get transferred to his division. His manager asked him to teach his methods to others in the corporation. For me, it was a joy to see others gravitate toward these positive changes.

Guides for Management

- In line with the Tao, managers should manage exactly as they would fry a delicate fish—lightly. Restrictions, rules, and regulations should be used sparingly. Too many controls are not only difficult to enforce, they create counterreactions from those being controlled. As a manager you, paradoxically, lose control.

- Remember the Golden Rule: "Treat others as you would like to be treated." If you follow this rule, your problems at work or at home will be minimized. Harshness gets you nowhere—why use it? When you are kind to others, you win their hearts and cooperation, which is what you really want and deserve. Remind yourself that we are all more similar than we are different.

- If you act as if you are willing to help and serve others, they will approach you for advice and guidance. If you are willing to be influenced by others, they will be attracted to you and partake in a wonderful exchange of ideas.

- Create environments where setbacks, mistakes, errors, and failures are permissible. In this way people will take risks to explore their unlimited potential, without fear of judgment or criticism from you, their manager or parent, if they fail.

- Avoid manipulation at all costs. As a managerial style, it creates anger, resentment, and loss of respect on the part of those it's used against. Power plays are a form of manipulation that creates an environment of distrust and suspicion. Motivation and team spirit diminish with the use of such tactics.

- With children, watch their reactions when they are given choices and options for carrying out tasks. Their sense of self-worth ("I count"), as well as their loyalty and commitment to completing the task, are noticeably strengthened. Say, for example, "Danny, you have a choice. Do your homework now and watch the game when you are finished, or play now and do your homework later, but not watch the game." The child feels empowered, with a sense of control over his life. For the parents, the goal of getting the child to do the homework is achieved. Here's another example: "Mary, you can eat your dinner first and have a snack later, or eat nothing now and have your dinner for snack time." The parents get their wish, and the child learns to make decisions and feels involved and important.

- In disciplining your children, remember that if you use physical force, they will leave you emotionally forever. You may win the battle, but you will lose the war. Talk to them firmly about acceptable boundaries. If they continue to disregard your policies, a short time-out may be appropriate to get them to listen.

- Encourage others to discover their own greatness. Give them opportunities to see how much they count, how important they are. When leading a group or talking at a convention, remind yourself that you need those people as much as they need you. This will keep you humble, thankful, and in touch with their needs.

Affirmations for Effective Management

Use these affirmations as touchstones to help you focus on remaining effective, as a manager at work or as a parent at home. Write them on three-by-five-inch index cards, and post them in highly visible places to be read at a glance.

- *"Followers follow when I don't force them to swallow."*
- *"Productivity is a function of people who understand and respect each other."*
- *"Build and nurture partnerships for productivity."*

With good leaders
when their work is done
their task fulfilled
the people will all say:
"We have done it ourselves."

TAO TE CHING no. 60

VI

THE
FINISHING TOUCHES

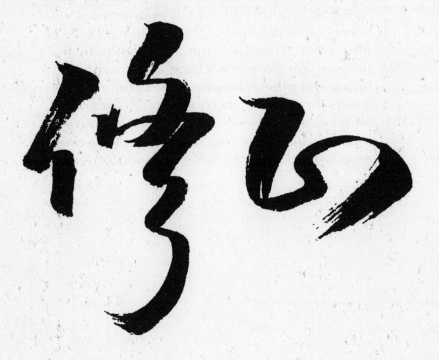

ADVANCED TAOSPORT VIRTUES

The finishing touches on a TaoAthlete are the attainment and practice of five advanced virtues—integrity, adaptation, persistence, balance, and simplicity. These principles will serve you as anchors of stability in the cycle of life's tides. They are sources of strength that protect you from the chaos and fluctuations that could otherwise affect your performance. As in other parts of this book, basic Tao guides, techniques, and tools are provided to help you practice and maintain these virtues for a more empowered sense of self, the TaoSport self.

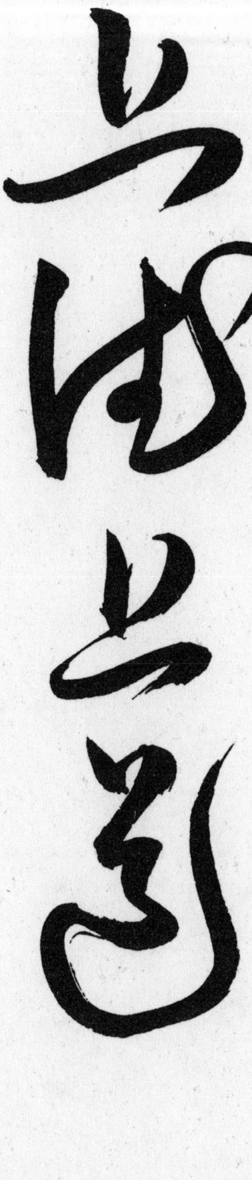

INTEGRITY

Hold to your ethics and principles and do not for
a moment consider compromising what you believe
to be right. Acting with integrity is the key.

I CHING no. 29

The heights you achieve in sport are strongly influenced by the depth of your
integrity. Integrity is the refusal to compromise your talents, your inner sense
of self, and your undergirding values and attributes regardless of the score,
the outcome, or different levels of ability between you and your opponent.

If your sense of self is one of mental toughness, resilience, consistency,
strength, health, courage, confidence, reliability, enthusiasm, commitment,
talent, and wholeness, you play with integrity. When you do perform in this
way, your opponent and the event are irrelevant; you show up and hold on to
this powerful self, and extraordinary performance follows.

An NCAA all-American athlete came to me complaining that he always
"backs off" his game against an inferior opponent, particularly if he is totally
in command. "Jerry, I just seem to 'open the door' for the other player to
walk in," he said. "I lose interest. My intensity deserts me. I see no purpose
to playing the match."

I suggested that he identify a new purpose, one that creates meaning and
motivation to continue playing well. I asked that he see himself as a teacher,

a model, who demonstrates how to play "clinic" tennis. In so doing, he would maintain his integrity while helping to teach his opponent a lesson in how to "close out" a set. I said that to play otherwise would be dishonest and unsportsmanlike.

Acting "as if" he were the perfect model of championship play, this athlete was able to maintain control and demonstrate high levels of athletic integrity.

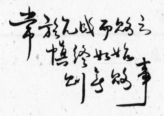

People often spoil their work at the point
of its completion.
With care at the end as well as the beginning,
No work will be spoiled.

TAO TE CHING no. 64

By contrast, an NCAA champion expressed difficulty staying with a set once he got down 5–love. His attitude was, "I can't win this one, so why put any energy into it? Let's go on to the next set." This, too, is a blatant misrepresentation of the spirit of sport. To give up your effort to play well detracts from your integrity as an athlete and diminishes your opponent's triumph. When you "roll over and die," the winner loses the satisfaction of having a victory over someone who gave his best. More important, however, you lose the opportunity to teach your opponent how champions play after they fall behind. To stay on top of a losing situation, force your opponent constantly to prove that he deserves to be as good as the score indicates by not letting up.

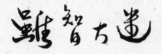

Therefore a good person is the teacher of
an inferior person;
And an inferior person is the resource of
a good person.
One who does not treasure a teacher, or
does not cherish a resource,
Although intelligent, is greatly deluded.

TAO TE CHING no 27

TAOSPORT TRAINING FOR ATHLETICS

So many talented athletes compromise their integrity by turning away from their true self and selling out because of intimidation and fear. They give other people permission to make themselves feel inferior, undeserving, or less than they are. Others resist this, as happened at a national championship cross-country race in Houston. A very talented but relatively unknown runner was in command, leading a pack of athletes whom he had not been expected to beat. Running the race of his life, thoughts of doom entered his mind. "Maybe they know something that I don't," he thought. "Am I crazy out here alone? Why don't they lead? They're better runners." Immediately, he caught his negativity and told himself, "I'm great too. That's why I was invited to run. I deserve to win." He held on to his integrity and outkicked all but one, for a stellar second-place finish in this event.

Follow his example, and feel powerful as an athlete. Know that you are a winner when you exhibit your integrity as a TaoAthlete, even if it doesn't show up in the score.

Visualization: Maintaining Integrity on the Road

The "home court advantage" in sport may very well be a myth. Believing in it may cause athletes on the road to accept an underdog status too readily by giving the crowd permission to make them feel unwanted and, therefore, less capable than they are. But many teams refuse to be intimidated by this psychological edge. You can silence hostile fans by playing with your utmost integrity.

The crowd was strongly rooting for Memphis State to upset the highly favored UCLA Bruins in the 1973 NCAA basketball championship game. The noise level in the arena favored Memphis State, but this didn't rattle all-American Bill Walton of the Bruins, who finished the game with forty-four points, a standing ovation from the antagonistic crowd, and a UCLA victory.

This visualization will help you reinforce your integrity as a TaoSport athlete on a daily basis.

> In your state of relaxation, affirm: "I am a terrific
> athlete. I refuse to give anyone permission to

strip me of my integrity." See yourself in a
competitive situation where you begin to
question your validity as an athlete. Catch
yourself, and switch your attitude from self-doubt
to self-confidence. See yourself beginning to play
exceptionally well as you exhibit your
integrity—those characteristics that make you
the athlete you are. Feel the joy of being in
control of your level of play.

The message of the *Tao Te Ching* is clear: Trust in the power within, and use it. Lao-tzu believed that when people (athletes) do not feel this power (integrity), they feel fear. Fear creates tension, anxiety, and stress, which limit performance. The Tao teaches you to become aware of your inner power and integrity. Staying in touch with it will provide you with consistent excellent performance.

Exercise: Contacting Your Integrity in the Heat of Competition

During an event in which it is difficult for you to maintain your integrity on the spot, you can recall your power by using a predetermined "anchor" or cue to bring you back. Do the above "Maintaining Integrity" visualization, and the moment you get in touch with the feeling of integrity, your strong, fluid, talented, confident, courageous self, make a firm fist and say: "This is the fist of my integrity. Whenever I clench my fist, I exhibit my integrity as an athlete. The fist re-creates this feeling strongly and I play accordingly." Practice this seven times, and use it in a difficult situation during the next game.

Guides for Performing with Integrity

- Whether you're the favorite or the underdog, ahead or behind, you can stay in touch with your integrity by focusing not on the outcome but on your willingness to exhibit a championship level of play. Imagine yourself putting on a "clinic" as if people wanted a demonstration of how well you can play in this particular moment.

- When confronted by fear of an opponent or the possibility of failure, do not compromise what you possess as an athlete. Deal with the confrontation by exerting the influence you have rather than fighting the force head-on. Simply do what you can do. Show yourself and others your greatness, even if it is less powerful than your opposition.

Affirmations for Integrity

- *"The depth of my integrity determines the breadth of my achievement in sport."*
- *"My performance is related to my willingness to play with integrity."*
- *"Nothing can diminish my true greatness as an athlete."*
- *"I deserve to be here—I deserve to win."*
- *"There is no home court advantage unless I give it to them."*
- *"I maintain my self-worth as an athlete with the highest integrity."*

TAOSPORTS FOR BUSINESS AND LIFE

In an ancient Chinese story, a stonecutter was dissatisfied with his position in life. On seeing a wealthy merchant, he wished he too could be rich and successful and set out to become a merchant himself. He did and became wealthier by far than anyone in the land. Even with all of his money and power, however, one day he realized he still had to bow before the king. Not liking to be subordinate, and having worked his way up from stonecutter to rich merchant, he set out to become king himself. This he did and was the most powerful king in the land. One day, however, he noticed how uncomfortable the sun could make him with its heat. How powerful the sun is, he thought, so he became the sun and shone with a bright splendor. One day, however, a cloud covered up the sun, making him wish to be that cloud. On becoming that cloud, however, he was pushed around by the mighty wind. He then became the wind, which could do all except blow the powerful stone. He became the stone, more powerful, he thought, than anything on earth. As he stood proudly in the wind, he asked himself what could be more powerful than a stone? As he looked down, he saw a stonecutter, his own first self, pounding him with a chisel.

You have within you at this very moment all that you need to feel good about who you are. The following will help you get in touch with this inner value during moments of doubt.

- When you feel down on yourself, remember that it's not how you feel that matters as much as what you do about how you feel. Exercise directly affects self-image. When you're "down," try going for a bike ride, swim, run, or play tennis. Eating good healthy foods and avoiding toxic substances like alcohol or refined sugars will enhance your image of self.

- To turn around negative self-portraits, try remembering the Tao of paradox. Acceptance of self has a lot to do with your acceptance of others. Try keeping your images of others positive. Avoid harsh criticism. Be quick to point out positive attributes that you appreciate in them. By doing this, you will immediately begin to feel better as you take attention away from your own negative sense of self. Also, you create the environment where they can reciprocate.

- Avoid, at all costs, name calling. Self-images based on negative labels from the past continue to cause problems for many of us. A young boy was referred to me because he was "acting out" uncontrollably in school. Teachers remarked that his craving for attention and approval was the by-product of low self-esteem. When his mom came for the appointment, I asked where her son was. "He's out in the car; I'll get him," was her reply. The next words I heard were: "Hey, Shorty, you can come in now." I immediately thought how I, too, would act out if "Shorty" were my name. Such an albatross becomes a heavy cross to bear for anyone. And, as you can see, we tend to act according to our self-image . . . most of the time.

Exercise: Strength Assessment

To help you assess your strengths realistically, go to a friend and ask that person to help you select specific words that describe who you are in each of the following categories: physical self, professional self, intellectual self, social self, spiritual self. Try to identify four or five for each category. Take these objective qualities and use them as you did in the visualization exercise for Tao training with water bottles.

Many companies and businesses experience a lot of pressure to abandon their code of ethics. The dollar dominates their every decision, influencing them to go in directions that reflect financial gain. They create and sell products that pollute the environment, and they disregard the health and wellness of consumers.

Not so, however, for Tom and Kate Chappell, owners of a hygiene products business in Kennebunk, Maine. Often referred to as the "saints of social responsibility," the Chappells act with integrity and sell recyclable toothpaste tubes, biodegradable detergent, and products that contain no preservatives, synthetic colors, or artificial colors—all their products are designed not to pollute the environment. Because the price of these items is significantly higher than those of less environmentally conscious competitors, establishing the demand for them was a risky undertaking. Would people be willing to spend the extra cash to support a company with environmental concerns? They obviously are because Tom's of Maine has since become an international success, supplying countries in North America, Europe, and Asia.

Creating personal power and success in daily life is a matter of acting with such personal honesty that you create emotional independence for yourself, free of the critical, judgmental influence of others. Your level of self-trust is enhanced as you refuse to let those around you control your behavior, how you think, or what you believe.

Guides for Maintaining Integrity

It's easy to compromise your integrity in environments where many others see things another way. These TaoSport strategies will help you to keep on track.

- Remember that you are "good enough." You deserve the best, so act "as if" this were true. Regardless of anyone else's stature, you have value, something to contribute, something to teach. You deserve the opportunity to display your attributes and qualities when it is appropriate.

- When you become aware of your deep-rooted values and act according to them, you behave with greater integrity. Review, in your mind, how you feel about your friendships, health, wealth, shelter, closeness, intimacy, sharing, community, exercise, education, and other items of value. Are you acting in concert with your feelings about these? If so, you are acting with integrity. Follow your dreams and visions based on these values. This is the best way to be honest with yourself.

- As a parent, you wish to pass on basic values and principles of living to your children. Be firm yet fair in upholding these values. Refuse to compromise what you believe is good for their overall mental and emotional well-being. Notice that when you say no to something they do, you are really saying yes to the integrity of your home, to those values that come from a deep sense of caring. If you value health, acting with integrity may mean saying, "No, Jennifer, you can't go out in the cold dressed like that." This is saying yes to health, even though she doesn't know that. You might add, "I love you too much to see you risk getting sick with no protection."

- When you are at work, take on the responsibility of working with integrity. Model excellence for those above you as well as for those lower in the hierarchy of the corporation or business. This will help others to trust and respect you, as well as encourage them to raise their level of performance.

- Refuse to let age be a criterion for determining who your teachers are. Many famous teachers—Jesus, Martin Luther King—were younger than the majority of their students. Children, although intellectually inferior to adults, are emotionally our superiors. Be open to learning from them. Everyone has a purpose and fulfills a function. You contribute to their growth, and they contribute to yours. When you act in this way, you exhibit integrity, much as the tennis players in the stories above teach their opponents.

- Winning the approval of others in social situations may require you to compromise your values. But it is totally irrational to think that you can gain everyone's approval—many people, naturally, will disapprove of you and your values. Remain true to yourself. Try to show others the validity of your ideas by demonstrating the positive effects of your choices based on your integrity. They may not agree, but they will respect you for upholding your beliefs. Through your consistency, you lead and inspire others in their own lives.

Visualization: Maintaining Your Code of Ethics

There's much pressure in today's world to abandon codes of ethics and behave in ways that contradict your basic beliefs. Use this visualization when you reach such a crossroad in your life to remain true to your integrity.

> Think of a situation at work, at home, or with friends that is about to test your code of ethics, your integrity. Take a minute, and feel the tension and anxiety from having to face this uncomfortable challenge. Now, free yourself from this pain. Affirm: "The consequences of acting without integrity are greater than acting with it." Choose to follow your beliefs and code of ethics at the risk of rejection. Feel the tremendous personal power you receive from being true to yourself. See others responding to you with deep respect and admiration because you act with integrity. They are proud of you. Feel strong and whole. Know that you made the best decision; you can now live with yourself, even if others can't. Practice this over and over until you feel the strength to act according to your convictions.

ADAPTATION

Those who are firm and inflexible
    are in harmony with dying.
Those who are yielding and receptive
    are in harmony with living.
The position of the highly inflexible
    will descend;
The position of the yielding and
    receptive will ascend.

TAO TE CHING no. 76

The Tao emphasizes the importance and power of flexibility in our lives. Adaptation to unpredictable changes is essential for optimal performance and excellence in sport. While centering is a Beginner's Mind state of remaining true to yourself and your capabilities regardless of external distractions during a performance, adaptation is a process of making specific adjustments in your attitude, approach, and strategies when confronted by unpredictable changes before or during a performance. It is the Beginner's Mind state of centering that enables a TaoAthlete to adapt.

By its very nature, sport is predictably unpredictable. Injury and illness can halt your efforts instantly. Events change quickly and without warning.

Mother Nature has a way of infusing a cold blustery wind, a downpour of rain, or a blazing heat wave that can ruin months of preparation for a big event. Just when you feel things are under control, the rug is pulled from under you.

Rarely does your preparation take into account all possible changes that could occur. Surprises spring upon you without warning or concern from your opponents or officials conducting the event.

In 1988, a very talented track and field athlete was on her way to Seoul to compete in the Summer Olympics. At the time, her performances were close to the American record, and she was in an excellent position to contend for a medal. After she arrived in Seoul, the days leading up to her event were filled with drastic changes in the food and housing available. Fifteen minutes prior to the start of the finals race, the officials announced that there would be a long delay. The athletes, already warmed up on the track and ready to go, were marched back into a tunnel holding area for quite some time. When the race was finally run, she was distraught, unfocused, cold, and nervous. Her failure to adapt to the changed circumstances resulted in a lackluster performance. Looking at the top three finishers' times, she realized a medal would have been hers had she just been able to run her normal race.

> Adapting is knowing when to act and when to
> rest . . . It is a peaceful, accepting frame of mind
> willing to adjust to the existing circumstances.
>
> *I CHING* no 17

Regardless of external changes, athletes need to maintain a flexible "go with the flow" posture. Pliability, fluidity, and softness to change help an athlete develop a clear mental advantage over those who become psychologically rigid or resistant. Resistance to change causes tension, anxiety, and stress, which obstruct one's potential. While rigid tree branches crack during a storm, pliable limbs bend softly and bounce back unharmed. In Chinese lore, bamboo signifies great strength, yet bends easily in the wind. It flourishes during winter, the hardest of seasons, and it happens to be the most versatile of plants, used for food, paper, shelter, and healing in China.

A vivid metaphor for helping us flow with change is leaves falling from a tree. They follow the wind. If they land in water, they flow with the direction of the stream. They don't complain about how dirty or cold the water is and go back to the branch. Like leaves, we need to follow the winds and currents of life by adapting to the changes.

TAOSPORT TRAINING FOR ATHLETICS

It was a comfortable sixty-five degrees with low humidity, and Herb was wearing a rubberized sweatsuit during a fast run four days prior to an important race. His friends all thought he had lost his mind. When they asked what he was doing, he replied, "I'm trying to simulate and adapt to race conditions on Saturday. They're predicting a heat wave." Sure enough, it was eighty-eight degrees with ninety percent humidity at the start of the race, which Herb eventually won. Once he had driven four hours to run in wind and rain to learn how to adapt to these conditions, too.

Visualization: Mental Simulation Training

You can train your mind to respond favorably to unpleasant changes during an event with a TaoSport technique called mental simulation training. It is a visualization exercise that will help you become more adaptable to unfavorable conditions during competitive situations.

> Think of every possible change, negative or positive, that could occur during your performance. These unforeseen circumstances could be weather variations, equipment failures, obnoxious crowds, unfair calls by the referee, or tactical mistakes in your performance. See each change occur, feel your disappointment, and immediately see yourself responding in a flexible, adaptive way. Affirm: "The hallmark of a champion is the ability to adapt. I am a champion." Feel yourself having the advantage over the opponent who failed to plan for such circumstances. Your performance is superb under the conditions.

Some situations do occur that are genuinely unpredictable. It's impossible to simulate all eventualities. Use the foregoing affirmations as touchstones to help you adapt during times of surprise change.

Affirmations for Adaptation

From a TaoSport point of view, athletes must adapt their attitudes to a change. It's not the change that causes turmoil; it's your attitude or view of the change. Flexible attitudes toward changes lessen their impact. Refuse to give unpredictable events the power to control your reactions. The Tao encourages us to accept, incorporate, and embrace change; the athlete who adapts will triumph and become a powerful force in sport. These affirmations will help you to accept change and adapt to gain the advantage.

- *"Inflexible athletes descend; flexible athletes ascend."*
- *"When the flow doesn't go, I go with the flow."*
- *"Like bamboo, I am strong, yet I bend with the wind."*
- *"Adaptability creates opportunity."*
- *"I am adaptable to the unpredictable."*
- *"Change is not strange. I am ready for it at all times."*

TAOSPORTS FOR BUSINESS AND LIFE

You hear of it every day: An investor pulls out of what was once believed to be a sure thing; a toy manufacturer stops producing its big seller; food chains are changing their produce to organic. These and myriad other examples point to the necessity for adaptation to change in a rapidly changing marketplace. Failure to read trends accurately and adjust to them can lead to your demise in business. One example of failure to adapt to industry demands is the story of the Cuisinart company. They refused to develop smaller machines, and as a result they lost huge shares of the market to competitors who produced mini–food processors.

So it is in all of life. Ralph Waldo Emerson once said that a foolish consistency is the hobgoblin of little minds. Gandhi claimed that he was committed to truth, not consistency. He would not be afraid of acting in a way that contradicted what he believed yesterday, provided the change represented what was right for today.

An example of successful adaptation in business is Mountain Network Solutions, a computer hardware and software firm in Northern California. In business since 1977, Mountain survived numerous slumps in the economy when other companies folded or were forced to downsize drastically. Mountain's management cites its adaptability to the changing computer market as a major reason for the company's success. The company began as Mountain Hardware, a manufacturer of printed circuit board products for Apple computers, but when the market for these products began to decline, the company turned to the emerging hard disk technology for IBM computers and experienced immediate growth. It also diversified to include a line of diskette duplicators and certifiers, and it changed its name to Mountain Computer to indicate its ties to the computer industry. As the capacity of hard disks increased, the need for a reliable form of data backup was created. Mountain quickly got into the tape backup business. Eventually, the Apple board products and hard disks disappeared from Mountain's price list, but it became a heavy contender in the tape backup business. When the company noticed that computer networking environments needed reliable data management systems, it adapted once again by creating several software tools for this purpose. That was the birth of Mountain Network Solutions. In a time when other companies are feeling the effects of yet another recession, this almost chameleonlike company is posting record-high profits.

Guides for Adaptation

These guides will help you practice being more flexible in everyday situations.

- If you are a political leader or are running for office locally or nationally, the I Ching states that only leaders who adapt their vision to the sentiments of the group they represent will be successful. You can communicate with others to get their opinions clear in your mind. Be sure to remain true to your deepest principles and values.

- As a manager, supervisor, teacher, or parent, seek out opportunities to harmonize with the wishes of the group. This can be frightening, but if it serves the interest of all and the outcome is not threatening, give up your preference for that of the others. You will experience greater joy and more cooperation from the group.

- Examine the old beliefs, prejudices, and opinions that may be holding you back at home or at work. Perhaps your views are out of sync with society or the group—self-adjustment may be beneficial. Adapting to the realities of change in the world will make your life happier and more peaceful. Of course, you want to be sure that such flexibility doesn't infringe upon your integrity as a person.

- When anything happens at work, home, or school that is different, see it as an opportunity to become flexible, and adapt quietly. Notice how others cope with the change. Follow those who seem to do well, and ignore the behavior of those who don't.

- Each day, when the opportunity arises, change the way you normally get dressed, go to work, where you have lunch. If you read, choose a book entirely unrelated to what you usually read. Choose to eat food that is unfamiliar.

- When trying to decide which movie or restaurant to go to with friends, avoid trying to control the situation by insisting that your choice is best. Be flexible, and adapt to the suggestions of others. Notice how well things work out and how much better you feel.

Visualization: Adaptation

Imagine yourself experiencing some changes that go against the normal patterns of your life and that clearly indicate real changes. As you begin to feel anxious, tell yourself, "*Stop*," and affirm: "I flow with the Tao by adapting right now." Ask your inner guide, "What do I need to know, what do I need to do to remain open and flexible with the change?" Hear the answer. Thank your guide, and see yourself following the advice. Let go of the old, and welcome the new. Feel the peace and calm that comes over you by adjusting to these new situations.

PERSISTENCE

Deliberate and slow cultivation . . . is the path to success and good fortune. Only by gradually developing your relationship with the area of your concern can you make the progress you desire. Calmness and adaptability along with good-natured persistence will see you through.

I CHING no 53

Persistence, according to the Tao, is key to attaining most worthwhile objectives: "If you persevere in constructive and positive thought, you will experience great good fortune" (*I Ching* no. 39). With persistence as your frame of mind, you will not be denied on your journey of excellence. Realizing your goals and attaining success are the by-products of persistence and perspiration. Talent accounts for a mere five percent of most achievements. Those who appear to have much talent were once struggling beginners. It was persistence and hard work that led them to achievement and excellence.

In sport, there is an expression that refers to the importance of persistence in learning a new skill or accomplishing a goal: "It's all possible— you just need time in the saddle." Becoming proficient as a cyclist requires hours of riding—in the bike saddle. Hitting a good serve is simply a matter of putting in hours of practice, persisting through any and all setbacks.

It took a number of years and many setbacks before I won my first distance race. Following many second- and third-place finishes, I became discouraged and resigned to the thought that I might never cross the finish line first. Then someone happened to say to me, "Jerry, every dog has his day—you just need to keep at it." I believed him and began to relax and be more patient. My very next race was the first of a string of five consecutive victories, including the Western Regional 5,000-meter track championships. When I stopped pushing and decided to persist with patience, I had freed up a bundle of energy. More exhilarating than the victories was the gift of knowing that with persistence, the sky's the limit in all of life.

I can't help but think of those old steam engines that will not budge when their boilers are 211 degrees Fahrenheit. Add one more degree of heat, and they race to their destination, lugging a hundred cars behind them. Many a great tennis star has been behind two sets and 5–love in the third. By persisting patiently, they wore away their opponent to win the match.

Those familiar with professional football remember the heroics of quarterback Joe Montana in the 1980s. He repeatedly carried his Forty-Niners back from huge deficits to become victorious in the waning seconds of many contests. He is the classic model of athletic persistence.

The key to maintaining the Beginner's Mind with respect to persistence in sport is to focus on your own excellent abilities and trust that if anything is to come of the situation you must remain patient, calm, and relaxed. In his beautiful book *The Zen of Running*, Fred Rohé eloquently makes the point:

> It's your choice of whether
> to run to PUNISH your self
> or to experience your self.
> If you choose, with me, the latter,
> then every run can be joyful.
> The key words are, TAKE IT EASY!
> Create your self as a runner gradually,
> patiently, relaxedly.

TAOSPORT TRAINING FOR ATHLETICS

Ray and Shirley Triplett took on one of the most difficult endurance athletic events possible. Over a period of eight years, they sailed by themselves one and a half times around the world. Facing violent storms, groundings on coral reefs, wars, pirates, shipwrecks, severe illness, and near drownings, they persisted to its completion. According to Ray, "We were tormented by the demons of the temptation to quit." Yet those harsh lessons taught them the wisdom of taking things one day at a time. They knew that with persistence, they would realize their goal. Giving up was not an alternative for them because both felt that they couldn't have lived with that decision later in their lives.

Affirmations for Persistence

Champions in sport are cultivated one day at a time. It's an illusion to think that they are born or come out of nowhere. These affirmations will help you focus on persistence for achievement in athletics.

- *"If I persist each day, I'll eventually get my way."*
- *"I expect success when I persist."*
- *"The path may be long, but I persist with a song."*
- *"All things come to those who wait."*
- *"Don't stop if I want to be on top."*

Visualization: Persistence

To help develop patience, determination, and persistence, practice the following visualization exercise daily when you are faced with situations that require you to persevere:

> In your state of relaxation, think of an aspect of your sport that makes you impatient and anxious. Perhaps you haven't been able to win a race; you still struggle with your backhand; your team has come close but never won the championship; your dismount is still awkward. Get in touch with the frustration of waiting for fulfillment. You are no longer tolerant of

delaying gratification, and you want to "throw in
the towel" and quit. Now, in your mind, "shout"
the word *stop* and begin to feel gratification from
simply pursuing your goal. Each day, in every
way, you get closer to your destination,
regardless of any delays or setbacks. Affirm: "I
persist each day and in time, I have my way."
Feel the excitement when your persistence pays
off, and know that it is all worthwhile.

TAOSPORTS FOR
BUSINESS AND LIFE

Jack Zeff, president of a Southern California–based water purification research firm, is a wonderful model of persistence in the corporate world. After
years of working for industrial giants, Jack decided to follow his dream of
starting his own business. He had discovered a way to use ultraviolet light
and ozone to treat waste waters, and in 1973 he incorporated. To obtain the
necessary equipment and space, he borrowed enormous amounts of money.
But then he realized that he had overlooked one important detail: The
market for his concept was nonexistent. He didn't know it then, but he was
twelve years before his time.

Jack persevered. He hired some consultants to help raise more money,
educate people about the benefits of his product, and develop markets that
could benefit from his ideas. This tactic failed as well, and after a few years of
effort his business went into bankruptcy.

With still greater determination and persistence, he started a new company with partners who fronted three million dollars. To help generate
interest and funds, they took their company public in the penny stock
market. Once again, he experienced a setback. As fate would have it, the
penny market was exposed for fraud around this time. It was a matter of bad
timing, according to optimistic Jack.

Continuing to persist, he landed on his feet once again—this time with
the support of a seven-billion-dollar company that believed in his product.
Now, with enough money and patience, Jack's dream has finally come true.
According to this entrepreneur, perseverance and persistence always
pay off.

Guides for Persistence

Most of us struggle with the problem of delayed gratification. We want the best home, the greatest career, the most wonderful family—and we want it *now*! To cure an illness, we prefer an instant pill that offers the promise of wellness immediately, rather than developing a lifestyle of health over a period of time. Forgotten is the cliché, "Rome wasn't built in a day." I have personally discovered, after many years of "fighting and screaming," that most worthwhile experiences take time. When I persist, all the best seems to evolve naturally. These thoughts will keep you aligned when you get off track.

- The task of persisting becomes easier when you can change it from being a chore to being fun. You can do this by focusing on the opportunities that come your way when you persist. The people you meet, the places you go, the things you learn, and the small positive improvements are all part of persisting on the journey. It's also fun to have a sense of purpose, something that keeps you going. Because of your choice to persist, life is fuller.

- Try to remember that great contributors to society like Thomas Edison, James Joyce, Richard Bach, Albert Einstein, Albert Schweitzer, and Jonas Salk were very persistent on their up-and-down journeys. Edison had more than five thousand major setbacks before the light went on. One of Bach's books was rejected for publication eighty-two times. When your path seems obstructed, persist, as other great people have.

- When you are tempted to take a shortcut with work, avoid it. There is no such thing as a shortcut. Refuse to sacrifice quality for time—all great products are the result of hard work. If something seems to be taking too long, know that you are probably on the right path.

- In his beautiful translation of Liu I-Ming's *Awakening to the Tao*, Thomas Cleary reflects on patience and persistence: "Climbing from lowliness to the heights, penetrating from the shallows to the depths, gradually applying effort in an orderly manner, not counting the months and years, not losing heart, eventually one will reach fulfillment. . . . Don't give up halfway."

Great men accomplish significant deeds through an enduring effort in a consistent direction. When you wish to achieve an important aim, direct your thoughts along a steady, uninterrupted course.

I CHING no. 57

Characteristics of People Who Persist

These major characteristics define those who persist. Develop these traits in yourself on your journey of achievement, and you, too, will persist along the way. People who persist tend to:

- Create fun in the process of accomplishment.

- Have a strong sense of self and feel that, regardless of the outcome, they will be still worthwhile.

- Have the courage to act and take risks.

- Make changes gradually and patiently.

- Reward themselves periodically for small gains they make.

- Seek the support of others when times get tough.

- Use variety as a means of maintaining interest.

- Expect positive outcomes.

- Focus on the joyous aspects of the journey.

- Know that progress is always two steps forward, one step backward.

BALANCE

Evolved individuals
>Avoid extremes,
>Avoid extravagance,
>Avoid excess.

TAO TE CHING no 29

The *Tao Te Ching* teaches that unbalanced energies are unstable extremes that detract from personal power and performance. A balanced life enables us to perform with increased excitement and motivation, with the potential for higher levels of output.

A national-class athlete was having difficulty with his sport. Constantly getting injured and mentally fatigued, he did little else but train. He worked out two, sometimes three times a day.

"Marty, Marty," I told him. "Have you considered being more balanced? Surely you have work, family, friends, and hobbies?" "Twelve hours of working out, twelve hours of sleep," he replied. "Perfect balance."

Marty, unfortunately, is not the exception—he's the rule. Many athletes, to excel in sport, seem to devote every waking hour to training. It's not uncommon for young tennis stars, dynamic skaters, and gymnasts to become unbalanced in their approach. They skip school, opting for correspondence courses so they can eat, drink, and sleep their obsession. Theirs becomes an artificial existence, an excessive emotional wasteland far away from the crucial natural maturation process of adolescence. Few of these young athletes go on to succeed; many more wind up wasting their lives. Even for those who do well, success takes its toll.

In a recent olympiad, a U.S. gold medalist in swimming was asked, "Where do you go from here?" "Far away from pools," was the instant response. He proceeded to relate how much he had sacrificed on his road to fame and intimated that it might not have been worth it. He complained about the lack of balance in his life.

Being out of balance does take its toll. Personal success has rarely made up for what I lost by being excessive. As a nationally competitive athlete, I became so self-absorbed in my sport that the rest of my life suffered or was put on hold. I succeeded at competing, but I lost friends and family in the process. My asymmetrical existence was unfulfilling; the applause, awards, and recognition for my hard work were satisfying yet ephemeral.

Over the past several years I have learned that I can actually perform at higher levels when my life is balanced. After the birth of my first son, I ran the fastest times of my life at all distances up to the marathon. After the birth of my second son, I continued to perform well, not only in sport but professionally. As I write this, my five-week-old son is sleeping on my bed. One more child would put me out of balance—I believe I'll settle for three.

TAOSPORT TRAINING FOR ATHLETICS

Many athletes say that having families, careers, and hobbies has enabled them to compete with less tension and anxiety. Loss and failure aren't so devastating when you have other points on your star that shine. Then again, you might not be as motivated to excel in sport if you have something to fall back on.

But great athletes seem to be able to handle lives of variety and balance. World-class marathoner Mark Plaatjes, who won the Los Angeles Marathon in a stunning time of two hours and ten minutes, believes in diversion from sport. To create balance, he works as a physical therapist and is an active, devoted father of two girls. According to Mark, when you become totally engrossed in your sport, you overanalyze everything. He says that leading a full life outside sport helps to avoid such unhelpful analysis.

Nancy Ditz, a member of the U.S. marathon team in the 1988 Olympics, experienced a wide life in addition to her vigorous training prior to the Olympic trials, where she ran a personal best, finishing second overall. Now, after giving birth to a child, she is still in contention as a world-class athlete.

Of the thousands of athletes I have worked with, those who have been successful feel that a balanced life was responsible for their good fortune. They have divided their precious time among training, education, social activity, hobbies, family, and part-time work. Balance and excellence go hand-in-hand.

Excess and extremes lead to injury, burnout, and fatigue. If you try to establish a balanced approach but exhibit excessiveness in each area, you will walk the path of personal destruction. Moderation enables you to create balance.

In leading people and serving Nature,
There is nothing better than moderation.
Since, indeed, moderation means yielding early;
Yielding early means accumulating Power.

TAO TE CHING no 59

According to the Tao, yielding early is knowing when you have had enough. When you are training for a competition, it may seem that you can't do enough. You may have to increase the hours you work out and thereby disrupt the balance in your life, but remember that this period of preparation is not forever, and you can return to a more moderate approach when competition season is over. Consider that you may not even need to do as much as you think to compete well. The concept of what is enough needs to be reevaluated constantly.

Olympian and author Jeff Galloway seems to understand the concept of moderation. After megamiles of running, doing daily double workouts, Jeff now runs only once every other day. Yes, he is getting older, and some may conclude that age has taken its toll. But he recommends a program of moderation for everyone. Jeff's concepts were adopted by the famous L.A. Leggers running group. They trained diligently yet moderately for three months prior to the recent Los Angeles Marathon. Using Galloway's program of "stress and rest," they alternated running days with complete days off from activity. The result—500 out of 503 of them finished the twenty-six-mile event.

These participants say that what they enjoyed most about the program of moderation was that it afforded them time to do other things in their lives while training seriously for a demanding event. They appreciated a balanced existence because it kept them motivated on a daily basis.

Do not indulge in extremes of any sort. . . . Strive for moderation in all you do. . . . In this way you use the balancing tendency of the current forces to center yourself. This aligns you with the Tao, thus bringing you into harmony with forces that can work for you.

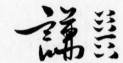

I CHING no 15

Besides being moderate with your training program, consider being less excessive with

- *Social activities.* It is important to balance your sport with social activity. If taken to extremes, you will become distracted and fatigued.

- *Work.* Excess in this area will tire you too. Consider ways to streamline your work so that you accomplish what's necessary. Know what is enough.

- *Diet.* A good balanced diet is important for athletes. Moderation here means not exceeding the required caloric demands your workouts produce. Endurance athletes need more calories than those in sports like golf, tennis, baseball, and archery. Determine what you expend on a daily basis, and try to adequately replace them. Excessive eating leads to weight gain, which may hinder performance.

Affirmations for Balance

These affirmations can be used as touchstones to remind you of the importance of maintaining balance as an athlete.

- *"Balance is power!"*
- *"Excel without excess!"*
- *"Excellence and balance are compatible partners for achievement in sport."*
- *"Moderate, don't proliferate!"*

- *"I realize my dreams when I avoid the extremes."*
- *"I come up short without balance in sport."*

TAOSPORTS FOR BUSINESS AND LIFE

Somehow, if you lack balance in your life, nature has ways to help you learn how to create it.

One client I had got the message the hard way. John worked constantly for many years. Saturday and Sunday became "catch up" or "stay afloat" days, to use his words. He admitted that work was really the only important thing in his life, and he claimed that he would go to his grave working at his desk. He almost did—he suffered a massive heart attack while he was at the office.

This is a common scenario with many people, although the outcome is not. Forced to curtail his work when the doctor said he'd die if he didn't, John decided to see this crisis as a message to relax. His recovery took place at his daughter's beach house, where he was surrounded by the love of his grand-children. He read books, and he did things he never knew could interest him. Exercise became a daily routine to which he quickly became addicted. At the age of sixty-eight, John has discovered a wonderful balance of body, mind, and spirit. He has returned to work, but only for ten days a month. He devotes the extra time to living a full, balanced life with his family.

Guides for Balance

The extent of your fulfillment and success is directly related to the balance you create among the nutritional, social, familial, professional, physical, mental, and emotional-spiritual aspects of your life. Concentrate on one at the exclusion of the others, and you will experience inner turmoil, dissat-isfaction, and unhappiness. These TaoSport strategies will help you establish a more balanced existence:

- Professionally, discover ways to create a smorgasbord, a balance among various ways to achieve your objectives. Many jobs allow oppor-tunities to unite, speak, consult, teach, and supervise. Others are more restricted but offer opportunities to create balance in scheduling, breaks, and arrival and departure from the office. Hardworking days can be balanced with easier ones. Some people find that two or three unrelated part-time positions give them the variety and balance they need to remain excited about work. Others seek to work less to free up the time to create a balance with other parts of their lives.

- Nutritionally, a healthy, balanced diet with much variety will improve your overall wellness and outlook toward life. Choose fresh, clean produce and unprocessed products that fulfill each of the major food groups. Notice, too, that food cravings are usually nature's way of balancing your nutritional needs. Pay attention to them.

- Athletically, maintain a balance by "cross-training." Try biking, swimming, running, or any other aerobic exercise on an alternating basis to keep motivated, excited, injury free, and in good shape. Weight training and stretching may round out your program. Remember that all of these are possible with moderation.

- Prioritization is a wonderful process to help you create a balance. Focus your daily activity on what is important, and eliminate the insignificant. With less to do, you'll have more time to maintain balance.

- Avoid trying to fill every open space of the day. Remember that time alone to reflect, visualize, meditate, or do nothing at all is a very important component of maintaining balance.

- As you try to develop the important aspects of yourself, remember that moderation in each will enable you to create the time you need to attend to all. Moderation will serve as a hedge against resistance, burnout, and fatigue. Each day, create opportunities to attend to body, mind, and spirit with moderation.

Tips for Healthy Moderation

- Use moderation when you make promises, and you will have less to live up to. As a result, you will create peace and calm in your life.

- Use judicious moderation when restricting children, and they will be moderate in their rebellion.

- Use moderation in friendship. Choose to put your energies into a few worthwhile people, and create greater depth and meaning in those friendships.

• Use moderation with your self-imposed limits. Question and transcend them for greater opportunity.

• Use moderation when making changes in your diet, exercise, and lifestyle. That makes it easier for your body to adjust.

• Use moderation when you are in doubt as to "how much" of anything. You can go back for more later.

Visualization: The Balanced Person

Use this visualization exercise to help you maintain balance in your life.

> Affirm: "I am a very balanced, fulfilled, happy person who attends to all aspects of living." See this being so. Imagine a day when you relax, work, play, socialize, and are spontaneous. Feel the exhilaration and joy from living in a full range of being. As part of being balanced, imagine how it would feel to be open to new experiences. Choose a new experience and imagine how it feels. Affirm: "A life of balance is a life fulfilled."

SIMPLICITY

見素　Perceive purity;
抱樸　Embrace simplicity;
　　　Limit desires.

TAO TE CHING no. 19

The Tao teaches us to follow nature's law of simplicity: Less is more. Some of the greatest performances in athletics have come when things are kept extremely simple: simple defenses and offenses, simple routines, simple strategies, simple training programs. All of these uncomplicate the way to excellence and provide a sense of harmony within and without. Simplicity, according to the Tao, is freedom—freedom to focus, concentrate, and be totally harmonious and present during a performance. Many outstanding accomplishments in athletics are truly basic, coming in moments of the purist simplicity.

American distance star Mark Nenow set a national record in the 10,000-meter run, ascribing his success to the precepts of simplicity. In an age of high-tech equipment and sophisticated physiological feedback equipment, Mark chose to embrace a less complicated way, virtually avoiding scientific training programs. He ran while "listening" to the natural messages of his body.

Another runner, Ethiopian Abebe Bikila, won an Olympic gold medal in the marathon and other victories running barefoot. Fancy clothing and digitally timed runner's watches were not part of his world. He simply ran.

Today, sport is big business. An entire industry is devoted to distracting us from the pure joy of a game—witness the scene at any downhill ski resort, triathlon, or other major athletic event. Training regimens are becoming quite involved and complex and strongly influenced by a Westernized attitude of "more is better."

The great Willie Mays of the New York Giants used to finish a Sunday home game at the Polo Grounds, then continue his heroics on the streets of his neighborhood playing "stick ball" with some of the kids the same day. Life was a bit simpler then, but the basic motives for participation—love of and excitement for the game—haven't changed. We have just lost touch with these values. The emphasis on salaries, signing bonuses, specialization, and other peripheral realities carry the focus away from our original motives for playing. If we devoted as much time to working out as we did coordinating our attire or purchasing the latest equipment, we'd all be better performers.

A national-class runner was constantly hooked up to pulse meters and pace keepers to monitor her progress. One day when she was cruising on a trail in the Santa Cruz mountains, her high-tech equipment malfunctioned, as it had so often before, and she stopped to repair the gadget. It was an unfortunate place to stop—she was soon attacked by a swarm of yellow jackets. After two vicious bites she continued her run. Technological failures don't always end this way, but her lack of simplicity took away so much quality from her workouts that the gains from her gadgetry were hardly noticeable. Running had become so complex that she ceased to experience any joy from it.

The problem with complexity is that it creates not only distraction but pressure, anxiety, and tension. Performance is hindered. But nature, by its very essence, is simple. So it is with greatness in sport.

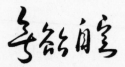

Nameless Simplicity is without desire;
And without desire, there is harmony.

TAO TE CHING no 37

TAOSPORT TRAINING FOR ATHLETICS

In times of difficulty, stress, and turmoil, or when things seem to slip backward, become simple. Avoid the tendency to overcompensate in a slump. Go back to basics. Shed the need for fashion, and focus on function instead.

Perhaps the epitome of TaoSport simplicity in my athletic career came while I was training at altitude in the foothills of the Colorado Rockies with my workout buddy, Gordon. One of the more exhilarating runs required that we run six miles up and six miles down on beautiful turn-of-the-century horse trails with gorgeous vistas of the incredible snow-covered 13,000-foot Indian peaks. In our descent, we traversed fifteen creeks supplied by the runoff from the high snows and encountered deer, coyote, mountain lions, eagles, and other birds of prey. Not once did we see another human. We were truly at one with the essence of nature, the simplicity of sport. We ran completely naked on each journey, except for a pair of seven-ounce running shoes. Gordon and I referred to these exhilarating jaunts as our "low overhead runs."

More socially acceptable attire was worn by world-class marathoner Bill Rodgers during his very first victory in the Boston Marathon. His plain white T-shirt with the initials of his track club printed on the front with Magic Marker didn't blemish his victory as he set a course record in the process.

Affirmations for Simplicity

- *"Embrace simplicity."*
- *"Less is more."*
- *"Simplicity is the freedom to focus on only that which is truly important."*
- *"Moments of greatness are experienced during times of pure simplicity."*
- *"When things get out of hand, simplify."*
- *"Function, not Fashion."*
- *"Keep it simple—get back to basics."*

Visualization: Simplification

Use this visualization exercise to help you simplify your approach to your sport.

Get in touch with the essence of your sport. Why do you like it? Why did you choose this particular event? Once you're aware of this basic essence, affirm: "I am now open to anything that will add to my performance as an athlete, and I place aside all that will complicate the way." See yourself performing excellently, with lightness and freedom. Detach from fashion, and focus on function. Ask the question and wait for an answer. "How much do I really need?" See yourself shedding unnecessary externals. Focus on the excellence of play. Feel the sense of purity that accompanies the process of simplification.

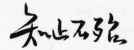

The more that is hoarded,
  The deeper the loss.
Know what is enough.

TAO TE CHING no 44

TAOSPORTS FOR BUSINESS AND LIFE

Lao-tzu constantly reminds us in the *Tao Te Ching* of the importance of returning to simplicity. The greatest happiness in life comes during times of pure simplicity. The Chinese word *p'u* appears throughout the Tao—it means "simple" or "plain," the uncomplicated way.

A young entrepreneur wanted to become very rich. He owned a small yet very successful athletic goods store. After three years, he reached his goal of earning a million dollars. Elated with his progress, he began to complicate his life through financial investments. He was proud of his new Porsche, yet he worried constantly about someone scratching it. He parked it far away from his office just to have it in the empty section of the lot. He constantly complained about the outrageous bills for its upkeep. His beautiful new house, big enough for a family of ten, kept him and his wife captive with cleaning, repairs, and outlandish mortgage payments. Going to the slopes to ski with his state-of-the-art equipment was impossible because he had to tend the store nine hours a day. Did he own that car, house, and other goods, or did they own him? He inadvertently answered this question one day when he remarked to a sales clerk, "I was richer when life was simpler." Six months later, he sold the business. He purchased freedom and simplicity in its place.

Guides for Simplicity

Happiness, freedom, and fulfillment in life result from limiting desires, not from having more. Your performance in all aspects of life will improve when you understand that less is more. Start by shedding the unnecessary externals. Ask yourself, "How can I streamline my life in every respect and embrace simplicity?" These guides will help you to begin.

- Slow things down—meditate, visualize, pray, take a walk each day alone, and ask yourself, "Do I really need ———?" "Will I be free if I get rid of ———?"

- Donate clothing to a good cause, thereby simplifying your wardrobe. Giving things to others makes life simpler for others, too, as they don't have to worry as much about how to get what they need.

- Simplify your diet, and create a simplistic exercise program. Eat basic nutritional food, free of chemicals, additives, and preservatives. Exercise need not be a complicated, expensive venture. Walking up and down a good hill in your neighborhood could easily replace expensive athletic machines.

- Shed unnecessary items in your home; get rid of clutter. Do you really need those curtains? Are rugs really essential? Some people have discovered the joy of reading, storytelling, and family togetherness by eliminating the television.

- Question the frequency of cleaning, washing, sweeping, vacuuming. These activities complicate your daily schedule. Do things really need to be so clean? Is it just a habit that has been passed down from your parents? If these things must be done frequently, try delegating work to create more time for simple pleasures. Divide the tasks among family members.

- Simplify work. Ask yourself if you could work fewer hours and still earn a living. How much money is enough for you? Wouldn't life be simpler if you had more free time?

- Consider being more honest and direct in your communication. This keeps it simple. Ask for what you want. Tell others how you are feeling rather than let bad feelings stew to the point of explosion. Try to avoid gossip and idle chatter—listen attentively to others. Life gets complex from miscommunication.

- Regulate the noise levels of the phone and television. Don't become a slave to ringing phones and doorbells. Life is simpler when it's not interrupted by outside intrusions. Try to screen incoming calls using the answering machine. This is one machine that can actually simplify things.

- Consider the various ways to simplify your friendships. You do not need to spend enormous sums of money together on dinner or entertainment. The idea is to spend time together, not to feel the pressure to cook lavish meals or eat at fancy restaurants. Once in a while it's fun to splurge, but on a regular basis it gets terribly complex. A simple, home-cooked meal, followed by a home movie or a table game, makes for a wonderful evening. There's also much to do in the community that involves little or no planning; outdoor music, university theater, picnics, and nature hikes are simple yet meaningful ways to spend time with those you love.

- During times of grief, pain, sorrow, high stress, and inner strife, seek simplicity by doing less. Refuse to make major decisions if possible. Slow down and become quiet verbally and mentally. Eat less. Avoid the normal tendency to fill your life with possessions and purchases. Alcohol and drugs will only complicate your life and detract from the clarity of mind so necessary during tumultuous periods in your life.

- Use the following rhyme as a touchstone:

> When you want to fly—simplify;
> When in doubt, throw it out.

I do not think that any civilization can be called
complete until it has progressed from sophistication
to unsophistication, and made a conscious return
to simplicity of thinking and living.

Lin Yutang, THE IMPORTANCE OF LIVING

EPILOGUE

You will find as you look back upon your
life that the moments that stand out, the moments
when you have really lived, are the moments
when you have done things in the spirit of love.

Henry Drummond

Perhaps the most important challenge for any of us is to live our daily lives in
the spirit of love and with passion. The force of love was described by
philosopher-theologian Teilhard de Chardin as the second discovery of fire
by humans in the history of the world. We hope that the TaoSport of this
book will stoke your passion, elevate your soul, and enliven your body. By
being true to your passions, the voice of your heart, you support and encourage your own journey, your attempt to make sense out of what you do and
how you do it, in a world where most people doubt themselves and fear to
change.

You are a great spirit, and great spirits have always encountered resistance
and obstacles along their way. You will experience self-doubt and aloneness,
but the Tao will comfort you. You may appear strange to others, but you will
know that we all are one with the Tao. With the age-old strategies and
wisdom of TaoSport, you can be truly strong and transcend all obstacles.

The key to following your passion is learning to listen closely to the inner voice of your own being. When you must make choices between what is practical and lucrative and what truly is your heart's desire, go to a deep place inside yourself and ask, "Who am I? What do I really want out of life?" Do what comes to you through your own existence, through being in touch with yourself. Doors will open to those who follow their passion; and the world will also move to help those who live a life of authenticity and integrity.

The ultimate and the simplest TaoSport is a deep understanding of the process of living, thinking with our whole body and dancing with our whole mind. This is the condition that T. S. Eliot described as "complete simplicity, costing not less than everything."

We now offer you this closing meditation in motion and e-motion:

Affirm: I am a passionate being with a fiery zest for life.
I feel within an extraordinary passion for being alive.
My energy is exuberant and joyful.
Energy is eternal delight.

Hear yourself say:

It's wonderful to be alive. Life is full. And I am full of life!

Stand up, stretch your body.

Let the impulse of living extend and expand your
whole mental and physical being.

OPEN your mind, your heart, your body.

Celebrate BEING ALIVE!

INDEX

A

Adaptation
affirmations for, 271
athletes and, 268–71
businesses and, 271–72
everyday situations and, 272–73
mental simulation training, 270–71
visualization for, 273

Affirmations
for adaptation, 271
applications of, 24–25
for assertiveness, 162, 164, 166
for balance, 283–84
for belief in self, 33–34
beyond fear of success, 105–6
for centering, 68
for coming out of slumps, 112
for competitive partnership, 202
for confidence, 155, 156
for conscientiousness, 196
for detachment from results, 176–77
for effective management, 253
for egolessness, 183–84
for expanding beliefs, 35–36
for fearlessness, 90
for focusing, 63
for gaining the advantage, 217
for goal setting, 228
going beyond the perfectionism trap, 147
guidelines for creating, 25
for health and healing, 127
for integrity, 263
for intuition, 73–74
in life, 23
for nonforce management, 114–15
for parents with expectations, 135
for persistence, 276
for positive thinking, 40

for reframing failure, 96
for relaxing, 49
for risk taking, 169
for self-image, 42
for self-improvement, 233
for selflessness, 189
for self-love, 140
for simplicity, 289
for synergy, 242
for "tuning in" to your life, 81–82
for unexpectedness, 133
for winners, 207
Ahmann-Leighton, Chrissy, 129
Aikido, 47, 89, 95, 201
Allegheny College, 205
Allen, Mark, 38, 60
Anatomy of an Illness (Cousins), 128–29
Anchors, 21–22, 49, 53–54
Anderson, Bob, 182
Archery, 231
Art of Strategy, The (Wing), 34
Art of War, The (Sun-tzu), 211–12
Assertiveness
affirmations for, 166
vs. aggression, 159–61
in athletics, 161–63
coping assertively with aggressive people, 165–66
guides for in business/life, 163–65
with sexual harassment, 165–66
Athletes, 9–14
behavior patterns of Western, 6–7
confidence of, 153–54
ego involvement, 181–82
injuries, stages of adjustment, 123
mindsets of, 31–32
motivation, 218–21
natural ability, 39
slumps, 109–10

297

About the Authors

Chungliang Al Huang is the founder-president of Living Tao Foundation and the director of Lan Ting Institute. An internationally recognized Tai Ji master and authority of East/West cultural synthesis, he has been a research fellow at the Academia Sinica and a member of the World Academy of Art and Science. He is the author of the best-selling classic *Embrace Tiger, Return to Mountain* and *Quantum Soup: Fortune Cookies in Crisis*, and coauthor with Alan Watts of *Tao: The Watercourse Way*.

Dr. Jerry Lynch has a master's and doctorate from Penn State University, and has taught at the University of Colorado and Stanford. He is a teacher, lecturer, consultant to major U.S. corporations, author of *Living Beyond Limits: The Tao of Self-Empowerment*, and founder of The Tao Center for Human Performance in Santa Cruz. His clients there have included NFL athletes and Olympian competitors. Dr. Lynch, a marathoner and father of three sons, is married to Jan Zeff, a natural medicine physician, and lives with his family in Santa Cruz, California.

Chungliang Al Huang and Jerry Lynch are available for workshops and information on *Thinking Body, Dancing Mind* at the Living Tao Foundation, Box 846, Urbana, Illinois 61803, (217) 337-6113.